APARTHEID

Apartheid

A geography of separation

ANTHONY LEMON
Fellow of Mansfield College, Oxford

with a contribution by
OWEN WILLIAMS
Professor of Geography
University of Natal

SAXON **SH** HOUSE

Published by
SAXON HOUSE, Teakfield Limited,
Westmead, Farnborough, Hants., England.

ISBN 0 566 00106 3
Library of Congress Catalog Card Number 76-20214
Printed in Great Britain by Biddles Ltd of Guildford

Contents

List of tables

List of figures

Glossary

AAAG	*Annals of the Association of American Geographers*
Afn Aff.	*African Affairs*
Geog. Rev.	*Geographical Review*
IBG	*Transactions of the Institute of British Geographers*
J. for Geog.	*Journal for Geography (South Africa)*
SABRA	South African Bureau of Racial Affairs
S. Afn Geographer	*South African Geographer*
SAGJ	*South African Geographical Journal*
SAJ of Afn Aff.	*South African Journal of African Affairs*
SAJE	*South African Journal of Economics*
SAIRR	South African Institute of Race Relations
SPRO-CAS	Study Project on Christianity in an Apartheid Society

Acknowledgements

This book was conceived in 1973 whilst I held a Visiting Lectureship at the University of Natal, Pietermaritzburg, and came nearer fruition during a second stay in 1975. To Professor Owen Williams and his colleagues in the Geography Department I am most grateful for the warmth of their hospitality and the stimulating working environment which they provided. Owen Williams has kindly contributed chapter 5 and the section on Transkeian elections in chapter 11. Bruno Martin, also of the Geography Department at Pietermaritzburg, drew Figs. 1.1 and 7.1–11.5, and himself obtained the information on which Figs. 11.2–11.5 are based from the Department of Bantu Administration and Development in Pretoria. Figs. 5.1 to 5.3 and 11.6 and 11.7 were drawn by Raymond Poonsamy of the same Department.

Many South African academics in other departments have helped at various stages of my research. I should like to mention particularly Professor S.P. Cilliers of the Sociology Department at Stellenbosch and Dr Gavin Maasdorp of the Economics Department at the University of Natal, Durban, both of whose ideas and approaches influenced my own thinking.

To Norman Pollock of St Edmund Hall, Oxford, I shall always be grateful for stimulating my interest in Southern Africa. I should also like to thank Diana Steer for her skilful typing, Penny Timms for drawing Figs. 1.2 to 4.2, and Tim Filkin for his careful reading of the manuscript.

Introduction

Geographers in South Africa itself have investigated many aspects of the geography of apartheid, or separate development as it is officially known, at all scales and levels of generalisation. Some of their work is to be found in the *South African Geographical Journal* and the *South African Geographer* (formerly the *Journal for Geography*). This book is an attempt to build on such research, as well as a considerable volume of relevant work by historians, economists, sociologists and others, to provide an overview of the geography of apartheid.

It is hoped that this will be useful not only to geographers, both within and outside South Africa, but also to practitioners and students of other disciplines who are interested in South Africa. The latter may be inclined to question whether there can be such a thing as a geography of apartheid, and it is to them that an introductory word concerning the perspective of the geographer may be most useful.

The history of geographical thought encompasses several distinct traditions, of which three of the most enduring are the ecological, spatial and regional approaches.[1] The ecological tradition, emphasising man–environment relations, has its origins in the 'classical' geography of Ritter and Von Humboldt. This approach has been revitalised by the broadening of the concept of environment to include man-made and psychological elements (the human and perceptual environments, respectively). The spatial view of geography, with its emphasis on location and spatial organisation, is currently tending to dominate the discipline, at least in English-speaking countries, although certain of its deficiencies have not escaped critical scrutiny. Haggett's recent attempt to synthesise the whole field of geographical enquiry admirably exemplifies this spatial approach.[2] The regional or area study approach stresses geography's synthesising or integrative role in the form of areal differentiation or areal interrelationships.[3] This tradition, whilst subject to much criticism for its holistic approach, its concern for the unique or the ideographic, and its subjectivity (ably defended by Paterson[4]) has shown a remarkable capacity for survival and adaptation, and continues to make a major contribution to geographical literature and research.

Each of these geographical perspectives lends itself well to a study of apartheid. The relevance of man–land relationships, and of man's perception of the environment, is variously illustrated by a study of the peopling and settlement of South Africa (Part I), the problems of White farmers in the 1930s, and the economic development of the African homelands today (chapters 9 and 10). Equally, few historians would deny the contribution of environmental factors in the emergence of a distinct Afrikaner nation with a recognisable set of social, religious and political attitudes.

Apartheid by its very nature creates spatial divisions, both macro-scale (the homelands) and micro-scale (urban group areas). From these basic divisions and laws relating to them arise a whole range of spatial and locational patterns of great interest to geographers. Social geographers study the geography of segregation and intergroup relationships, the migrant labour system, population pressures in the homelands, rural–urban migration, residential and commuting problems in cities, and the distinctive urban morphology of an apartheid society. Economic geographers are concerned, *inter alia,* with the spatial characteristics of the various sectors of the White economy and its dependence on non-White labour, policies of industrial decentralisation, the economies of the homelands and their potential development, and the effects of urban segregation and influx control on the economic geography of both urban and rural areas. The political geographer, broadly defined, is interested in many of these things too, for any geographical expression of political policies is legitimately his concern. More specifically, the emerging homeland map is of obvious interest to political geographers in terms of, *inter alia,* the resource base of the state (including its people), the organisation and control of territory, problems of small size and landlocked position, the application of a state's functions at its boundaries, the state idea and the importance of race, language and nation, external relations and participation in supranational and international groupings. Most of these subjects are equally important in relation to South Africa as a whole and her relationship with other states in and outside Southern Africa.

Underlying these spatial and environmental perspectives is concern for the geography of a specific area of origin in its totality. The regional geographer is concerned to provide 'accurate, orderly and rational description and interpretation'[5] of a particular part of the earth's surface. 'Accurate' does not necessarily mean 'scientific', for in dealing with problems of human creation and problems which require human solution the regional geographer must necessarily embark on what Wright has called 'realistic (objective?) subjectivity',[6] in much the same way as a historian who considers controversial actions, decisions and policies of the past in relation to their context. Minshull rightly regrets the tendency for regional geography to become an 'emasculated science' in its concern to avoid allowing any human aptitude, failing, emotion or interference affect its work.[7] This has unfortunately led to the neglect of many problems of vital significance to the countries concerned, even in otherwise detailed and scholarly works of regional geography. There is neglect of the personal viewpoint which is essential in regional geography. Thus the whole subject of race relations in South Africa, and apartheid in particular, receives little attention in Wellington's *Southern Africa*, which is in other respects a model work of regional geography.[8] The same author's *South West Africa and its Human Issues* is, on the other hand, a splendid example of the fruits of combining a scientific approach with 'realistic subjectivity' in the application of a geographical approach to human problems, and deserves to become a classic.[9]

The present work makes no claim to be a comprehensive regional geography of South Africa. Instead it takes for its central theme a subject which might justifiably be placed at the heart of a modern regional geography of South Africa, and to the understanding of which the geographer can make an important contribution.

References

[1] E.J. Taaffe (1974), 'The spatial view in context,' *AAAG* 64, pp. 1–16.
[2] P. Haggett (1972), *Geography: a modern synthesis,* Harper and Row, New York.
[3] R. Hartshorne (1960), *Perspective on the Nature of Geography,* John Murray, London.
[4] J.H. Paterson (1974), 'Writing regional geography: problems and progress in the Anglo-American realm', *Progress in Geography* 6, pp. 1–26.
[5] R. Hartshorne, op. cit., p. 21.
[6] J.K. Wright (1947), 'Terrae incognitae: the place of the imagination in geography', *AAAG* 37, pp. 1–15.
[7] R. Minshull (1967), *Regional Geography: theory and practice,* Hutchinson, London.
[8] J.H. Wellington (1960), *Southern Africa: a geographical study,* (2 vols), Cambridge University Press, London.
[9] J.H. Wellington (1967), *South West Africa and its Human Issues,* Clarendon Press, Oxford.

PART I

HISTORICAL BACKGROUND

1 The peopling of South Africa

In 1904, the year of South Africa's first official population census, the inhabitants numbered 5,175,000, and all the major elements of an unusually complex plural society had been assembled. The rate of growth in the present century has been such that the 1970 census recorded 21,448,000 South Africans, of whom just over 15 million (70 per cent) were Black Africans. The 3,750,000 Whites constituted the second largest group (17·5 per cent), followed by just over 2 million Coloureds (9·4 per cent) and 620,000 Asians (2·9 per cent). When the total population passed the twenty-five million mark in 1974 the African component was approaching 18 million.

The social, economic and political problems which confront this plural society cannot be understood without reference to the past. It is necessary to know something of the origins, movements, characteristics and early development of the various population groups which are the subject of the present chapter. The contacts and conflicts which have occurred between these groups and sub-groups in the past three centuries have had a direct bearing on the attitudes and policies which prevail today. Chapter 2 examines these cultural contacts in the context of evolving spatial patterns of economy and political organisation, to which they are closely related.

A word of caution is necessary. It was only towards the end of the fifteenth century, when Columbus was discovering America, that Portuguese sailors rounded the southern tip of Africa and found a new trade route to the East. The absence of written records prior to this time explains much of the confusion which prevails concerning the origins and extent of the various peoples already present within the borders of what is now South Africa. The picture is only gradually being made clear using archaeological evidence and anthropological research based on the oral traditions of present day inhabitants and genealogies, where these survive. This short introductory account of the peopling of South Africa can therefore only outline the present state of knowledge, without attempting to present the detailed evidence on which these conclusions are based.

The earliest inhabitants: Bushmen and Hottentots

Much confusion surrounds the use of the terms 'Bushman' and

3

'Hottentot', owing to the mistaken assumption that physical type, language and economy are necessarily correlated.[1] It is by no means the case that all Bushmen were small in stature, hunters, and spoke a distinct language (San), nor that all Hottentots were taller people, pastoralists, and speakers of a different language (Khoikhoi). Indeed physical anthropologists argue as to how to differentiate Hottentot from Bushman.

Equally mistaken is the assumption that Hottentots, Bushmen, Bantu and Europeans each occupied, at least in the seventeenth and eighteenth centuries, a specific area, where they remained isolated from the others. Such territorial separation was equally uncharacteristic of physical, cultural and linguistic groups. The assumption that it existed appears to reflect present day preoccupations with race and the existing social structure rather than historical reality.

The first people to inhabit South Africa were almost certainly ancestors of the Bushmen and Hottentots. The latter were both yellow-skinned and physically much alike; early European accounts do not distinguish between them on physical grounds, though it is likely that the herders were taller than the hunters, for whom shortness of stature was a physical asset. There is a marked similarity in the techniques and material culture of all the hunters and herders, and some similarity in their religious ideas, which argues long interaction. Khoikhoi speakers did not, however, share with San speakers a proclivity for painting.

The nomadic hunters and gatherers had no collective name for themselves, but were called 'Bosjesmannen' (Bushmen) by the Dutch. Their social organisation consisted only of hunting parties, numbering between fifty and a hundred people in most cases. Only the rudiments of tribal organisation and chieftainship existed. Amongst the herders, on the other hand, the number acknowledging one chief might reach 2,500. The long-haired cattle and fat-tailed sheep of the herders must have been introduced, since there were no potential wild ancestors in Southern Africa. This has been one of the major reasons for the widely held traditional belief that the herders migrated from East Africa, but it has been demonstrated that there is little anthropological or archaeological evidence to support such a hypothetical pastoral migration.[2]

Linguistic and other evidence indicates that contact between Khoikhoi speakers and the Nguni group of Bantu peoples began before the seventeenth century. There is also ample written evidence of continual interaction between cattle-owning Xhosa and one Khoikhoi group, the Gona, in the country between the Kei and Gamtoos rivers.[3] Interaction between Xhosa and Khoikhoi further west appears to have been more restricted, to judge from the difference between their respective breeds of cattle.

There is likewise evidence to show that Nguni and San long occupied the same territories, living side by side in some sort of symbiotic relationship. Periodic conflicts between the two groups may have reflected population pressure leading to competiton for grazing and hunting grounds. The San generally occupied the more arid areas and the high mountain grasslands where buck abounded, whereas the Nguni sought the better watered and less frostbitten grass and forest land suitable for cultivation as well as grazing. They were clearly conscious of the ecological boundary to the west, since they settled neither beyond the hills marking the eastern boundary of the dry Karroo, nor on the very sour veld west of the Gamtoos. It was the transition between these different habitats which was disputed between Xhosa, Khoikhoi, San and Dutch settlers in the late eighteenth century.

Neither Khoikhoi nor San are significant elements in the population of South Africa today. The hunting groups were forced by the combined pressures of Khoikhoi and Nguni herders and Europeans to retreat north and west into semi-desert regions from the beginning of the seventeenth century. Today most surviving Bushmen are found in the central and northern parts of the Kalahari, largely in Botswana, and in southern Angola and the northern part of South-West Africa. In the latter territory Bushmen numbered 22,000 in 1970, of whom just under 7,000 lived in the 'homeland' which has been allocated to them.

Two major epidemics of smallpox during the seventeenth century killed a large proportion of the so-called Hottentot herders. The remainder were largely absorbed by racial admixture with incoming Europeans and East Indian slaves, and have contributed to the groups known as Griquas and Rehoboth Basters (the latter have been allocated a 'homeland' in South-West Africa, where they numbered 16,500 in 1970), as well as the far more numerous Cape Coloured community.

Africans: the Southern Bantu

Africans known as Bantu occupy the southern two-thirds of sub-Saharan Africa. They are defined primarily on linguistic criteria, most simply as those Africans who use the root 'ntu' for human being. With the plural prefix this becomes 'ba-ntu' (Bantu) meaning simply 'men' or 'people'. It is because the term has such a general meaning that its official use in the Republic of South Africa is disliked by the people concerned, who prefer to call themselves Africans or simply Blacks. Bantu peoples in South Africa fall into two main language groups, Nguni and Sotho, and two much smaller ones, Venda and Tsonga.

The Nguni are a people who can understand one another's speech. Two of the more distinct dialects were written down by missionaries in the nineteenth century – Xhosa as spoken on the Eastern Cape frontier and Zulu as spoken north of the Tugela River – and these have stabilised into the two main forms of Nguni speech. In 1970 Nguni speakers in the Republic numbered just under nine million; others were living in Swaziland and Rhodesia.

The Nguni are herders and cultivators with a deep attachment to cattle, which were shifted from one pasture to another so long as land was plentiful; the new growth on sour mountain grassland was burnt in winter and used for spring grazing. They also kept dogs, goats and sheep, whilst other animals were introduced by Europeans. At least until the early nineteenth century the Nguni also depended for food and clothing on hunting and collecting, but avoidance of fish is an important characteristic. Sorghum was the major crop until the early nineteenth century, by which time maize, today by far the most important crop, showed signs of displacing it.

Scattered homesteads are a distinguishing feature of the Nguni. Among commoners each homestead was composed of two to forty huts. Those of chiefs were larger, and with the development of Zulu military power a population of 2,000 may have been reached in exceptional cases by military concentration at royal homesteads.

The precise distribution of the Nguni in space and time has long been debated. It now seems clear that the Nguni speakers have reached their present wide distribution in Southern Africa within historical time, spreading northwards from the area which lies between the Drakensberg and the sea, from the Fish River in the south-west to Swaziland in the north-east. Monica Wilson cites detailed evidence to disprove the long-held theory of a relatively recent migration of Nguni peoples (in association with other Bantu) southward from Central Africa.[4] A much more ancient migration to the country south of the Drakensberg now seems more likely.

The widespread scattering of Nguni-speaking peoples in the first half of the nineteenth century resulted from internecine strife associated with the consolidation of Zulu power under Dingiswayo and Shaka. Increased population pressure to the south-west of Natal was a direct result of this dispersal, and undoubtedly accentuated conflict with Europeans along the 'Eastern Frontier' of the Cape Colony (chapter 2).

Sotho peoples include those who speak 'southern Sotho', 'northern Sotho' or Pedi, and Tswana. In 1970 there were rather less than five million Sotho speakers in South Africa, and well over a million in Botswana and Lesotho. In the early nineteenth century the Sotho were hunters, herders and cultivators much as the Nguni were. Some of them eat fish, but many avoid it as do the Nguni. The main distinction between the economy of the Sotho and that of their neighbours was the skill of the Sotho as craftsmen. They mined and smelted iron, copper and tin, and traded extensively in metal goods. They were also skilled in leatherwork and in carving wood and ivory.

The remains of stone buildings are widely distributed over the areas the Sotho occupy. It seems likely that all or most of these were built by the Sotho, and in Lesotho at least they continue to build in stone. Most of the Sotho lived in large settlements of several thousand people, each of which was a capital in which an independent chief lived with his followers. Concentration of settlement has continued in Botswana, where it is explicitly linked with the authority of chiefs. Beyond the larger settlements there were cattle posts, whilst more distant areas were occupied by small groups of hunters who owned no cattle and became clients of those who did.

Traditions point to the well-watered and well-wooded Magaliesberg and to the watershed between the Limpopo, Malopo and Hartz rivers as the area of earliest Sotho occupation and as the centre of dispersion. Successive waves of Sotho immigrants from the north crossed the Limpopo, the first possibly in the thirteenth century or even earlier. Each group in turn either absorbed the earlier inhabitants or forced them to move westwards into the desert. By the early nineteenth century the Sotho were concentrated between the Limpopo and Orange Rivers, north and west of the Drakensberg, and across the upper reaches of the Limpopo.

The Venda are a small but linguistically distinct people, whose speech shows close affinity with Shona as well as clear connections with Sotho. They are a fusion between a lineage of incoming chiefs which did not cross the Limpopo until about the end of the seventeenth century and the Ngona and other earlier inhabitants. Like the Sotho, the Venda built in stone; their villages were sited in inaccessible places for protection, and were similar in size to the smaller Sotho settlements. The economy was based on cultivation, hunting and metal-working, including the mining and working of gold. In 1970 the Venda numbered only 358,000, many of whom continue to occupy the lush, wooded Soutpansberg range which runs east-west to the south of the Limpopo.

Several dialects are spoken by Tsonga people, who are known by several names. The most common in South Africa is Shangaan, which was derived from one of Shaka's warriors, Sashangane, who conquered the Tsonga in 1820–21. Oral tradition confirms that the Tsonga have long lived on the coast between the Save River and Kosi Lake, and at one time they stretched considerably farther south, beyond Lake St Lucia, until they were driven out. The Tsonga were deeply influenced by their Zulu conquerors, but remain culturally and linguistically distinct. One effect of the nineteenth century wars was to drive many Tsonga westward, so that they came into much closer contact with the Sotho and Venda, with whom they already traded. Their economy differs radically from that of the other peoples discussed, as fishing in coastal lagoons and rivers is an important activity. The rural Tsonga live in small, scattered homesteads like the Zulu. In 1970 they numbered 737,000, but more than twice that number were living in Mozambique.

Whilst Nguni, Sotho, Venda and Tsonga are real and significant subdivisions of the Bantu peoples of South Africa, none of them should be thought of as a homogeneous group. Nguni and Sotho are further subdivided by the government, which recognises ten Black 'nations', but each of these shows great economic, social and cultural variation. Fragmentation of political power into many chiefdoms has been the norm. Strong tribes frequently subordinated and incorporated weak ones, but consolidation into larger units (as with the Zulu under Shaka) was exceptional and generally temporary. Today, after a great deal of consolidation, there are still 624 tribes organised as tribal authorities, although there are constellations forming large blocks of territory, notably the 138 Transkeian tribes.[5]

It is equally important, however, to stress the common ground between the four main peoples. Whilst they must have lived in relative isolation to grow so different in language and custom, there was certainly movement between them, each absorbing remnants of the others. The chiefdom was always made up of peoples of diverse descent; strangers, even those who spoke another language, were accepted. There are marked similarities between the four groups in terms of symbolism, ritual and law. All thought in terms of kinship, and assumed the dependence of the living on their dead ancestors. The existence of the chief was assumed by all; his health was seen as related to the general well-being, and his function was primarily to settle disputes.

To this traditional common ground must now be added a common and growing experience of urban, industrial life (chapter 4).

The White population

The European contribution to the peopling of South Africa consists of two distinct elements, Dutch and British, which have largely absorbed other European groups. Each element has its historic 'core area' of settlement, which is still reflected in present day patterns: the Dutch in Cape Town and the south-west Cape, the English in the eastern Cape, including Grahamstown and Port Elizabeth.

The Dutch East India Company first sent Jan van Riebeeck to establish a refreshment station for its ships at the Cape in 1652. It was never regarded by the Company as anything more than this, although attempts to contain the areal extent of the settlement and to avoid trouble with the Khoikhoi and San inhabitants were quickly frustrated (chapter 2). The first few non-official Europeans came to settle as 'free burghers' in 1657, and their numbers increased slowly but steadily. Soon cattle farmers began to move across the Hottentots Holland mountains to become semi-nomadic *trekboere*.

The Company made only one significant effort to encourage immigration to the Cape. About 200 French Huguenots who had fled from France to the Netherlands subsequently emigrated to South Africa between 1688 and 1700. As they were interspersed with Dutch farmers and Dutch was the only medium of instruction in public schools, the French language soon began to disappear. The Huguenots intermarried with Dutch burghers, helping in the process to stabilise the 'free' White population.

During the eighteenth century more Germans than Dutchmen entered the Cape, but the pressure towards cultural uniformity continued to be strong. Burchell, writing of the 'Dutch part of the community' in 1810, described them as 'Africaanders, whether of Dutch, German or French origin.'[6] By the end of the century the Colony consisted of four districts with a total population of about 30,000. The Cape district was inhabited by the Company's officials and a non-official population that lived by keeping lodging houses, by fishing, brickmaking and market-gardening. At Stellenbosch there were well-to-do farmers who cultivated vines and corn, kept sheep and cattle, and built splendid 'Cape Dutch' houses. In Swellendam and Graaf-Reinet lived the stock farmers, occupying 6,000 acres or more per farmer and trekking on when the need arose.

When the French revolutionary armies invaded Holland in 1795, Britain occupied the Cape by arrangement with the Dutch King. By the Treaty of Amiens (1802) the Cape was restored not to the Company, which was now bankrupt, but to the (Dutch) Batavian Republic. The latter ruled the Cape for only three years before Britain realised that it would endanger her trade with the East if the Cape were to remain in the hands of an ally of France. She therefore occupied the Cape and retained it until the Act of Union in 1910.

The British government's initial attitude to emigration appeared apathetic, if not antagonistic. Its change of heart in 1820 is commonly attributed to the high unemployment prevailing in Britain after the Napoleonic Wars, but Hockly gives greater weight to the need for an inexpensive way of securing a safe eastern boundary for the Cape: to plant a dense European population in the Albany district west of the Fish River seemed the only such way.[7] Certainly the number of settlers involved (5,000) could effect no appreciable change in Britain's economic position.

These small numbers were, however, equal to about one-sixth of the existing European population of the Cape Colony, on which they had far-reaching effects. Because the settlers were English-speaking and had friends and relatives in Britain, the British government was compelled to pay greater attention to the Cape, and to institute a whole series of reforms. Later, when the Dutch frontiersmen trekked northwards (chapter 2), men of British stock found themselves engaged in frontier wars: 'it was as if the old garrison had moved and a new one was left to man the frontier.'[8]

Similar motives explain a further scheme of assisted immigration. This time it was not the defence of Albany but the consolidation of British Kaffraria (see Figs 1.1 and 1.2) that the British government desired. Members of a German legion which had fought with the British Army in the Crimea were granted land in the present Stutterheim-King William's Town area between 1857 and 1859. Nearly 3,000 settlers arrived, although more than 600 legionaries amongst them subsequently failed to return from the suppression of the Indian Mutiny. In the interests of social stability 1,600 German peasant settlers were also established as small farmers in the same area.

These German settlers were dispersed among a predominantly English-speaking population, but in small nuclei rather than on isolated farms. Like the Huguenots they gradually lost their cultural distinctiveness: the British authorities saw the importance of language as a means of preserving the identity of a cultural group, and in various steps compelled the public use of English in schools, courts and Parliament. The legion itself was disbanded in 1861, and German place names like Berlin, Potsdam and Hamburg mark the site of military posts from which the legionaries dispersed.

A third scheme of assisted immigration was privately organised by

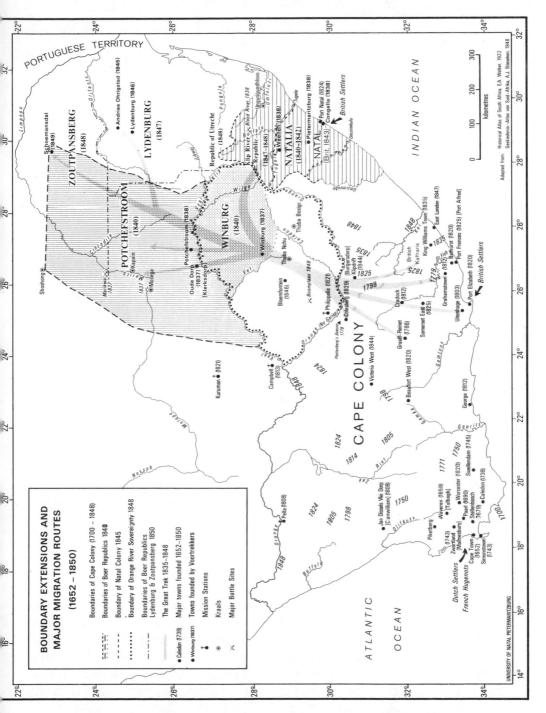

Fig. 1.1   Boundary extensions and major migration routes, 1652–1850

11

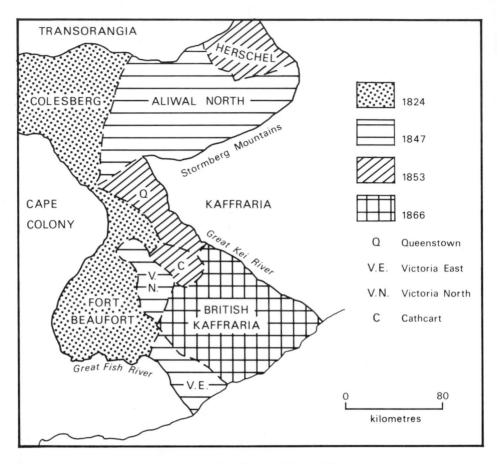

Fig. 1.2   Territory annexed to the Cape, 1824–66
Source: N.C. Pollock and S. Agnew, *An Historical Geography of South Africa.*

Joseph Charles Byrne with the sanction of the Colonial Office. In the late 1840s some 5,000 British emigrants were attracted to Natal, which was then only a district of the Cape Colony. They went to take up twenty-acre farms, which proved utterly inadequate in what was essentially grazing land: blocks averaging 6,000 acres had already been taken up by the Boers. The scheme was in most respects a failure. Nevertheless, most of the Byrne settlers stayed in Natal, whose European population increased from about 3,000 in the 1840s to 7,500 in 1852: thus the foundations of Natal's predominantly 'British' character were laid.

The low numbers involved in these settlement schemes reflect the generally small volume of migration to South Africa in the nineteenth century and subsequently. In the period 1820–60, when over a million people emigrated from Britain to Canada, Australia, New Zealand and the USA, only 40,000 emigrants of all nationalities went to South Africa. Likewise between 1860 and 1945 South Africa was relatively unaffected by the waves of non-British migrants who went to the other Dominions and the USA. Environmental conditions alone are insufficient to explain these differences. The real reason was the existence of a large indigenous population. More than half the people who emigrated from Britain were crofters and agricultural labourers, but in South Africa agricultural labour was performed by slaves, Hottentots, Coloureds and Africans at rates of pay too low to attract labourers from Europe. South Africa, unlike the other Dominions, had room only for those who could immediately become members of the employing class.

Slaves and the Coloured peoples

In the first ten years of European settlement at the Cape, a few hundred slaves from the west coast of Africa were brought in. After 1662 slaves were imported from Mozambique and Madagascar and from the Dutch East India Company's sphere of influence in the East. Many of these eastern slaves were Mohammedans, and some were highly skilled in various arts and crafts. Some of the Malays still form distinctive communities in the Cape Peninsula, Paarl, Stellenbosch and one or two other towns. The African slaves were a grade lower, working on the settlers' farms. Shiploads of African slaves continued to arrive throughout the eighteenth century, especially from Madagascar. The eastern supply of slaves, which was never large, ceased in 1767. In the period 1807–21 the import of slaves gradually ended, and with the arrival of the 1820 settlers slaves ceased to be a majority of the non-indigenous population. There were 39,000 slaves at the time of emancipation (1839), the vast majority of them in Cape Town and its agricultural hinterland.

The fact that 'White South Africa' started its career as a slave-owning community is historically important. The Afrikaners, even had they wished to work in urban trades, were denied such opportunities by the presence of skilled slaves. Consequently farmers' sons shunned the town, and the tradition grew up that, except in one of the learned professions (to which hardly any rural colonist could aspire in the seventeenth and eighteenth centuries), there was no occupation worthy of an Afrikaner but that of landholder. Thus the White farmers spread rapidly inland and away from civilisation, whilst the slaves and their freed descendants continued to do all the unskilled work as well as some of the skilled work in the western towns.

The Coloured population owes its origin to the seventeenth century slave population. During the first twenty years of settlement, 75 per cent of children born of slave mothers had European fathers. Intercourse and marriage with slave women were prohibited in 1685, but miscegenation continued owing to the predominance of European males over females. Intercourse between slaves and colonists became rarer as the Dutch farmers developed pride of race, but soldiers and sailors still had intercourse across the colour line. Children of these mixed unions could not hope to join Dutch society, and by the second half of the eighteenth century they were becoming a people apart. They tended increasingly to marry amongst themselves and also to have larger families than the Europeans.

Numerically, the most important type of miscegenation in the history of the Coloureds is that of slave and Khoikhoi. In 1708 the proportion of adult male slaves to adult females was 6:1, and even in the 1830s men still outnumbered women considerably. Since many farmers had both slaves and Khoikhoi on their farms, it is not surprising that miscegenation took place. San peoples also made a minor contribution to the Coloured population, as some of them, especially the children, were captured in skirmishes and apprenticed by White farmers. Later, San were hired as herdsmen by Boer pastoralists on the northern frontier, where they again contributed to the Coloured population.

The infusion of European blood continued, on a small scale, long after that of Khoikhoi and San had ceased, and was still occurring in the 1930s, according to Marais.[9] In the present day Coloured population of South Africa the slave strain is most important, particularly in the Western Cape. It is less prominent in the Cape Midlands and northern districts, where Khoikhoi and Bantu labour was much more important than slave labour. The Hottentot–Dutch 'bastards', who were fewer in number, tended to concentrate along the Orange River, where their descendants can still be found.

Four-fifths of South Africa's Coloureds still live in the Cape Province. Most of the rest came originally from the Cape, either in the days of the Voortrekkers or subsequently.

Indians in Natal

In Natal Coloured labour was lacking, and the coastal planters who were trying to create sugar and cotton industries required workers with skills and interests which were remote from the experience of African men, who left most of the field work to their womenfolk. At first the planters sought a break-up of the locations (chapter 2) in order to force more Zulus to work for them, but when the chances of this faded they eventually turned to India, following the precedent set by sugar planters in Mauritius and the Caribbean. The indenture system was duly extended to Natal in 1860. After five years' service the Indian became free to make a private arrangement with an employer, or to branch out on his own; many were offered land as an inducement to reindenture. After another five years they became entitled to a free return passage to India, but there was nothing to prevent them staying in Natal. This, combined with the requirement that at least twenty-five women were shipped with every 100 men, encouraged the establishment of a permanent Indian population in Natal, although this was not foreseen at the time. Between 1860 and 1866 over 6,000 Indians arrived, mostly low-caste Hindus drawn from areas of poverty and unemployment in India's south and central provinces. A major element was thus added to the Natal population, which included only 7,000 Europeans in 1860. Altogether 140,000 Indians came between 1860 and 1911, some of the later immigrants working on the railways, in the coalmines and in domestic service. About 10 per cent were 'passenger' immigrants who entered South Africa at their own expense to trade and serve in commerce.

The Indians were the final element of South Africa's plural society to enter the country, and for a long time their permanence was questioned. Prohibition of further immigration and strict controls on movement have ensured that they remain numerically the smallest and geographically the least dispersed of the major population groups.

References

[1] M. Wilson and L. Thompson (eds) (1969), *The Oxford History of South Africa, Vol. 1, South Africa to 1870,* Clarendon Press, Oxford, p. ix.
[2] R.R. Inskeep (1969), 'The archaeological background' in M. Wilson and L. Thompson, ibid., pp. 23–9.
[3] M. Wilson (1969) in M. Wilson and L. Thompson, op. cit., p. 103.

[4]   Ibid., pp. 78-102.

[5]   J.H. Moolman (1974), 'Consolidation', paper given at the 44th annual council meeting of the SAIRR, Cape Town, January 1974.

[6]   W.J. Burchell (1953), *Travels in the Interior of South Africa, 1822* (2 vols), ed. I. Schapera, The Batchworth Press, London, vol. 1, p. 21.

[7]   H.E. Hockly (1949), *The Story of the British Settlers of 1820 in South Africa,* Juta, Cape Town.

[8]   L. Marquard (1955), *The Story of South Africa,* Faber, London, p. 108.

[9]   J.S. Marais (1939), *The Cape Coloured People 1652-1937,* Longman, London (reprinted by Witwatersrand University Press, Johannesburg, 1957).

2 Spatial patterns of political and economic development, 1652–1948

Contradictions of Company rule

The Dutch East India Company instructed van Riebeeck to build a fort and lay out a vegetable garden, and to obtain sheep and cattle from the natives by barter, but to retain good relations with them. These orders soon led him to pursue contradictory policies. To produce supplies of meat as economically as possible he wanted the Hottentots to drive the cattle to market at Cape Town, but when they did so thieving and quarrelling occurred. The Company's servants, discontented with an arduous life in a desolate spot, were inefficient workers. They saw in the presence of the Hottentots an opportunity for private trade, which led to more quarrelling and dissatisfaction with the Company for prohibiting such trade. When supplies from the Hottentots proved insufficient, van Riebeeck began to establish his own herds and, from 1657, to encourage 'free burghers' to farm. This meant that Europeans occupied grazing lands which the Hottentots regarded as their own; after a small scale war in 1658 they were compelled to accept the loss of these lands. Above all, the Company wanted to limit its occupation at the Cape to what was strictly economic, but the very establishment of a class of non-official free burghers and the introduction of slaves were bound to lead to the expansion of settlement.

Partly to contain the settlement and partly to guard against Hottentot thieving, van Riebeeck planted a bitter almond hedge enclosing an area of about 2,400 hectares. Significantly, this early attempt at separation failed because the very economic demands which van Riebeeck tried to serve broke all boundaries.

The first free burghers were given holdings of only 11·3 hectares on which they bound themselves to live for twenty years. Their freedom was very limited: they retained certain military duties, and were not allowed to grow tobacco (a Company monopoly) or to trade with the natives. They suffered from lack of capital and labour, and when in 1664 South African farming endured its first depression, the burghers 'cried out aloud at the poverty of their lives and the smallness of their opportunities';[1] this was to be a familiar cry for many generations faced with environmental difficulties. The monopoly and restrictions of the Company were exasperating to a population which was still experimenting with its natural environment. The real failure of the Company in these early decades, however, was in its effort to insist on a type of settlement more suited to the climatic conditions of Europe, one which faced the sea and carried out an intensive agriculture which could be easily supervised from the castle. The task of the eighteenth century at the Cape would be to find a level of economic activity appropriate to the Colony's environment and geographical position in the world, and to produce a community adapted to its environment.

The size of the settlement grew slowly. By 1697 there were sixty-two families of colonists, but by then the first generation of children of colonists was petitioning the Company for farms in Hottentots Holland, forty-eight kilometres inland across the sandy Cape Flats. Simon van der Stel, van Riebeeck's successor, sanctioned expansion, although he attempted to control it. By 1685 there were about 125 settler families on the land and the Company began actively to encourage immigration to the Cape as a means of holding on to what had become a strongly fortified strategic post guarding the Dutch trade routes to the East. The Huguenot immigration was part of this policy. Van der Stel established South Africa's first village at Stellenbosch, granting freehold farms there and to the north-east at Drakenstein and Paarl in the Berg River valley. This policy of close settlement was seen as a means of checking illegal cattle barter and obtaining an easily mobilised militia, as well as guaranteeing cheap provisions. By the year 1700 the European population of the colony was 1,300 but there was no further Huguenot immigration and after 1705 the Company sent out no more Dutch settlers.

The end of the seventeenth century found the Colony unable either to pay its own way or to satisfy the needs of the forty-odd ships which called annually. Yet the Company's limited economic aims in promoting free agriculture were in sight of success: the Cape was becoming self-sufficient in cereals, as the first export of wheat in 1684 showed, and gradually viticulture was combined with cereal growing on many farms. At the same time the colonists' flocks and herds increased rapidly, partly as a result of continued illegal barter, and in 1700 the government was successfully petitioned to allow grazing outside the existing settlement.[2]

The Trekboers

Small as the population was in 1700, it successfully challenged the personal monopoly which Simon van der Stel's son, Willem Adriaan, was building up for himself during his governorship. A new period of colonisation was opened by the outcry of the colonists which finally led to Willem Adriaan's dismissal in 1707. The independence of the Afrikaners, as they were soon to be known, was foreshadowed by this incident: they regarded the function of government as 'protection', in the sense of ensuring that farmers had sufficient labour and that farm prices were high.[3]

The eighteenth century was the century of the Trekboers (trekking farmers) who were large scale cattle ranchers. The increasing demands of the Cape market for meat encouraged cattle farming, but more fundamentally the Trekboers were people who turned their backs on the difficulties and frustrations of life under Company rule. On a slowly widening frontier they developed an economy in which self-sufficiency was more important than profit. Three or four generations of unhindered movement with little effective government encouraged the Trekboers to regard all government as interference with personal liberty, and to believe that possession of ample land – not less than 6,000 acres – was an inborn right of all free men.

The Company was unwilling to spend money on extensive land surveys, and in 1717 halted the issue of freehold land. Instead 'loan farms' could be obtained for an annual rent which, if paid, entitled the farmer to sell or bequeath his land. This permitted the colonists to acquire land without capital and therefore enormously stimulated their rapid dispersal. It also encouraged farmers to overgraze and then move on to still more distant pastures. Theoretically the frontiersmen could not move on to fresh land without the sanction of the administration, but the Trekboers soon availed themselves of land without heed to anyone, those on the farthest frontier not always registering their farms or paying their dues. The precise doctrine of Crown Lands which was so important in the history of settlement in Australia, New Zealand and Canada was thus utterly lacking in South Africa.

The physical environment has a dual importance in understanding the rapidly widening frontier of the eighteenth century. On the one hand, it was permissive: the terrain was relatively easy to cross, without great mountain ranges, wide rivers or dense forests, and the climate posed none of the formidable obstacles which faced pioneers in Australia and Canada. In addition, the very mildness of the climate rendered intensive effort unnecessary: adequate homes were easily built. Yet on the other hand the environment was also limiting. South Africa's rainfall diminishes from the east coast, where it is plentiful, to the west where near desert conditions prevail. Over half the total area of the present Cape Province receives an annual rainfall of 250 millimetres or less, and as this falls in the summer months, the rate of evaporation is much higher than in the narrow belt of winter rainfall around Cape Town. Such a régime precludes arable farming and severely limits stocking densities. When Boers and Africans finally met in the last third of the eighteenth century, the latter had already penetrated beyond the area of comparatively high rainfall which lay behind them, further east: this circumstance alone, according to de Kiewiet, was enough to force the Boers to take the offensive.[4]

Isolation from the forces of civilisation, emphasised by distance, poor communications, and the lack of further immigration in the eighteenth century, was as important a formative influence as the physical environment. Tenacity, endurance and self-respect were the qualities developed by the Boers, but in the face of isolation these qualities could all too easily degenerate into obstinacy, resistance to innovation, suspicion of foreigners and contempt for those regarded as inferior. Lichtenstein, travelling in South Africa between 1803 and 1806, comments on the 'joyless existence' of the lives of the Boers, which is mirrored all too vividly eighty years later in Olive Schreiner's *The Story of an African Farm*.[5] They were isolated even from one another, coming together only in time of crisis or danger. In the absence of formal education and sufficient pastors, the Boers found justification for their beliefs and way of life in the Old Testament, particularly in the experiences of the Children of Israel in their search for the Promised Land. Such attitudes have far from disappeared today, especially in the rural Platteland.

The Eastern Frontier

By 1770 the Boers had reached the Gamtoos and Sundays Rivers and the Bruintjeshoogte (Fig. 2.1). Five years later they had reached a line stretching from Bushmans River to the upper Fish River. By the end of the century they had crossed into the Zuurveld (sour veld) and were facing Nguni tribes across the lower Fish River. The Eastern Frontier, so named in relation to Cape Town, was the scene of the so-called 'Kaffir Wars' which began in 1778. Each had its storm centre a little further east than the one before, beginning near the Gamtoos River, moving through the Zuurveld and the Fish River bush to the Keiskama, the Amatolas, beyond

20

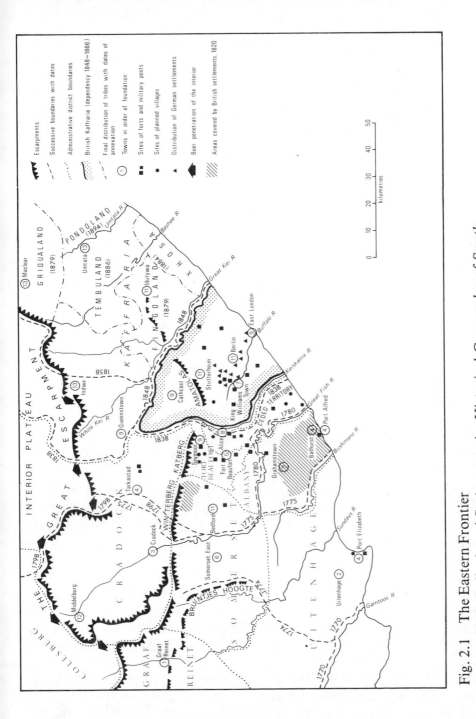

Fig. 2.1 The Eastern Frontier
Source: N.C. Pollock and S. Agnew, *An Historical Geography of South Africa.*

the Kei, and finally, in the rebellion of 1878 which ranks as the last war, to the Bashee River country. A detailed geographical interpretation of events on the Eastern Frontier has been made elsewhere,[6] whilst Macmillan's work is outstanding amongst studies which attempt to explain the historical complexities.[7] Only the broad environmental circumstances and men's responses to them need be noted here.

Within the border region, as it is known today, there is a threefold territorial division which clearly reflects past struggles. West of the Great Fish River and its tributary the Kat lies the land which was occupied by Boer farmers before 1780. To the east, between the Great Fish and Kei Rivers, largely hemmed in by the Katberg and Amatola Escarpment, lies the Ciskei. It is clear that Nguni tribes were in effective occupation of this area long before the Europeans, and were forced to withdraw spasmodically before the pressure of better armed White peoples. Parts of this territory were variously known during the 'Hundred Years War' (see Fig. 1.2) as the Ceded Territory (from 1819), Queen Adelaide Province (1836–37), and British Kaffraria (from 1847). This belt remains today an area of heavily populated African reserves and large, virtually empty, White farms. East of the Great Kei and its tributary the White Kei is the third division, the Transkei. This almost wholly African territory is amongst the most densely populated and closely settled rural areas in South Africa.

Differing attitudes to the land were a fundamental source of conflict. In the subsistence economy of the Nguni tribes, it was to no-one's advantage to claim exclusive rights to *property* in land. Colonial farmers, on the other hand, regarded tribal areas as wastefully used for intermittent grazing, and readily planted themselves on unoccupied sites where there seemed to be room, without asking about grazing or hunting rights. But the wide dispersal of the colonists themselves made their cattle an easy target for tribesmen who felt they were being dispossessed and had the advantage of being grouped more closely together in the bush country which afforded ample cover. Both the colonists and their rulers in Cape Town failed to see how the increasing disorders arose directly from the devastating effects of the colonial advance on the social and economic life of the dispossessed tribes. Meanwhile the expansion of the Colony merely intensified the Boer disposition to trekking and superficial agricultural methods.

For the Nguni tribes the problem was essentially one of 'lebensraum'. This was partly an internal problem: the territorial expansion natural to pastoralists, and indeed necessary in the face of population growth, had reached its environmental limits. The Highveld was uncongenially cold,

22

whilst the Karroo, which lay ahead, was so dry as to make the normal Bantu way of life impossible. The resulting struggles may well have contributed to the Shaka wars in Natal, which resulted in successive waves of displaced people pouring into Xhosa territory. All through the 1820s the Xhosa had to come to terms with organised hordes or broken tribes such as the Fingos and the Tembu killing, stealing and seeking new homes. Yet in the same decade the Xhosa were faced with the problem of accommodating other groups from the west. The clearing of the Zuurveld in 1812 had involved driving 20,000 Ndhlambi and Gqunukwebe tribesmen across the Fish River. After an attack on Grahamstown in 1819 the same people were pushed into the hands of hostile kinsmen further east beyond the Keiskama, and out of the Ceded Territory. The latter was not returned until 1836 ('on loan' during good behaviour), only to suffer military occupation in 1844. Meanwhile the position of the Xhosa and other claimants to territory became increasingly desperate. Violence against the colonists was their inevitable response to droughts which hit the border country in 1834 and 1846.

Despite these pressures, peaceful intercourse was by no means absent on the frontier. New slave laws in the 1820s made the labour shortage acute, and Ordinance 49 of 1828 provided for the granting of passes to tribesmen who wished to enter the service of colonial farmers. Trade across the frontiers increased in the same decade; the attractions of the Grahamstown fairs which had been established in 1817 proved so great that they were moved to Fort Wiltshire, a frontier post on the Keiskama. In 1830 this method of controlling trade was judged to be no longer necessary, and colonists were allowed to trade freely in tribal territory. This relaxation of restrictions and the 1828 Ordinance suggest that peaceful co-existence on the frontier was by no means impossible, given an equitable apportionment of land between rival claimants. Unfortunately, despite growing tension in the years after 1829, there was no hint of measures calculated to meet the essential problems of the frontier. Dr John Philip of the London Missionary Society was almost alone in arguing the need to establish the authority of law and ordinary civil government on the frontier.[8] Instead, the colonists continued to resort to patrols and commando raids, whilst the government attempted a series of solutions involving a neutral belt (the Ceded Territory), the shortlived Queen Adelaide Province, and a collection of unsatisfactory treaties in the late 1830s.

Drought and war had already done much to ruin the tribal system when 'British Kaffraria' was annexed in 1847. Two years later tribesmen were forced to choose between assigned 'locations' and service on colonial farms, thus initiating the modern search for work caused by shortage of land. At the time no-one could foresee the cumulative ecological effects of the continuous application of extensive agricultural methods to increasingly restricted locations. The best of the Ceded Territory and the Amatolas was lost for ever in the peace of 1853 which followed yet another war. Many of the forfeited districts were allocated to Europeans, an act described by Macmillan as 'the first deliberate exploitation of the plan of making South Africa a chess-board of black and white.'[9]

In 1856 the Xhosa were induced by an 'itola' (war-doctor) to kill their own cattle and destroy their crops, in the belief that their dead ancestors would rise and drive the White men into the sea. At least 150,000 cattle were killed, and by February 1857 the whole countryside was starving. The government chose to regard the cattle killing as rebellion. It confiscated much of the land remaining in the hands of the chiefs and planted it with Europeans, especially Germans. The spontaneous dispersal which followed the cattle killing itself was thus confirmed, and the reunion of fragments of Xhosa territory finally prevented. Thus it is that under the 1973 consolidation proposals the Ciskei consists of four widely scattered pieces of territory (see chapter 11, Fig. 11.2).

The Northern Frontier and the Great Trek

The human barrier to further coastal movement was extremely disappointing to the Boers, who were forced to turn northward instead of eastward, away from the well-watered grassland of the Transkei and beyond. Small scale northward movement occurred well before the 1830s, but the volume of movement from 1836 onwards was such that in the course of a decade between 12,000 and 14,000 people trekked out of the Cape Colony. The distribution of these Voortrekkers by the end of the 1840s foreshadowed the extent of South Africa today. Amongst the many consequences of the Great Trek, two are absolutely fundamental to an understanding of the country's subsequent development. First, the frontier between European farmers and Bantu-speaking tribes was extended from about 320 to more than 1,600 kilometres in a great horseshoe-shaped curve. From the middle of the nineteenth century onwards these tribes were progressively confined to the arid western periphery of the Highveld or the malarial northern and eastern subtropical and tropical plateau slopes and lowlands. This successful occupation of the Highveld is the second great consequence of the Trek, for not only was Afrikaner nationalism bred there, but the region also proved to be 'the richest parcel of real estate in the world'[10] and as such became the economic, demographic and political core area of South Africa.

The Great Trek has been the subject of extensive historical study, notably by Nathan[11] and Walker,[12] and its causes have been intensively scrutinised. Tactically, it represented a decision to give up the frontal attack and to undertake an outflanking movement, with Natal as the ultimate objective. Politically, the Great Trek was an essentially conservative movement, an attempt to preserve a way of life and the manner and thought of an age which elsewhere was quickly passing. More specifically, the Boers were retreating from a government which interfered with the relationship between master and servant, and was responsible for the freeing of the Hottentots in 1828 and of the slaves in 1833. Environmentally, the underlying cause of the Trek was land hunger: this was inevitable in a colonial economy characterised by a lack of agricultural markets and poor communications, and therefore dominated by subsistence pastoralism despite the dry climate and lack of winter feeding. By perpetuating and accentuating the dispersal of population, the movement made Boer isolation more extreme than ever.

The first people encountered by the Trekkers were the Griquas, weakly organised groups of mixed-breed refugees from the Colony, who had with the aid of missionaries built up small, unstable states north of the Orange River. Conflicts arose from the fact that the Griquas had settled upon the most desirable land along all the parched southern border, where crumbled layers of shales and jaspers beneath the soil held moisture, thus enabling the survival of permanent pasture. The government refused to extend the colonial boundary beyond the Orange, but made ineffective efforts to protect the Griquas which engendered violent Boer antagonism. By obstructing the way northwards at a critical period these weak states attained disproportionate importance. They forced the Boers further afield into the better watered country of the upper Vaal River, true Highveld, where grass replaced scrub.

The horseshoe shaped curve of dense Bantu population extended from Kaffraria, through Basutoland, Natal and Zululand, and Swaziland, to the northern Transvaal and its western border. Within this curve the wide open spaces of the Highveld were unquestionably capable of supporting many more inhabitants. Their exposure to cold winter winds, the want of shelter for cattle, and the difficulty of hiding from human enemies made them unattractive to Bantu tribes except for summer grazing. In addition the regiments of the Zulu king, Shaka, had crossed the Drakensberg and left a trail of destruction in the Transvaal, whilst one of Shaka's former lieutenants, Mzilikazi, who had broken away and established his own following (the Matabele), had laid waste vast areas in the eastern Transvaal. Tribes such as the Hlubi and the Mantatees, which moved north, exterminated other tribes or drove them further northwards. The charred remains of huts and villages understandably reinforced the Boer impression of an empty Highveld, which became firmly entrenched in the Afrikaner interpretation of history.[13]

The truth was more complex: from the beginning Boer and Bantu were intermingled. The open plains of the Highveld are frequently broken by low ridges, shallow depressions ('leegtes') and clefts ('kloofs') which, particularly where they have a northerly exposure, have patches of bush and often permanent water. Refugees sought security in such spots, which were precisely those likely to attract Boer farmers, and emerged when the latter had broken the power of their enemies. These scattered fragments of Bantu tribes were powerless against the Boers, and were in time reduced by trekker 'protection' to a large landless proletariat of farm 'natives'.

There was encroachment along the Zulu border, although the Transvaal escaped a Zulu war. Further north, in the direction of the Swazis, the Pedi and the tribes of the Soutpansberg, fever and broken country aided the Bantu in opposing European settlement, which helps to explain the extent of homeland territory in the northern Transvaal today (see chapter 11, Fig. 11.2). On the western border of the Transvaal, the struggle was less for land than for the springs and water courses without which the land was useless. The Bantu in these areas found their access to water, and hence the area of land in which they could live, severely limited. It was only at British insistence that formal rural locations were finally established in the Transvaal in 1907.

The Orange Free State came to regard Basutoland as the 'location' for its Bantu population, although two other small areas were set aside for groups who found favour with the government.[14] These survive as the only homeland territory in the Free State today, amounting to 0·4 per cent of the area of the province. The Free Staters had to struggle for many years to clear the east of tribes professing allegiance to the great Basuto chief, Moshesh, who was strongly ensconced in the foothills of the Drakensberg. In 1866 the Basuto were finally forced to yield well over half of this arable land, notably the fertile Caledon Valley cornlands. Many tribesmen became squatters on the new Boer farms, whilst this nineteenth-century Boer victory has left the Lesotho of today over-populated and impoverished, with much of its population crowded into the narrow lowlands bordering the Free State.

Britain's attitude towards the Boers was dominated by her reluctance to assume greater colonial responsibilities. Independence was thrust on the Transvaal Boers in 1852 despite their reluctance to shoulder responsibility for defence against Bantu tribes. The independence of the Orange Free State followed in 1854, thus destroying the land bridge between the Cape and Natal. Political isolation reinforced the aloofness of the Boers, whose fundamentally different view of the status of dependent peoples became a great unifying bond. Political unification was more difficult to achieve in the Transvaal than in the Free State, owing to its extent (over 250,000 square kilometres) and poor communications, but its four constituent republics merged in 1864.

The underlying assumption remained that Britain could resume full sovereignty if necessary, which she did over the Transvaal in 1877 because of the anarchy prevailing there. Unfortunately this did little to alleviate Black–White conflict and the distress of tribes on the various borders. The Boers themselves successfully rebelled in 1880 and regained their independence under the Pretoria Convention of 1881, which also defined the Bechuana frontier to their advantage. The Transvaalers, having found themselves master of more Bantu than they at first realised, had begun to insist on their right to manage these people in their own way, thus contributing to the mounting strain between Britain and themselves which ultimately led to the Anglo-Boer War of 1899–1902.

Meanwhile Britain remained watchful of her interests, especially the Cape sea route. Fear of the Free State gaining access to the coast was a major motive in the annexation of Basutoland in 1868, in addition to the protection of the Basuto against further displacement. Similar anxieties in relation to the Transvaal encouraged the insertion of a guarantee of the independence of Swaziland in the Pretoria Convention, and the proclamation of Bechuanaland as a British protectorate in 1885. Together these moves prevented the Transvaal from gaining access to the coast either eastwards through Portuguese East Africa or westwards through the newly proclaimed German protectorate over Damaraland and Namaqualand.

Natal and Zululand

The Voortrekkers hoped that, after the devastation of the Shaka wars and despite the presence of the Zulus, there would be room for many of them in the more genial climate of Natal. By 1840, less than three years after crossing the Drakensberg, the Trekkers had broken the military power of the Zulus under Dingaan. But they soon found the country far from empty. Away from the great stretches of Highveld seen by early travellers there are many secluded, inaccessible bush valleys such as the Umkomaas and the rugged upper valleys of the Mooi and Tugela rivers. Dingaan's overthrow allowed the weaker tribes who had found refuge in these valleys to move more freely once more, but the Boers mistakenly assumed that these natives – reputedly 50–80,000 in number – were 'filtering' from Zululand into Natal. Although they were glad of a labour supply, it was found necessary to restrict the number of squatters on any one farm to five families in 1840.

British annexation of Natal in 1843 was both a humanitarian gesture and a strategic move. The Colonial Office was uneasy over reports that Boers were capturing and apprenticing native children, but it was also alarmed when the Trekkers found their way to the coast at Port Natal, a small British trading settlement established a few years earlier. Annexation turned whatever republics the Trekkers might erect into landlocked states, economically dependent on British ports.

Britain's first problem was to provide for 'surplus' natives created by the usual Boer claims to farms of at least 6,000 acres. A Land Commission appointed in 1846 to delimit reserves included farms claimed by Boers in the native areas. Many Trekkers withdrew rather that abate their full claims, thus giving way to the anglicisation of Natal, which was firmly established in the 1840s by the Byrne settlers.

The demarcation of the reserves made no provision for population growth. At first this mattered little, as extensive Crown Lands were only gradually swallowed up by new White settlers, whilst White farmers welcomed labourers or share-paying squatters. In later years, however, as commercial agriculture prospered in Natal, the days of unrestricted squatting gradually ended: the coastal belt was thickly planted with sugar-cane, subtropical fruit and vegetables, whilst mixed farming spread over the Highveld districts. Thus a growing population of physically insecure Africans existed in 1893 when Natal became a self-governing colony. The problem was hardly reduced by the annexation of an overwhelmingly Black Zululand in 1897, despite previous British promises to the contrary. This led to the confinement of the Zulus to reserves within their own territory east of the Tugela, and the opening of the rest of Zululand to White settlement in the years 1902–4. This process of alienation, together with the much earlier loss of land to the Boers in Natal proper, explains why KwaZulu is today the most fragmented of the ten officially recognised homelands (see chapter 11, Fig. 11.2).

Kimberley, the Witwatersrand and the Anglo-Boer War

It was not until the mid-nineteenth century that South Africa's White population reached 200,000. By that time the country's first large export commodity, wool, was beginning to introduce a commercial element into Boer pastoralism. Wool exports increased in value from £178,000 in 1846 to £2,082,000 in 1866.[15] Hopeful though this was to a struggling colony, sheep-farming was hardly likely to attract capital investment from abroad or a large number of immigrants. However, the discovery of diamonds in 1867 in Griqualand West (annexed by Britain in 1871), followed by the discovery of the world's greatest goldbearing reef on the Witwatersrand in 1886, drew South Africa's patriarchal subsistence economy into the full stream of world economic development with dramatic suddenness. Investment and White immigrants poured into the country, much internal migration of both Blacks and Whites occurred, and South Africa faced modern problems of capital and labour for the first time.

The diamond fields were South Africa's first industrial community. The major fields around Kimberley were in Griqualand West, but the Orange Free State benefited considerably both from its proximity to Kimberley and from its own small diamond mines at Koffiefontein and Jagersfontein. By 1871 Kimberley had about 50,000 inhabitants, and the number of Whites exceeded that which had taken part in the Great Trek. Some 10,000 Africans worked in the mines each year, although the numbers decreased somewhat as diggers formed partnerships, partnerships gave way to companies, and companies were swallowed up by Rhodes' De Beers Consolidated Mines. Experience gained on the diamond fields paved the way for even more rapid growth on the Witwatersrand goldfields, which were proclaimed public diggings at the end of 1886. Johannesburg had a population of 102,000, half of them Africans, in 1896, whilst nearly 100,000 Africans were employed altogether in the goldmines on the eve of the Anglo-Boer War.

The distinctive characteristics of South African labour economics also derive from the circumstances in which these early mining operations took place. Labour was from the beginning divided into two classes: a large body of African labour earning very low wages, and a much smaller group of White workers earning high wages. This enduring division was not in the first instance simply the result of colour prejudice, although this certainly existed, as was shown by opposition to the attempted application of the more liberal labour laws of the Cape Colony. African labourers were unskilled, and left their kraals only for the duration of their contracts, whereas the Whites who came formed a permanent population,

29

bound by many ties to their place of work. They were also a compact, self-conscious community in a way that the Africans, drawn from every tribe south of the Zambesi and many farther north, could not be. The special position of skilled labour was further strengthened because it was, of necessity, imported labour: except for the wagonbuilders South Africa simply had no skilled workers on whom the mines could draw. An important consequence of this emphatic separation of Black and White in the mines was, and remains today, the elimination of an area of semi-skilled occupations which in most industrial economies offer the possibility of upward mobility based on effort and experience.

The cheapness of African labour was crucial to the development of the Rand. Whilst its goldbearing deposits are the most extensive in the world, they are also the poorest in gold content per ton. The major problem has always been one of payability, and it is unlikely that the goldmines would have been developed so extensively if only White labour had been available. In this sense the African contribution in laying the foundations of South Africa's present economic strength was a crucial one.

At the same time White farms were demanding much more African labour than hitherto, as industrial and urban demand created the base for a major extension of commercial agriculture. An important fact which has not been widely realised is that these same market demands equally opened up new opportunities for African commercial agriculture, which resulted in a virtual explosion of peasant economic activity in the early 1870s and a period of prosperity in the locations and reserves which stands in marked contrast to the predominantly subsistence agriculture prevailing in the homelands today.[16] Colin Bundy quotes ample evidence of this from the observations of magistrates in the late 1870s and early 1880s, as well as impressive recorded statistics of African production.[17] Even in the Transvaal and the Orange Free State, despite the minimal land allocation made to Africans, they found means of entering the market economy. The tenuous rule of the republics was insufficient to prevent Africans occupying, tilling and grazing nominally White lands. In areas of the Transvaal where land appropriation had been more effective, African peasants even succeeded in using the money acquired from the sale of agricultural surpluses to buy back land. Closely related to this emergence of a peasantry was the growing degree of differentiation and social stratification occurring within it.

The African's participation in the cash economy on his own terms threatened to reduce the availability of labour on mines and farms, particularly in view of failure to raise wages. The Whites used various methods to ensure a sufficient supply of cheap labour. Land under

30

African occupation was reduced, and the accepted systems through which Africans farmed White-owned land (labour tenancy, share-farming, renting of land) came under attack, as for instance in the Location Acts of 1876 and later years in the Cape. Likewise one of the goals of the Native Land Act of 1913 was to increase the supply of African labour.[18] The introduction of taxes was also designed to force peasants to enter the labour market.

Amongst various less calculated factors which adversely affected African commercial agriculture the most important was the relative ease of access by White and peasant farmers to markets. This was essentially a consequence of the development of the railway network associated with mineral discoveries, urban growth and greater commercialisation of European agriculture. Although the railway network grew from 101 kilometres in 1870 to 4,067 kilometres in 1891 and to 11,095 kilometres in 1909, most reserves were circumvented or entirely missed even by the many branch lines built during the latter period.[19]

Nothing could better illustrate the way in which the distance between the races in terms of economic development was actually widened by the capitalist development initiated by mineral discoveries. With less land in the face of an increasing population, and a greater need for cash income, Africans inevitably became increasingly involved in migrant labour. This in turn depleted the intensity of economic activity in the peasant areas (chapter 9), thereby reproducing the necessity for more migrant labour. The first steps had been taken towards creating the detribalised and landless proletariat which is characteristic of South African towns today, and which represents the greatest single problem facing the architects of separate development.

Meanwhile the great influx of Whites to the Rand caused more immediate political problems. Resentment at British annexation, triumph over the subsequent regaining of independence, and justifiable anger at the selfish refusal of Natal and the Cape to share import dues had stimulated Transvaal patriotism. The Boers inevitably felt their rural lifestyle and homogeneous society to be threatened by the arrival of cosmopolitan, aggressive immigrants (Uitlanders) in such numbers that by 1895 they outnumbered the Boers themselves by seven to three. President Kruger responded with measures which made it virtually impossible for Uitlanders to obtain the franchise, and also imposed other disabilities upon them. The Transvaal, no longer struggling financially, was also able to punish Natal and the Cape for their previous selfishness by imposing its own tariffs, constructing a railway to Delagoa Bay in Portuguese East Africa, and forcing the railway line of Rhodes' imperial vision to skirt the

Transvaal through the unproductive scrub of Bechuanaland. Rhodes in turn sought to foment dissident elements in the Transvaal, and planned the disastrous and ill-conceived Jameson Raid from Bechuanaland, after which war seemed inevitable.

In 1897 the Transvaal concluded a firm alliance with the Orange Free State, which until President Brand's death in 1888 had managed to champion republican independence yet remain within the orbit of the Cape Colony. Thus the war of 1899–1902 became essentially one between British power and Afrikaner republicanism, and one which destroyed Britain's long-cherished hopes of achieving federation in South Africa by peaceful means (an objective which is being discussed in a new context today: see chapter 12). The prolonged duration of the war and the memories it left inevitably cemented the unity of the Afrikaner people, which was to make its political comeback in 1948 and – in the eyes of some – to win the last battle of the Anglo-Boer War when South Africa became a Republic in 1961 and subsequently left the Commonwealth.

Agricultural problems after Union

Soon after the Act of Union in 1910 an attempt was made to bring some order into the African land situation. With the passing of the Native Land Act (1913) practically all existing reserves and locations were registered as 'scheduled Native areas' which might not be disposed of to non-Africans. Such areas amounted to 7·3 per cent of South African land, at a time when Africans constituted 67 per cent of the population (according to the censuses of 1904 and 1921). The Act also made it illegal for any African to be on European land unless he was a hired servant. This caused an immense upheaval in African life, forcing thousands of tenants into the reserves.

The 1913 Act was regarded as a temporary measure until the position could be reconsidered. The Beaumont Commission, set up to do this, recommended in 1916 that a further 6 per cent (6·7 million hectares) should be added as 'released areas'. The Commission's map suggested a considerable degree of consolidation, and included much European land within the proposed released areas. The denunciation of its recommendations by White public opinion and their rejection by Parliament were significant pointers to future White attitudes.

The distribution and extent of the reserves remained more or less stable for twenty years. By 1936 rural population densities per square kilometre were as high as 204 in the Transkei, 244 in the Ciskei and 106 in

Zululand.[20] Under such pressures the carrying capacity of the soil was clearly decreasing. The Report of the Native Economic Commission warned that:

> Unless precautionary measures are taken against overstocking, the condition in the Transkei and Native areas in the rest of the Union will be tomorrow what that of the Ciskei is today. The same causes are at work there, and they will inevitably produce the same effects in the near future – denudation, donga-erosion, deleterious plant succession, destruction of woods, drying up of springs, robbing the soil of its reproductive properties, in short the creation of desert conditions.[21]

The government responded by passing the Native Trust and Land Act (1936), which earmarked a further 6·1 million hectares, a little less than had been recommended by the Beaumont Commission, for transference to the Native Reserves over a period of ten years. In practice the purchase of these additional areas was slow, especially with the rise in land prices after 1945, but it is to the letter of the 1936 Act that the government adheres today, forty years later, in its homeland consolidation policies (chapter 11).

Meanwhile the reserves continued to deteriorate. In 1946 the Social and Economic Planning Council produced a report on the position of the reserves which observed that:

> Not only is the deterioration of the Reserves affecting the European areas through the drying up of watersheds, the spreading of soil erosion and so forth, but the general debility of the Reserve population means that the major portion of the Union's labour force is attaining only a very low degree of efficiency.[22]

It even appeared that the reserves were producing less food than a generation before. The Council stressed the need for improved farming practice, but urged that this should go hand in hand with diversification of the economy of the reserves. Meanwhile the African population found relief not by adopting intensive farming methods but in further large scale migration of workers to industrial centres.

European agriculture in South Africa was also beset with problems at this time. The instability of agricultural prices in the 1920s and the low level to which they fell during the Great Depression, together with very imperfect knowledge of sound husbandry under South African conditions, combined to produce a critical situation. White farms as well as the reserves were badly eroded as the result of overstocking, burning the veld, and insufficient care for maintaining the humus and water content of the soil. Farming had degenerated into 'Räuberwirtschaft' (a 'robber economy') in the 1930s, when South Africa was probably the most eroded country in the world.

These conditions were partly responsible for the plight of between 200,000 and 300,000 'poor Whites' in the 1920s and 1930s. The legacy of the Anglo-Boer War and the reconstruction of agriculture as it sought to produce for urban markets and export were also important factors. Drifting into the towns, this mainly Afrikaner population lacked experience of urban life, possessed no industrial skills, and found mining and industry largely controlled by English interests and conducted in what to them was a foreign language. They were forced to compete with Africans and Coloured people whose wages were too low to support a civilised way of life.

Such degradation of their fellows was unacceptable to the Whites generally. The seriousness with which they viewed the problem is reflected in the fact that the Carnegie Commission Report of 1932 runs to five volumes.[23] The government embarked upon a policy of encouraging manufacturing industries to provide a new field of employment for poor Whites, and introduced labour legislation designed to protect White workers. The Industrial Conciliation Act (1924), the Wages Act (1925) and the Mines and Works Amendment Act (1926) laid the foundation upon which subsequent policy has been built.

Industrialisation

The South African gold mines, unlike those in other countries, lasted long enough and were sufficiently large to sustain regional economic growth. The geological conditions were such that much machinery and equipment was needed and many 'backward' linkages developed to supply the industry's needs, particularly during the First World War when South Africa suffered from shipping difficulties and the inflated costs of European suppliers. With coal nearby, the Witwatersrand was the natural location for the development of heavy industry, whilst its growing population provided a large consumer market. The Transvaal overtook the Cape as the leading industrial area of the Union during the war, and continued to increase its share of industrial output until 1934–35, when it reached 46·6 per cent; since then it has remained approximately stable. The ports gradually became the 'servants' of this virile industrial interior.[24]

Tariff barriers, first erected in 1914, were strengthened after 1925, whilst the establishment of the South African Iron and Steel Industrial Corporation (ISCOR) in 1928 and a higher gold price further contributed to rapid expansion of manufacturing in the latter half of the 1920s and in the post-Depression 1930s. The powerful anti-cyclical effect of the goldmining industry helped South Africa to weather the Great Depression more easily than almost any other country. The number of workers of all races in manufacturing increased from 115,000 in 1924–25 to 245,000 in 1939–40, by which time secondary industry provided 18 per cent of the national income.[25]

The 1933–45 period is seen by Hobart Houghton as one of take-off into self-sustained growth.[26] The general boom attracted foreign capital, and domestic capital formation also increased markedly. Employment of Whites in industry rose rapidly after the Depression, and employment of other groups still more rapidly. The movement of Africans out of low-productivity subsistence farming into the modern sector of the economy was accelerated. During the Second World War, the manufacturing sector exceeded the share of mining in the national income. Manufacturing employment reached 361,000 in 1945, by which time the functioning of the South African economy was irrevocably dependent on the economic integration of all races.

References

[1]   C.W. de Kiewiet (1957), *A History of South Africa: social and economic,* Oxford University Press, London, p. 6.
[2]   M.F. Katzen (1969), 'White settlers and the origin of a new society 1652–1778', in M. Wilson and L. Thompson (eds), *The Oxford History of South Africa: Vol. 1, South Africa to 1870,* Clarendon Press, Oxford, p. 197.
[3]   L. Marquard (1969), *Peoples and Policies of South Africa,* 4th ed., Oxford University Press, London, p. 4.
[4]   C.W. de Kiewiet, op. cit., pp. 24–5.
[5]   O. Schreiner (1883), *The Story of an African Farm,* republished by Penguin, Harmondsworth, 1971.
[6]   N.C. Pollock and S. Agnew (1963), *An Historical Geography of South Africa,* Longman, London.
[7]   W.M. Macmillan (1963), *Bantu, Boer and Briton,* Clarendon Press, Oxford.
[8]   Ibid.

[9] Ibid., p. 339.

[10] O. Ransford (1972), *The Great Trek,* John Murray, London, p. xii.

[11] M. Nathan (1937), *The Voortrekkers of South Africa,* Gordon and Gotch, London.

[12] E.A. Walker (1965), *The Great Trek,* 5th ed., Black, London.

[13] See, for instance, D. de Villiers (1970), *The Case for South Africa,* Tom Stacey, London, p. 26; and Republic of South Africa (1974), *Multi-national Development in South Africa: the reality,* Pretoria, p. 22.

[14] A.J. Christopher (1972), 'South Africa and the Nation State', *Zambezia* 2, no. 2, p. 24.

[15] C.G.W. Schumann (1938), *Structural Changes and Business Cycles in South Africa 1806–1936,* Staples Press, London, p. 47.

[16] S.T. van der Horst (1942), *Native Labour in South Africa,* Oxford University Press, London, pp. 103–5; also M. Wilson (1971), 'The growth of peasant communities', in M. Wilson and L. Thompson (eds), *The Oxford History of South Africa: Vol. 2, South Africa 1870–1966,* Clarendon Press, Oxford, p. 55.

[17] C. Bundy (1972), 'The emergence and decline of a South African peasantry,' *Afn Aff.* 71, pp. 376–7.

[18] S.T. van der Horst, op. cit., pp. 291–3.

[19] W.M. Macmillan (1930), *Complex South Africa,* Faber, London, p. 212.

[20] Lord Hailey (1957), *An African Survey,* Oxford University Press, London (revised 1956), p. 761.

[21] Union of South Africa (1932), *Report of the Native Economic Commission 1930–2,* UG 22/1932, para. 73.

[22] Union of South Africa (1946), *The Native Reserves and Their Place in the Economy of the Union of South Africa,* Social and Economic Planning Council, UG 32/1946, para. 98.

[23] Carnegie Commission (1932), *The Poor White Problem in South Africa,* vols. 1–5, Stellenbosch.

[24] L.P. McCrystal (1969), *City, Town or Country: the economics of concentration and dispersal with particular reference to South Africa,* A.A. Balkema, Cape Town, p. 53.

[25] R.T. Bell (1973), *Industrial Decentralisation in South Africa,* Oxford University Press, Cape Town, p. 27.

[26] D. Hobart Houghton (1973), *The South African Economy,* Oxford University Press, Cape Town, pp. 16–17.

PART II

WHITE SOUTH AFRICA

3   The economy

The strengths of the South African economy are well known. An extraordinary wealth of scarce mineral resources and abundant cheap labour have permitted an impressive rate of expansion despite low individual productivity. In the 1960s the country's economic growth rivalled that of Japan; the GNP almost trebled between 1960 and 1973, when it reached £11,468 million. GNP *per capita* in the same year was £472, greater than that of any other African country except oil-rich Libya. Manufactures still comprise well under 10 per cent of South Africa's exports: she may be classified as a developing primary producer, whose manufacturing, commerce and services have been built up extensively on the foundations of mining and farming. Although the contribution of agriculture to the GNP has fallen to below 10 per cent and that of mining to just over 10 per cent, primary products (including gold, which may be sold or added to the reserves) still account for three-quarters of South Africa's foreign exchange earnings.

Foreign investment has played a leading role in both mining and manufacturing. It amounted to £640·5 million in 1936, or 43 per cent of total foreign investment in Africa at that date. Another large wave of investment occurred after 1945, associated with the newly discovered goldfields in the Orange Free State and the western Transvaal (see Fig. 3.1). Subsequently foreign investment slowed down, and a net outflow of capital occurred between 1959 and 1964. This reflected some loss of confidence in South Africa, especially after the much publicised Sharpeville shootings in 1960. In 1961 the country faced a severe balance of payments problem, but restrictive measures led to a remarkably rapid recovery which indicated the inherent strength of the economy. A revival in international business confidence followed, and a massive and somewhat unexpected inflow of foreign capital began in 1965. It has continued since then, and in 1972 foreign liabilities stood at £4,768 million (£2,659 million to the Sterling Area, mainly the UK), whilst foreign assets (including gold reserves) were worth £1,881 million, concentrated mainly in Rhodesia, Zaïre and Malawi. Some 40 per cent of South African industry is still foreign controlled, and this is an important element in the capital flows which usually offset the deficit on the current account of the balance of payments. In 1973 the net capital inflow amounted to £72·2 million.

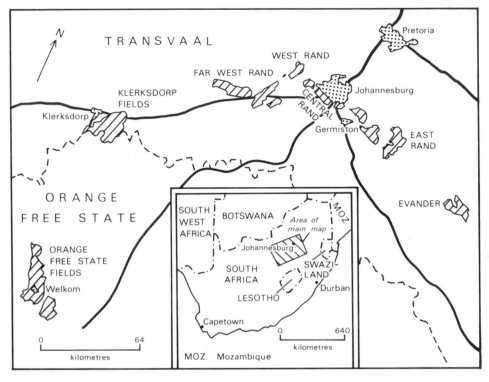

Fig. 3.1   South Africa's goldfields

South Africa has a mixed economy in which private capitalism
flourishes alongside growing state participation. As in the USA, the
individualistic capitalism and 'atomistic' economy of the nineteenth and
twentieth centuries are rapidly being replaced by the economy of the
larger private and public corporate enterprise. The twenty leading private
employers in South Africa provide more employment opportunities than
are totally available in either Cape Town or Durban.[1] It is estimated that
the top 100 companies provided employment for one in every six of South
Africa's economically active population in 1973.[2] At the same time the
government has established a number of state corporations which rival
those of the private sector, including the Electricity Supply Commission
(ESCOM, established 1923), the Iron and Steel Industrial Corporation
(ISCOR, 1928), the Phosphate Development Corporation (FOSKOR,
1950), and the South African Coal, Oil and Gas Corporation (SASOL,
1950). Most important of all is the Industrial Development Corporation
(IDC), with assets of over £240 million and at least 45,000 jobs under its

aegis.[3] Other state corporations are specifically concerned with the African homelands and with the Coloured population (chapters 7 and 10).

Labour problems

South Africa's economy is certainly not without its weaknesses, many of which stem from the use which is made of the country's labour resources. Whilst government policies have accentuated, if not created, many of these difficulties, they are in some respects merely a continuation or modification of practices which existed before the National Party came to power in 1948.

Prior to that date, Whites normally occupied the managerial and skilled posts, whilst other groups worked mainly as labourers. Exceptions included large numbers of Indians who ran their own commercial concerns and many who were independent market gardeners. Coloured artisans in the Cape, and to a lesser extent Indians in Natal, were employed in the building, furniture, leather and other industries. Coloured, African and Indian ministers of religion, teachers and nurses worked among their own people.

The first legal colour bar was introduced in terms of the Mines and Works Acts of 1911 and 1921, largely as a result of pressure from White trade unionists in the northern provinces. It was laid down that certificates of competency for many skilled occupations on the mines might not be issued to Africans or Asians. Strikes by African workers were made illegal. Shortly afterwards, even much unskilled work was reserved for Whites under the 'civilised labour' policy which was introduced in the public service in response to the 'poor White' problem. Private manufacturers were urged to follow suit.

Wartime and post-war mechanisation caused the fragmentation of many skilled jobs into several semi-skilled, operative jobs which were performed by Black workers. In addition, Coloureds, Africans and Indians were increasingly employed as drivers of heavy vehicles, clerks, salesmen, and insurance agents. White workers feared that such changes would mean lower wages or even redundancy if employees of other race groups entered a given occupation for the first time. These fears of competition were exaggerated, since South Africa's industrial expansion was probably sufficiently rapid for Whites possessing any ability to progress in the skilled and managerial field, but for the least able Whites the threat was real. As a result of these fears, job reservation was introduced in 1956. The Minister of Labour may reserve specified types of work for a given racial group, or he may lay down the proportion of employees of each race who may be employed in a stated industry. Job reservation determinations have since been applied in many industries.

Any restriction upon the full realisation of human potential is economically wasteful of the country's resources. Not only are individuals prevented from rising to positions which reflect their abilities, but the impossibility of doing so is a disincentive to efficiency in the jobs they actually hold. Conversely, the artificial protection afforded to some White workers also tends to lower efficiency, because they lack the incentive afforded by healthy competition. Job reservation has created shortages of skilled labour which have inevitably restricted the rate of economic expansion and resulted in artificially high wages. The government is understandably afraid of antagonising the very people on whom it relies for electoral support, namely the White working class. The grudging agreement of the White unions to relaxation of restrictions can usually be bought only by wage increases, thus further widening the overall Black–White wage gap. Nevertheless, the colour bar has shifted upwards in industries such as mining, steel and engineering, many exceptions to job reservation determinations have been made, and there has also been widespread underhand circumvention of job reservation, for instance by giving different names to identical jobs when performed by different races. The one enduring rule is that Whites do not work under members of other races, who are therefore not allowed to rise to supervisory and administrative positions.

Low activity rates are a further source of economic weakness. Only 37·3 per cent of Whites are economically active, compared with 42 per cent in Australia and 47 per cent in Britain.[4] This is partly due to the very low activity rate of White women, only 24 per cent. The overall activity rate of non-Whites is 35 per cent, which includes much barely productive work done by domestic servants and farm labourers.

The Human Sciences Laboratory at the Chamber of Mines has estimated that by 1980 South Africa will need 3·7 million skilled people, of whom Whites will be able to supply only 1·7 million.[5] Of the two million Blacks, 320,000 will need to be trained as managers, administrators and technicians. Yet South Africa entered the 1970s with fewer than 10,000 non-White graduates. In the face of these needs, industrial training of Africans is beginning to show signs of progress. In 1973 the government relaxed its ban on the training of Africans in semi-skilled jobs in White areas, although they still cannot become artisans, and decided to establish sixteen training centres in the main industrial areas. Generous tax concessions have been made available to industrialists establishing their own training schemes, provided that these are officially approved, but the private sector has been extremely slow to take up these concessions.

This reluctance in part reflects the attitude that it is the State's responsibility to train African workers. But it also reflects problems inherent in the migrant labour system, which is adapted to an economy based on extractive industries and agriculture that requires only a small percentage of highly skilled individuals in supervisory positions.[6] Increased training and dependence on African skills implies the stabilisation of the African labour force, but current policies are working against this in urban areas. It is officially intended actually to *reduce* the number of Africans permanently resident in White urban areas (chapters 4 and 8).

Low productivity is an inevitable consequence of the migrant labour system with its high labour turnover. More efficient use of labour is in any case discouraged by its very cheapness. Thus despite the generally impressive performance of the South African economy, increases in productivity have lagged behind those of most industrial nations. Output per worker in manufacturing increased by only 12 per cent between 1963 and 1970,[7] yet, as Horwitz points out, 'the South African economy is inescapably bound to the pursuit of growing productivity, which implies that economic rationality urges the polity beyond its ideology.'[8]

The migrant labour system and the restrictive nature of recruitment through labour bureaux has undeniably benefited the development of a modern economy in some ways. It has held Black wages at lower levels than would otherwise have been the case (which may be regarded economically as a mixed blessing), whilst it has averted the need to divert resources directly from productive investment to housing migrants and their families. Nevertheless, the economic disadvantages of the system now appear overwhelming. Many businessmen and industrialists oppose it, including the chairman of Anglo-American, Mr Harry Oppenheimer. The fundamental objection is the absence in South Africa, under present conditions, of a basic requirement of any complex capitalist system, namely a freely mobile labour force responsive to labour demands. The same criticism may be levelled at restrictions on the freedom of movement of the Indian population (chapter 6) and the restrictive effects of the Coloured employment preference area (chapter 7).

Wages and employment

For an industrial nation, South Africa's income disparities are extreme.

The country's four million Whites receive about three-quarters of the national income. In 1973 White:Black wage ratios were 5·1:1 in manufacturing and 14·5:1 in mining. The relative abundance of unskilled labour has kept Black wages down in the past, but the migrant labour system has held them at a lower level than would otherwise have been the case. Employers have been able to pay migrants less because their families remained in the homelands, whilst being 'footloose' has in turn undermined the migrants' bargaining strength. The migration of large numbers of Africans from neighbouring territories to work in South Africa has also had a depressing effect upon earnings in the Republic. The past advantages of cheap labour in developing the South African economy are obvious enough, but as industrial development plays an increasingly important part in the economy, the importance of raising African incomes to create a wider domestic market has become more and more apparent.

Between 1963 and 1971, non-White wage increases scarcely kept pace with those for Whites in percentage terms. In 1972, however, the situation began to favour non-Whites, whose percentage increases climbed to about double the rate for Whites in 1973 and 1974. In real terms, White incomes declined by 0·5 per cent in 1972–73, whilst non-White incomes increased by 2·7 per cent; in 1973–74 the corresponding figures were a 1·1 per cent rise for Whites and a 10·4 per cent rise for other groups.[9] Since July 1974 all groups have received large increases at a time of relatively high inflation. It has been argued that the large absolute increases in White wages arising from inflation redouble the urgency of further training schemes for non-White labour.

Several factors explain this recent improvement in non-White wages. The forces opposing investment in South Africa seem to have given way somewhat, first in the United States and subsequently in Britain, to the argument that investment is permissible provided that the foreign company concerned sets a good example in such things as wage rates, union recognition, and working conditions. The pressures on foreign companies were increased by a series of articles in *The Guardian* in 1973 about wages paid by British firms in South Africa, which led to an enquiry by the Expenditure Committee of the House of Commons. These events have undoubtedly contributed to the improvements which have taken place in African wages, but it is arguable that a second factor, industrial action taken by Africans themselves since the end of 1972, has been at least as important. According to official figures there were 246 strikes involving African workers during 1973 and 374 during 1974.[10] These strikes involved more than 75,000 workers and took place across a very broad spectrum of economic activity. The great majority were attributable principally to wage demands. The average number of hours lost per worker was only twenty, but the success of the strikes in pushing up wages is quite clear, and has spread beyond those concerns which were directly affected by strike action. The outbreak of strikes began in Durban but subsequently spread to other areas. In July 1974, for example, widespread strikes hit engineering firms on the East Rand and at Welkom in the Orange Free State. There quickly followed a wave of strikes in East London and the Border area. The government's response to the communication problem revealed by the strikes is the system of works and liaison committees, which by September 1975 represented 30 per cent of the African labour force (excluding gold- and coal-miners) according to the Minister of Labour.[11] However, official recognition of African trade unions continues to be ruled out.

Wage increases have been most dramatic in the mining industry. Average wages for Black miners rose by 78·8 per cent in the twelve months between the last quarters of 1973 and 1974 to R59 per month, whereas White mining wages rose by only 16·2 per cent (an absolute increase of R83 per month, however). This undoubtedly reflects the need for the mining industry to reverse the trend of the last decade, during which industry has been gradually outbidding the goldmines for African labour and the proportion of Black South African labour in the goldmines has fallen from almost 40 per cent to just over 20 per cent, with a corresponding increase in the proportion recruited from other countries (see Table 3.1). This is despite the fact that legislation restricting the movement of Africans into urban areas does not apply to mineworkers, a

Table 3.1
Foreign labourers in the goldmines, 1973

Country of origin	Number of workers
Malawi	109,723
Mozambique	83,387
Lesotho	76,114
Botswana	20,339
Swaziland	4,821
Angola	2,745
Rhodesia	2

Source: M. Horrell (1975), *A Survey of Race Relations in South Africa 1974*, SAIRR, p. 285.

factor which has hitherto diverted men who might otherwise have sought employment in other sectors into mining.

More recently, foreign recruitment has dropped considerably, and by early 1975 the goldmines' Black labour force had dropped to 300,000, only about 70 per cent of normal requirements. Malawi's suspension of mine labour recruitment in April, following an air crash in which seventy-four Malawian miners were killed, is partly responsible. Difficulties have also arisen in relation to recruitment from Lesotho, whose government has called for a meaningful labour agreement with South Africa based on Lesotho's needs and 'in line with civilised labour practices.'[12] Better wages and the possibility of Basotho mineworkers living with their families at mine compounds are the major issues. Further uncertainty has resulted from the change of government in Mozambique and the likely renegotiation of the existing Mozambique Convention of 1928. In November 1974 it was announced that the Rhodesian government had agreed to allow Rhodesian Africans to be recruited for work on South African gold mines,[13] but this source is unlikely to compensate for the loss of foreign recruits from other countries. Meanwhile outbreaks of unrest over wages and inter-tribal clashes at the mines, many of them involving foreign workers, have become disturbingly frequent since 1973.

White farmers will find it increasingly difficult to keep their African labour as mine wages continue to rise. In August 1973 the average cash wage paid to South Africa's 1,468,000 farm workers was a mere R11·50 per month. Most White farms are undermechanised and inefficient; they could afford to lose some African labour, given mechanisation and rationalisation, but this would require further government subsidies to an already heavily subsidised industry.

More competitive mine wages are also likely to induce the mining companies to cut the wastage of a high labour turnover, by encouraging African miners to acquire skills and stay in the mines. This will mean providing more of them with family housing: such housing exists for only about 1 per cent of Black mineworkers at the moment and is limited by current regulations to 3 per cent. If increasing pressures from the mining companies lead to a relaxation of restrictions, it will be increasingly difficult to regard the mining labour force as migrant workers in 'White South Africa' whose citizenship is in the homelands.

Certain forecasts in the Economic Development Programme (EDP) for 1974–79 also suggest that the demand for stabilisation of a greater percentage of the African labour force in 'White' urban areas will become increasingly difficult to resist. Much larger increases in Black employment

Table 3.2
Projected increases in Black employment

	EDP 1972–77	EDP 1974–79
Agriculture, fisheries, forestry	18,000	237,000
Mining	73,000	99,000
Manufacturing and construction	227,000	240,000
Services	406,000	600,000

are projected in several sectors than in the previous EDP for 1972–77 as is shown in Table 3.2.

An increase of 108,000 African workers is projected in the construction industry, whilst in manufacturing industries proper big increases are anticipated in metal products (43,000), non-metallic minerals (27,000), textiles (26,000), iron and steel (21,000) and clothing (19,000). These increases indicate the rapid advancement of Africans to more skilled jobs, and the relaxation of job reservation in many sectors. Overall, the non-White share of the manufacturing labour force has grown from 70 per cent in 1960 to 78 per cent in 1974.

Government support for the gradual closing of the wage gap has been emphasised in the mid–1970s. At the same time, economists recognise that wage increases must be related to increased productivity if they are not to impair South Africa's export position and result in serious unemployment. The need to maintain a high rate of industrial growth in order to absorb the natural increase of population of all races (chapter 8), and to give employment to those who are expected to move out of subsistence agriculture in the homelands (chapter 9), are important constraints on the rapidity of African wage increases. Quite apart from these and other constraints, it would require an absolute ceiling on White living standards and an economic growth rate averaging 6 per cent per annum to reduce the ratio of White to Black incomes from 10:1 to 2:1 by the end of the twentieth century.

Commercial agriculture and the rural population

Market-orientated farming, which accounts for 95 per cent of South Africa's agricultural output, is overwhelmingly in the hands of White farmers, whose land accounts for 72 per cent of the country's land surface. The contribution of agriculture to the GNP has declined from 22 per cent in 1920 to less than 9 per cent in 1972, but agriculture still accounts for one-third of South Africa's non-gold exports. White farming poses a number of problems in relation to policies of separate development.

In a pioneering contribution to the geography of apartheid, Brookfield published two maps jointly entitled 'The shrinkage of White South Africa.'[14] They showed that the areas in which Whites constituted 40 and 25 per cent respectively of the total population in 1951 were a mere skeleton of their 1911 extent. This was essentially a reflection of rural–urban migration, which was proportionately greater for Whites than for any other group except Indians. Huge areas of South Africa, chiefly in the Karroo and Western Highveld, had far smaller White populations in 1951 than in 1911. Whilst there has been no repetition of the exodus of 'poor Whites' since the 1930s, rural Whites have continued to decrease steadily in numbers. The number of White farmers has decreased from 117,000 in 1950 to 90,000 in 1969 and 82,000 in 1974, whilst the White farm labour force has dwindled to less than 20,000 workers. Between 1921 and 1971 the White rural population decreased by 166,000, whilst the African rural population increased by 1,842,000.[15] Cilliers observes that the pattern of internal population migration in South Africa's rural areas 'consists broadly of a population succession, in which the Bantu in particular act as successors to the White and Coloured occupants.'[16] Whilst such a process has certainly occurred as Whites and Coloureds moved to the towns, the overall number of agricultural labourers continued to increase substantially until the late 1960s, despite large-scale mechanisation and the decrease in the number of White farm units. The number of regular farm labourers increased by 5·4 per cent per annum between 1960 and 1969, whilst the number of casual African workers in agriculture increased by 11·3 per cent between 1961 and 1970–71.[17] These increases appear to have given way to a more stable situation in the 1970s; according to the Minister of Agriculture, the number of regular and casual African workers on White farms increased only marginally from 1,387,200 in 1968–69 to 1,391,300 in 1971–2.[18]

The rural Platteland has long been the Afrikaner cultural heartland and its declining White population has given rise to official concern over the 'verswarting' (blackening) of White rural areas. The Du Plessis Commission recommended that 'white agriculture must accordingly gradually be made less dependent on non-white labour and eventually be released from need of it as far as possible.'[19] As yet the government has done nothing to reduce the number of Africans on White farms, except in declaring a 'job preference' area for Coloureds in the Western Cape, where African numbers are anyway lowest. A policy of reducing African numbers in White rural areas might well improve agricultural efficiency by more effective use of the remaining labour force, but it would also pose severe problems in the absence of measures to relax urban influx controls and to enlarge the area of the homelands. It also seems strategically unnecessary from the Nationalist viewpoint since, as Dr. Verwoerd was quoted as saying, 'these widely separated Natives constitute no danger.'[20]

Economically there appears to be a strong argument for further reduction of the number of *White* farmers. As long ago as 1941 the Van Eck Commission argued that special assistance to agriculture 'often merely keeps inefficient farmers on the land and perpetuates or even accentuates unhealthy farming practices'; the Commission concluded that the movement of labour from agriculture to more remunerative industries was economically beneficial and in line with world trends.[21] More recently, the Du Plessis Commission found that the top third of White farmers produce over 85 per cent of total agricultural output and earn a return of R14·68 per R100 of capital invested, whereas the bottom third produce only 3 per cent of total output and earn a return of only R3·03.[22] The Commission concluded that the latter were uneconomic and recommended that they should be encouraged to move off the land. The government's acceptance of this recommendation marks the first public departure from the traditional South African policy of keeping Whites on the land at all costs. The United Party opposition, which has on more than one issue shown itself more conservative than the National Party, has urged increased government support for the bottom third of White farmers.[23] Although the proportion of farmers in the United Party is less than in the National Party, it does represent large numbers of English-speaking farmers in Natal and the Eastern Cape (chapter 5), and farming interests are strongly represented in the party hierarchy.

Farm workers have traditionally been amongst the lowest paid African workers. The agricultural sector was excluded from the protection afforded to African workers by the Wage Act of 1925 and the Bantu Labour (Settlement of Disputes) Act of 1953. The Natives (Urban Areas) Act of 1923 and subsequent amendments prevented Africans from freely seeking work in the towns, and has been administered in such a way as to direct labour and to keep it on the farms. No farm labourer can get a 'pass' to work in a town unless he has permission to leave from the district Labour Control Board, on which local White farmers and officials sit. Once familiar with these restrictive conditions, African migrant labourers often return to the homelands, whence they can go more easily to the White urban areas; this tendency has been increasingly noticeable in recent years.[24]

Controls and restrictions on African farm labour reflect the considerable political leverage long exercised by White farmers, who even managed to prevent the establishment of 'job reservation' in agriculture. Farmers replaced the White 'bywoners' (squatters) driven off the land in the 1920s and 1930s with cheaper African and Coloured labour, and today Africans and Coloureds do many of the skilled and even managerial jobs on White farms. In the 1950s the supply of farm labour was also swelled by convicts but, possibly as a result of widespread criticism, this has been reduced to around 13,000 workers,[25] and is likely to be phased out altogether.

There is considerable disagreement and confusion about the effects of growth and mechanisation on wages and conditions, and on the relative proportions of migrant and settled, and casual and regular workers in agriculture. Wilson[26] argues that mechanisation is leading to large-scale unemployment, and predicts that it will also result in a shift to more part-time migrant workers, pointing to evictions and removals from farms as evidence that this is already happening. He also believes that growth has brought no real benefits to the workers and that real wages have probably declined. Lipton[27] has demonstrated a number of flaws in this analysis. Mechanisation has increased yields rather than replaced labour, to the extent that if the index of agricultural production was equal to 100 in 1948, it rose to 149 in 1960 and 231 in 1970. Those being removed from the land were not labourers, nor, apparently, their families, but tenants or 'squatters', some of whom were the original owners of the land or their descendants. Farmers' labour needs in the 1970s have not so much diminished as changed: they are short of the able-bodied men who have gone to the towns, but on large, mechanised farms they no longer want large communities of women, children and old people. Thus while they still complain of labour shortages, farmers welcome the removal of 'squatters', and especially the elimination of 'Black spots', or areas of African-occupied land in the midst of White farmlands. The Du Plessis Commission found that mechanisation was reducing the need for casual labour in some areas, and anticipated a decrease in casual numbers accompanied by a switch to a smaller, better trained force of regular workers.[28]

Such a change in the size and composition of the labour force should enable farmers to pay, house and feed their workers better than hitherto. Lipton shows that the Black:White ratio, although extremely wide, was practically static in the 1960s: in 1968–69 the wage ratio of Whites to Coloureds was 7·5:1, and to Africans 13·7:1.[29] It is widely claimed that, with the extension of the system of labour bureaux during the 1960s, the controls over African labour have been tightened, and that their object is to keep wages down and differentials (favouring the low wage levels of the Orange Free State and the Transvaal) wide. In fact, wages rose and regional differentials narrowed in the 1960s as shown by Table 3.3.

Table 3.3
Average annual wages in cash and kind for Black farmworkers* (Rand)

	1961/62	1968/69	% increase
Cape	68	91	34
Natal	82	104	29
Transvaal	58	85	47
Orange Free State	50	74	47
South Africa	61·6	87	42

* Includes both regular and casual workers. Wages for regular workers in 1968/69 were on average 55 per cent above those in column two of the table.

Source: M. Lipton (1974), 'White farming: a case history of change in South Africa', *J. of Commonwealth and Comparative Politics* 12, no.1.

It appears that the prime object of the control system is no longer economic. Rather it has the political and strategic function of keeping down Black numbers and controlling the proportion of Africans permanently settled in 'White' areas. This is clearly compatible with the more efficient use of labour on White farms, but in itself such a policy makes no provision for the livelihood of the rapidly increasing African population (chapter 8).

Minerals and the economy

Despite growing industrialisation South Africa remains very dependent upon minerals, especially gold, for her foreign exchange earnings. Gold has, in the past, shielded South Africa from the effects of international recession. She produces more than two-thirds of the world's gold, but output has fallen from a 1970 peak of 1,000 tons to 758 tons in 1974. This has accentuated the effect of rising production costs: South African gold cost 28 per cent more per ton to produce in 1974 than in 1973.[30] Nevertheless, rising gold prices have ensured a continued increase in the value of gold output from R1,161 million (1972) to a record R2,560 million (1974). The increased revenues accruing to the government even led to discussion about how to spend the 'bonanza' in many South African newspapers early in 1974.[31] English-language newspapers such as the *Rand Daily Mail, Natal Mercury* and *Diamond Fields Advertiser* advocated greater spending on African education and training, and on homeland development. It was not expected that even the highest cost gold producers would cease production before 1980, by which time two new mines on the West Rand were expected to be in operation, and considerable expansion in the Free State goldfields would have occurred. A number of new sources of gold were also in prospect during 1975.

However, this pronounced optimism was severely curtailed early in September 1975, when the International Monetary Fund announced an agreement permitting substantial sales of its gold stocks. The subsequent slump in world gold prices led South Africa to devalue the Rand by 17·9 per cent, which demonstrated only too clearly the extent of the Republic's continuing dependence on gold.

Fortunately for South Africa, however, her mineral wealth is far from confined to gold as Table 3.4 shows.

Table 3.4
Principal mineral sales, 1972 ('000 Rand)

Gold	1,159,915·5
Coal	126,781·5
Copper (metal and concentrates)	116,591·3
Diamonds	90,028·8
Asbestos	38,031·0
Manganese (ores)	37,297·0
Iron ore	30,314·2
Nickel	25,887·5
Limestone and dolomite	21,788·6
Vanadium	21,576·7
Chrome (ore concentrates)	12,719·6
Phosphates	12,375·0
Antimony (ore concentrates)	11,063·9

Source: Republic of South Africa (1974), *South Africa 1974,* p. 613.

Consolidated Diamond Mines in South-West Africa continues to be the main source of gem diamonds; the production of South Africa *per se* is not separately disclosed. South-West Africa also figures prominently in copper production, but the largest producer is located at Phalaborwa in the eastern Transvaal (see Fig. 3.2), which is also important for phosphates. Another Transvaal town, Rustenburg, is the main source of platinum, the demand for which is closely related to the fortunes of the motor industry, platinum being used in catalytic converters in connection with American anti-pollution requirements. Nickel is a valuable by-product of platinum mining. South Africa produces about a third of the world's platinum metals, and a quarter of the world's antimony and chromite. Japanese markets are important for the former, as well as for manganese. Chromite is of strategic importance, as the principal sources outside South Africa are Rhodesia and the USSR: a British Steel Corporation plan to invest in a £20 million chrome-producing plant in South Africa was approved by Britain's Labour government amid backbench protests in 1975.[32]

South Africa and South-West Africa together contain a quarter of the western world's uranium reserves (more than any country outside the United States), and a pilot plant for the enrichment of uranium began production in 1975. The Republic's energy experts reportedly believe that large scale production of uranium for commercial purposes will put South Africa in the forefront of international energy production, adding significantly to her export earnings and strategic importance for the Western powers.[33] Uranium is partly produced as a by-product from goldmining, but there are indications of large disseminated uranium ore bodies in the Karroo, whilst possible further South-West African sources are also under investigation.

In view of South Africa's lack of known oil reserves, it is not surprising that she derives 80 per cent of her energy requirements from coal: following recent heavy increases in world oil prices this has been a source of strength (chapter 12). South Africa pioneered the technology of oil from coal production at Sasolburg in the Orange Free State, and in 1975 work began on a second plant, far larger than the existing one; together these plants should supply over 40 per cent of the Republic's needs for petrol and various derivatives. Such developments are made possible by the cheapness of South African coal, reserves of which are mainly found at shallow depths. In 1974 the pithead price was only R2 per ton, compared with an equivalent price of R6·30 in the United States and R12 in Britain.[34] Output has been steadily increasing and reached 58 million metric tons in 1972, whilst reserves are estimated at 80,000 million tons.

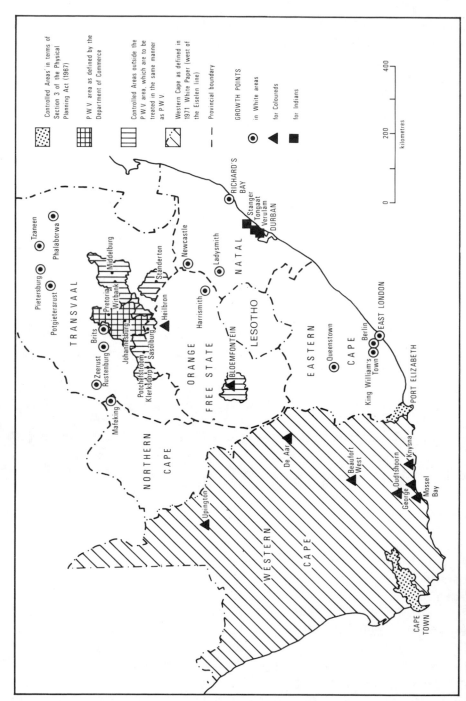

Fig. 3.2　Growth points and controlled areas

Legend:

Controlled Areas' in terms of Section 3 of the Physical Planning Act (1967)

P W V area as defined by the Department of Commerce

Controlled Areas outside the P W V area, which are to be treated in the same manner as P W V

Western Cape as defined in 1971 White Paper (west of the Eiselen line)

Provincial boundary

GROWTH POINTS

in White areas

for Coloureds

for Indians

kilometres

0   200   400

54

Iron ore reserves are likewise impressive. ISCOR owns large ore bodies in the north-west Cape, which are providing a steadily increasing share of local iron ore for its major plants at Pretoria, Vanderbijl Park and Newcastle. More than 4,000 million tons of high grade ore are known to exist.

The decline in gold prices and the relatively slow growth of industrial exports underline the need to export more basic minerals. Hitherto coal exports have been restricted to anthracite, but in 1974 a major contract was signed with eight Japanese steel mills to supply low grade coal, and a lesser contract with the United States to export bituminous coal. Iron-ore exports to Japan have also grown in the early 1970s. The limiting factor for exports of both coal and iron ore is the shortage of harbour facilities. Durban currently handles most of the coal (from northern Natal) and a little iron ore, whilst Port Elizabeth is the main iron ore port and Maputo (formerly Lourenço Marques) in Mozambique handles magnetite from Phalaborwa. The first stage of a major new harbour at Richard's Bay (see Fig. 3.2) is due to open in 1976, and will be able to handle all South Africa's coal exports. A new iron-ore port at Saldanha Bay in the south-west Cape has been under construction since 1973, and the first shipments should commence in September 1976, by which time the railway under construction from Sishen will be ready.[35] Meanwhile it has been decided to construct a further ore-exporting port on St Croix island, near Port Elizabeth. ISCOR plans large scale iron-ore export to Japan and the West – initially eight to fifteen million tons per year, rising eventually to thirty million tons per year. Sishen will develop into a major mining town in the late 1970s, although geographical isolation, the migrant labour system which will be used for African labour, and the capital intensity of operations will together keep any spillover effects of growth to a minimum.

Further evidence of South Africa's extraordinary mineral wealth is still coming to light. News of two major discoveries by American groups in the north-west Cape was announced in 1974. One is a complex ore body containing copper, lead, zinc and silver, and the other an extensive deposit of zinc with small quantities of lead. In 1975 preliminary news of important gold deposits in the Mafeking area was made public. This and other recent discoveries have brought good news for certain of the African homelands (chapter 10).

Industrial development and decentralisation policies

The early post-war years were very prosperous ones for South African industry. Factors favouring growth included the pent-up domestic demand of the war years, a large foreign demand and the discovery of new goldfields in the western Transvaal and Orange Free State. Import controls were introduced in 1948, primarily to restore equilibrium in the balance of payments. Between 1946–47 and 1956–57 exports of manufactures increased from 9·2 to 13·4 per cent of manufacturing output.[36] After the mid-1950s, the overall rate of manufacturing growth declined, principally because of the slackening of import replacement as a dominant growth force: it contributed only 16 per cent of growth in manufacturing production between 1956–57 and 1963–64, compared with 52 per cent in the preceeding thirty years. Although substantial import replacement potential still remained in the mid-1960s, it was confined largely to the heavy, intermediate and capital goods industries, which are dependent on large markets and economies of scale for their viability. Increased incomes for South Africa's non-White population would clearly widen the home market, and enable some industries at least to achieve the economies of scale which would make them more competitive in overseas markets.

Intending industrial exporters face another major problem, however. More than four-fifths of South Africa's exports are destined for markets over 5,000 miles away. A large proportion of them have to travel long distances from the interior to the ports. This does not matter too much when the product is a high value mineral or metal being disposed of in a perpetual seller's market, or a much sought-after commodity, but for manufactured goods seeking to compete in overseas markets the cost of transport as a percentage of the eventual price of the product can be crucial. The location of manufacturing industry in South Africa is, for obvious historical reasons (see chapter 2), not export-orientated. The Pretoria–Witwatersrand–Vereeniging (PWV) area alone is responsible for just over half of all secondary production by value.[37] The three other major metropolitan areas, all of them coastal, were together responsible for only 30 per cent of secondary production in 1968. The South African Railways (SAR) tariff structure has helped to discourage export-orientated location of industry. By favouring foodstuffs and raw materials over finished goods, it provides a locational advantage for regions with a large market, and therefore favours the PWV core area. SAR have now introduced export incentives for inland producers; reduced freight rates may be charged if a producer can show that payment of the full rate would prevent him from selling his products abroad at a competitive price. This will clearly encourage exports, but it will do nothing to alter the predominantly inland location of manufacturing industry.

56

A commission of enquiry into exports, under the chairmanship of Professor J.H.H. Reynders, recommended in 1972 that the government should provide incentives to exporters who move to growth areas near the ports.[38] This would have the additional benefit of creating employment in and near the homelands along the eastern seaboard where pressure for jobs is greatest (chapter 10). Existing growth points (see Fig. 3.2) include the following coastal locations: the Richard's Bay area bordering the KwaZulu homeland; the coastal belt north of Durban where three small Indian growth points are located; East London with the nearby growth points of Berlin and King William's Town, close to the Ciskei; the three Coloured growth points of Mossel Bay, George and Oudtshoorn (which are, however, far from any major port); and two further Coloured growth points of Dassenberg and Darling in the south-west Cape, designated only in 1974 and clearly linked with the projected growth of the Saldanha Bay area. The Reynders Commission also recommended other export incentives, almost all of which have been implemented, to overcome what is regarded as the complacency and lack of export-mindedness characteristic of South African businessmen and industrialists.

Incentives to export-orientated location of industry must be viewed within the wider context of government decentralisation policies. As Ratcliffe points out, 'the difference between industrial decentralisation in South Africa and elsewhere is not that it is to a high degree politically and socially motivated in South Africa (the same is true in other countries); but that in South Africa since 1960 industrial location policy has been directed largely towards palliating the adverse effects on income distribution of government policy towards the geographical dispersion of the population.'[39] The intentions of the Physical Planning and Utilisation of Resources Act (1967) and the 1971 White Paper on the decentralisation of industries were essentially concerned with limiting the growth of African urban population in 'White' South Africa, and with encouraging the decentralisation of industry to border areas and the homelands themselves. The success or otherwise of government policies in achieving these aims will be examined in chapter 10, but their implications for 'White' areas are relevant here.

The economic case for decentralisation on the grounds of excessive metropolitan growth has been examined in detail by Trevor Bell.[40] Whilst in a relative sense the concentration of economic activity in South Africa is high, in an absolute sense the degree of concentration and the diseconomies arising from it are small. The four major metropolitan areas, together with East London, Pietermaritzburg, Bloemfontein and Kimberley, had a total population in 1970 of 6·5 million, no more than that of Chicago alone.[41] If excessive urban growth is nevertheless accepted as sufficient grounds for implementing industrial decentralisation policies, then a limited policy based on the 'growth centre' concept might reasonably be implemented in respect of industries which are not 'locality bound'. Maasdorp[42] suggests a two-tier strategy utilising the existing urban hierarchy by focusing growth upon existing viable locations with a high potential for further expansion. In its initial stages growth would be concentrated on metropolitan centres, including Port Elizabeth–Uitenhage, East London–King William's Town, Bloemfontein, Kimberley, Vereeniging–Vanderbijl Park–Sasolburg, Orange Free State Goldfields, Pretoria and Pietermaritzburg. Subsequently, attention would shift to promote a few smaller centres such as Richard's Bay, Ladysmith, Newcastle and Witbank–Middelburg, rationally selected on the basis of accessibility to existing centres of production and consumption. Alternatively, if excessive urban concentration were rejected as sufficient grounds for government sponsored decentralisation, the need for more export-orientated industrial location would justify more limited decentralisation to what Rogerson calls 'export-processing zones.'[43]

Instead of either of the above strategies, South African decentralisation policy is designed to meet the goals of separate development. It leaves vast geographical gaps, such as the twenty-one magisterial districts of the Cape Midlands analysed by M.L. Truu,[44] who questions how much more of its population this region can afford to lose before it also loses its very development potential. Furthermore, some of Maasdorp's suggested growth points are actually treated as 'controlled areas', where industrial growth involving the use of African labour is restricted: this is true of Bloemfontein, Sasolburg and Witbank–Middelburg. Present policies also exert a negative or at best neutral effect on potential export locations. In terms of the 1971 White Paper, industrialists in the Cape Town, Port Elizabeth–Uitenhage and Durban–Pinetown metropolitan areas who plan expansion in decentralisation areas qualify for concessions in respect of the element of expansion involved.[45] In the Western Cape, employment of African labour 'will continue to be relatively restricted' and 'This area must be looked upon as mainly the employment sphere of Whites and Coloureds and the industrial development in the area will have to become adjusted to this pattern of labour supply.'[46] Port Elizabeth–Uitenhage is somewhat better treated, but the employment of additional Africans by existing firms is only allowed when registered unemployment amongst Coloureds drops below 2 per cent.[47] Durban–Pinetown is not a 'controlled' region, in view of its proximity to KwaZulu, although the planning of future industrial areas is to be restricted in order that

58

industrial development should 'proceed at a more moderate rate.'[48]

Present industrial decentralisation policies therefore give little encouragement to export-orientated industry, with the exception of the coastal growth points previously mentioned. They neglect ' "natural" growth locations which are situated at optimal points of potentially high interaction in terms of the total spatial system' in favour of the attempted creation of entirely new viable growth locations where none existed previously.[49] Such a policy ignores the fact that in an economy which is still undergoing industrialisation, spatial patterns of industrial growth will be constrained by economies of agglomeration.

Decentralisation also presents the government with a difficult dilemma. If it has an adverse effect upon the national economy, as the Opposition has alleged, the living standards of all groups will be affected and the overall rate of job creation will fall. This undoubtedly explains the very low refusal rate of applications for the establishment or extension of factories in controlled areas (see Table 3.5), although it has risen slightly

Table 3.5

Results of applications made under the Physical Planning Act between 19 January 1968 and 31 January 1975

Applications	Transvaal	Western Cape	Other areas	Total
Received	12,883	1,247	1,781	15,911
Granted	11,476	1,027	1,617	14,120
Refused	1,198	168	157	1,523
Under consideration	409	7	7	423
Percentage refused	9·3	13·5	8·8	9·6

Source: M. Horrell and T. Hodgson (1976), *A Survey of Race Relations in South Africa 1975,* SAIRR, Johannesburg, p. 182.

from 8·5 per cent in the period up to 31 January 1972 to 11·1 per cent between the latter date and 31 January 1975. The total number of potential African employees affected by refusals in the seven years to January 1975 was 182,183.[50] This represents an average rate of 11,740 per year, which can hardly have a significant impact either on the growth of the urban African population (chapter 4), or on the diversion of industrial employment to the homelands. It also seems probable that the Physical Planning Act and other measures restricting the geographical mobility of labour will tend to increase capital/labour ratios in the larger centres and so reduce the availability of African employment there,[51] without necessarily leading to the creation of an equivalent number of jobs elsewhere (chapter 10).

References

[1]   C.M. Rogerson (1974), 'The geography of business-management in South Africa', *SAGJ* 56, p. 87.
[2]   C.M. Rogerson (1975a), 'Corporations in South Africa: a spatial perspective', *S.Afn. Geographer* 5, p. 42.
[3]   Ibid., p. 44.
[4]   'Kruger's golden rand: a survey of gold and South Africa', *The Economist,* 22 March 1975, p. 32.
[5]   'South Africa', *Financial Times,* 25 February 1975, p. 22.
[6]   H. Adam (1971), *Modernizing Racial Domination: the dynamics of South African politics,* University of California Press, Berkeley, p. 154.
[7]   Republic of South Africa (1974), *South Africa 1974* (official yearbook), p. 558.
[8]   R. Horwitz (1967), *The Political Economy of South Africa,* Weidenfeld and Nicolson, London, p. 427.
[9]   South African Reserve Bank, *Annual Economic Report 1974.*
[10] M. Horrell (1975), *A Survey of Race Relations in South Africa 1974,* p. 325; M. Horrell and T. Hodgson (1976), *A Survey of Race Relations in South Africa 1975,* p. 210.
[11] *Financial Mail* (1975), p. 921.
[12] M. Horrell, op. cit., p. 287.
[13] *Rand Daily Mail,* 5 November 1974.
[14] H.C. Brookfield (1957), 'Some geographical implications of the apartheid and partnership policies in Southern Africa', *IBG* 23, p. 231.
[15] Republic of South Africa (1975,), *Geographical Distribution of Population: Population census figures on the basis of 1970 boundaries,* Department of Statistics (unpublished).
[16] S.P. Cilliers (1969), 'Social and demographic aspects of rural development', *Agrekon* 8, no. 2, p. 20.
[17] P. Smit (1976), 'The Black Population', in D.M. Smith (ed.), *Separation in South Africa: peoples and policies,* Queen Mary College, London, Department of Geography Occasional Paper No. 6, p. 56.
[18] M. Horrell, op. cit., pp. 278-9.

[19] Republic of South Africa (1970), *Second Report of the Commission of Enquiry into Agriculture,* RP 84/1970, p. 175.

[20] M. Legassick (1973), 'South Africa: forced labour, industrialization and racial differentiation', in R. Harris (ed.), *The Political Economy of Africa,* Schenkman, Cambridge (Mass.), p. 15.

[21] Union of South Africa (1941), *Third Interim Report of the Industrial and Agricultural Requirements Commission,* UG 40/1941, pp. 32-4.

[22] Republic of South Africa (1970), op. cit., p. 168.

[23] M. Lipton (1974), 'White farming: a case history of change in South Africa', *J. of Commonwealth and Comparative Politics* 12, pp. 56-7.

[24] P. Smit, op. cit., p. 56.

[25] M. Lipton, op. cit., p. 47.

[26] F. Wilson (1971), 'Farming 1866-1966', in M. Wilson and L. Thompson (eds), *Oxford History of South Africa: Vol. 2, South Africa 1870-1966,* Clarendon Press, Oxford.

[27] M. Lipton, op. cit., pp. 45-7.

[28] Republic of South Africa (1970), op. cit., pp. 158, 174-5.

[29] M. Lipton, op. cit., p. 48.

[30] 'South Africa', *Financial Times,* 25 February 1975, p. 25.

[31] *South African Press Mirror* 1, no. 6, pp. 8-11.

[32] *The Times,* 28 July 1975 *et seq.*

[33] *The Times,* 7 April 1975.

[34] *Report from South Africa* 12, no. 3, p. 13 (undated).

[35] W.H. Thomas (1973), *Greater Saldanha and the Development of the Western Cape,* Bureau of Economic Research, Stellenbosch, for the Syfrets–VAL Group.

[36] Republic of South Africa (1974), op. cit., p. 542.

[37] 'The Metropoles', *Focus on Key Economic Issues,* no. 11, March 1975, Department of Economics, University of Pretoria.

[38] Republic of South Africa (1972), *Report of the Commission of Enquiry into the Export Trade of the Republic of South Africa,* RP 69/1972.

[39] A.E. Ratcliffe (1974), 'Industrial decentralisation in South Africa', *SAJE* 42, pp. 166-7.

[40] R.T. Bell (1973), *Industrial Decentralisation in South Africa,* Oxford University Press, Cape Town.

[41] T.J.D. Fair (1972), *The Metropolitan Imperative,* Inaugural Lecture, Witwatersrand University Press, Johannesburg, p. 14.

[42] G. Maasdorp (1974), *Economic Development Strategy in the African Homelands: the rôle of agriculture and industry,* SAIRR, Johannesburg, p. 2.

[43] C.M. Rogerson (1975b), 'Export-processing zones and spatial planning in South Africa', *SAJ of Afn. Aff.* 5 no. 2.

[44] M.L. Truu (1973), 'Some effects of regional migration', *SAJE* 41, pp. 98–110.

[45] Republic of South Africa (1971), *White Paper on the Report by the Inter-Departmental Committee on the Decentralisation of Industries,* Pretoria, para. 88.

[46] Ibid., para. 34.

[47] Ibid., para. 35.

[48] Ibid., para. 36.

[49] C.M. Rogerson (forthcoming), 'Industrial movement and South Africa's decentralisation programme', *Journal of Southern African Studies.*

[50] M. Horrell and T. Hodgson, op. cit., p. 182.

[51] R.T. Bell (1973), 'Some aspects of industrial decentralisation in South Africa', *SAJE* 41, p. 422.

4   The towns

The urban spatial system

Whereas urban development in much of the world has been built on a firm agricultural base, in South Africa it is the industrial and urban demand which has created, and is creating, the agricultural response. The great urban industrial core of the southern Transvaal lies far inland in areas of limited agricultural potential. Its development has depended, in the absence of navigable eastward flowing rivers, on rail transport. Links to the coastal ports are of crucial importance. Those with the east coast ports – Durban, Maputo in Mozambique, and soon Richard's Bay – traverse areas of heavier rainfall and high agricultural potential, with the greatest densities of indigenous population which form labour reserves for industrialisation. For these reasons Mallows argues that links with these ports 'should be regarded as more than lifelines to the external world, but also as forms of valuable investment that should be optimised, with an increased urban and individual superstructure.'[1] He also notes, significantly, that the ports are exceptionally vulnerable, and only the relative inaccessibility of the Indian Ocean has for a long time prevented this vulnerability from being put to the test: this era may now be ending (chapter 13).

Early patterns of urban development in a few mining towns and ports have been reinforced by subsequent urban growth in these primate centres. During the period 1911–36, 77·2 per cent of the total positive net shift in the population of South Africa was registered in the seven primate and secondary urban nodes: Southern Transvaal, Cape Town, Durban, Port Elizabeth, East London, Bloemfontein and Kimberley.[2] Between 1936 and 1960 the figure was still 73·6 per cent, but there was some evidence of 'spilling out' by population increase into areas immediately adjacent to the Witwatersrand, Cape Town and Durban. In the 1960s much the same trends continued in relation to the White population, but upward shifts in the African population were more widely distributed.[3] In addition to concentration in major urban areas, they included a horseshoe shaped area of upward shifts stretching from the Swaziland border along the Vaal River and back across the middle of the Orange Free State between Kimberley and Bethlehem. This suggests that the spilling out of economic activity noted by Fair has extended with the progressive integration of this area and the southern Transvaal core region; it includes both recent industrial development and new mining developments on the eastern Highveld. The relative absence of upward shifts of African population in the western Cape suggests that the government has successfully restricted African population growth there, whilst shifts in the Coloured and Asian groups were mostly small, suggesting a general lack of mobility except for local reorganisation of their residential areas within conurbations under the provisions of the Group Areas Act.

This continuing pattern of urban concentration, albeit with a gradually widening base, is reflected in the peculiarities of the South African urban hierarchy (Table 4.1). South African cities appear considerably larger than the size predicted by Christaller's K = 3 central place model, whilst there are fewer centres than might be expected at the lower levels of the

Table 4.1

South African hierarchy of central places in comparison with Christaller's K = 3 model

Order		SA number of towns	K = 3 model number of towns	SA average size of towns	K = 3 model average size of towns
1	Primate metro-politan areas	1	1	2,180,914	1,000,000
2	Major metro-politan areas	3	2	754,352	300,000
3	Metropolitan areas	8	6	197,040	100,000
4	Major country towns	19	18	30,136	30,000
5	Country towns	57	54	11,131	9,000
6	Minor country towns	173	162	3,538	3,500
7	Local service centres	140	486	1,364	1,500
8	Low order service centres	200	1,358	1,047	800

Source: R. Davies (1967), 'The South African urban hierarchy', *SAGJ* 49, p. 9; R. Davies and G.P. Cook (1968), 'Reappraisal of the South African urban hierarchy', *SAGJ* 50, p. 120.

hierarchy because South Africa's less intensive pattern of rural development has never produced or required the dense network of villages and hamlets characteristic of Western Europe.

Physical planning and the urban system

The recently published National Physical Development Plan (NPDP), tabled in Parliament during March 1975, aims 'to regulate the settlement pattern in the Republic to the maximum benefit of all population groups,'[4] bearing in mind a probable doubling of the South African population during the next three decades. The principal physical development problems are seen as excessive population concentration in the larger cities, with resulting social costs of increasing congestion and pollution, together with the depopulation of many rural areas (presumably by Whites). The NPDP represents the translation into a spatial strategy of policies expressed by governments at least since the early 1940s, involving the achievement of a more evenly distributed settlement pattern which combines efficiency with equity, and reconciles a desirable degree of economic concentration with policies of dispersal.

To achieve these aims, a growth centre strategy is proposed within a regional framework. In the four major metropolitan areas, broad guidelines for land use are being provided by Central Guide Plan Committees. The rest of 'White South Africa' is divided into thirty-eight regions. Several categories of growth centre are identified (see Fig. 4.1), which 'the Government will concentrate upon and stimulate until sufficient momentum has developed for further growth to take place spontaneously.'[5] 'Planned metropolitan areas' include Saldanha and Richard's Bay, and the East London–King William's Town complex. 'Growth poles' are mainly middle ranking towns, together with a new centre in the north-west Cape tentatively located between Upington and Springbok. Development areas are envisaged, linking certain metropolitan centres and growth poles. In most regions without designated growth poles or planned metropolitan areas, 'principal towns' have been scheduled, although in some no suitable town has emerged, or more than one centre has fulfilled a principal role. 'Growth points' are those which the Board for Decentralisation of Industries has attempted to stimulate as border industrial centres adjacent to the homelands (e.g. Berlin, Potgietersrus, Rustenburg), as well as the new growth centres within the homelands. The new homeland capitals are omitted from the NPDP map of growth centres, as are the Coloured and Indian growth points.

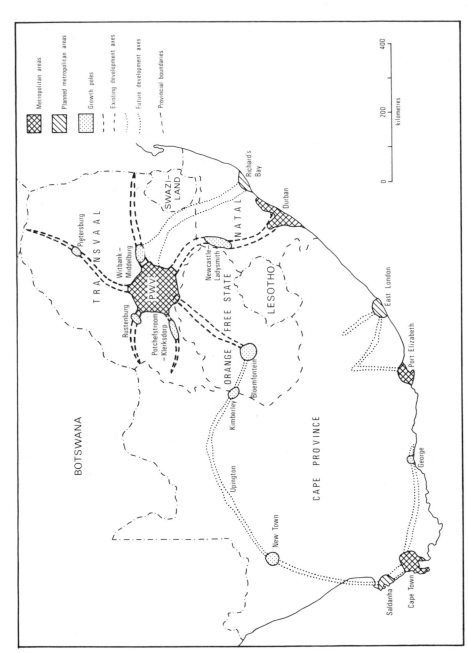

Legend:
- Metropolitan areas
- Planned metropolitan areas
- Growth poles
- Existing development axes
- Future development axes
- Provincial boundaries

0 200 400
kilometres

BOTSWANA

T R A N S V A A L

SWAZI-LAND

NATAL

Pietersburg

Witbank–Middelburg

Rustenburg

PWV

Potchefstroom–Klerksdorp

Newcastle–Ladysmith

Richard's Bay

Durban

LESOTHO

ORANGE FREE STATE

Kimberley

Bloemfontein

East London

Port Elizabeth

Upington

CAPE PROVINCE

New Town

George

Saldanha

Cape Town

Fig. 4.1   National Physical Development Plan proposals

Viewed in relation to separate development, there is a degree of ambivalence inherent in the NPDP. The most difficult problems of peripheral development in South Africa lie in the African homelands, yet these are omitted from the framework of planning regions, presumably because they are expected to follow the example of the Transkei in seeking independence. Yet the plan refers to the necessity 'to create new core centres [in the homelands] in places where there is little or nothing in the way of services or infrastructure.'[6] Fig. 2 of the NPDP gives the impression that the policy of more balanced development is confined predominantly to White areas. This may well prove to be the case, since the homeland growth points are locationally unattractive compared with the planned metropolitan areas, growth poles and principal towns in White areas where growth is to be encouraged. All the growth poles designated are already healthily growing towns, unlike the homeland growth points, whilst Richard's Bay and Saldanha are related rather to ongoing national economic expansion than to deliberate attempts to decentralise. Furthermore, the designation as growth poles of Klerksdorp-Potchefstroom, Witbank–Middelburg and Rustenburg, all within 150 kilometres of Johannesburg, will strengthen more than ever the PWV area as the nation's economic core.[7]

Professor Fair doubts whether the growth poles and planned metropolitan areas will be large enough to offset continued polarisation of the White population and of economic activity in the metropolitan cores, especially in view of the increasingly important tertiary and quaternary sectors.[8] Whereas in 1970 the four metropolitan cores had a combined White population of 2,454,000, the thirty-five planned metropolitan areas, growth poles and principal towns had a combined population of only 408,000. It may well be true, as Fair foresees, that the strategy will accelerate the present relative decentralisation of the system as far as the African population is concerned, as it will be implemented in association with continued influx control measures restricting the flow of Africans to metropolitan centres. But such relative decentralisation is occurring *within 'White' South Africa:* as such it cannot benefit the development of the homelands, nor can it reduce the urban African population in White areas.

Racial patterns of urbanisation

The semi-nomadic rural lifestyle of the original inhabitants of Southern Africa, based upon a subsistence economy, generated no urban settlement. The towns are thus an essentially European creation. The four coastal settlements of Cape Town, Port Elizabeth, East London and Durban remained the only notable urban centres for a considerable period, with a few minor inland market and administrative centres which were associated with the White migrations described in chapter 2. An intensified phase of urbanisation followed the discovery of diamonds and gold. As well as the mining centres themselves, small central places grew up on rail and road routes linking inland mining centres and ports. Initially it was mainly the English-speaking population which showed an affinity for urbanism, together with foreign Europeans attracted by mining prospects. The Boers considered urban life detrimental to their inherited, traditional ways of life, and Africans too were slow to exchange rural for urban life. Thus, as late as 1904–7, 54,000 Chinese 'coolies' had to be imported to fill the ranks of the permanent mining workers, especially in the Transvaal goldmining towns of Johannesburg, Springs and Benoni.

The first real urbanisation of the rural population started after 1902, as a result of devastations of land during the Anglo-Boer War, over-population on the reserves, cattle epidemics and long droughts. Further pressures to leave the countryside during the Depression years have already been described. But it is only since 1945 that intensified secondary and tertiary activities in the cities have provided a powerful positive attraction to rural Afrikaners. Since 1948 National Party governments have encouraged Afrikaner penetration of commerce, mining and manufacturing, to the extent that by 1970 Afrikaners controlled 40 per cent of total invested capital in manufacturing industry, 37 per cent of uranium, 32 per cent of asbestos, and 20 per cent of coal production, although still only 9 per cent of gold production.[9]

In 1904, 23·6 per cent of South Africa's population was urbanised, compared with 47·9 per cent in 1970. Urban Africans outnumbered urban Whites between 1936 and 1946, and now constitute the largest single element in the urban population. Africans as a whole are, nevertheless, by far the least urbanised group, and exhibit a degree of urbanisation (33·1 per cent in 1970) more characteristic of developing than of developed countries. African urbanisation has not even reached the level of the world as a whole, whereas the White and Coloured–Asian populations exceeded that level even at the first census in 1904.[10] Levels of White and Coloured–Asian urbanisation in 1970 (86·9 per cent and 77 per cent respectively) both exceeded the collective urbanisation figure for the developed countries. It is, however, the African urban population which has shown the fastest rate of growth since 1951 (see Table 4.2). Whilst the

Table 4.2

Table 4.2
Urban population growth, 1951–70

	Whites	Coloureds–Asians	Africans	Total
1951: Number	2,089,000	1,016,000	2,391,000	5,494,000
Urbanised (%)	79·1	69·1	27·9	43·4
1960: Number	2,575,000	1,428,000	3,471,000	7,474,000
Urbanised (%)	83·6	71·9	31·8	46·7
Annual increase (%)	2·3	3·8	4·2	3·5
1970: Number	3,258,000	2,033,000	4,989,000	10,280,000
Urbanised (%)	86·9	77·0	33·1	47·9
Annual increase (%)	2·3	3·5	3·8	3·3

Source: I.J. van der Merwe (1973), 'Differential Urbanization in South Africa', *Geography* 58, p. 338.

small decrease in the African growth rate in the 1960s may partly reflect the success of government controls, it is also influenced by changed census definitions. Even in terms of the census figures the ratio between urban Africans and Whites widened from 1·35:1 in 1960 to 1·53:1 in 1970.

Origins and development of urban segregation and influx control

During the early years of town growth in South Africa, African settlement was not controlled. Thus in Durban the mayoral Minutes of 1887 report a public meeting which discussed assaults and other crimes by Africans and asked that locations should be established at a convenient distance from the town.[11] Most Africans at that time lived in shacks and hovels and were not residentially segregated; the only planned accommodation consisted of barracks erected for male labourers by the city council and by private enterprise. Such hostels, as they are now known, remain a distinctive feature of the South African urban scene today. The general policy in Durban, as in most towns, was initially to achieve segregation without compulsion by attracting the population to segregated facilities. The Orange Free State was the most deliberately segregationist colony: by a law of 1893, only Whites could own or lease fixed property in Free State towns.

Regulations for the control of urban Africans, Indians and Coloureds were gradually introduced for a number of reasons: because of the obvious social, cultural and economic differences between Whites and other races in the early twentieth century; to cushion the unfamiliarity of other races with White urban culture; to control and channel labour; to deal with misfits and contain crime; and to prevent the spread of contagious diseases (the establishment of locations in Cape Town, Port Elizabeth and Johannesburg was precipitated by a frantic effort to limit bubonic plague).[12] By the time of Union, most Africans, Indians and Coloureds lived in special areas allocated to them, but the locations themselves quickly became a problem. Thus the Tuberculosis Commission reported in 1914 that the kinds of conditions in which tuberculosis flourished were the rule rather than the exception in locations throughout South Africa.[13] A bad influenza epidemic in 1918 revealed the distressing conditions in which Africans lived and the health threat which they posed. In Johannesburg this aroused the civic conscience and led to the first African housing schemes, but it is indicative of contemporary attitudes that 'Native locations' were the responsibility of the city's Parks Department in the 1920s.[14]

Official attitudes to urban Africans today are remarkably close to those expressed by the Report of the Stallard (Transvaal Local Government) Commission of 1922 in its oft quoted dictum that:

> . . . the native should only be allowed to enter urban areas, which are essentially the White man's creation, when he is willing to enter and minister to the needs of the White man, and should depart therefrom when he ceases so to minister.[15]

One of the most controversial proposals in debates leading up to the passing of the Natives (Urban Areas) Act of 1923 was to give Africans the possibility of freehold title to land in 'White' towns. In the event this right was denied: there was a widespread fear, especially among parliamentarians from the Orange Free State, that the extension of rights to Africans in towns might in the long term undermine the security of the Whites. This opposition from the Free Staters to freehold rights for Africans in urban locations in the 1920s was to be matched by their opposition to African trading rights in the 1930s.[16]

The 1923 Act was not a harsh one by later standards. It empowered urban local authorities to set aside land for African occupation in locations, and to house Africans living in the town or require their employers to do so. It stopped Whites from owning or occupying premises in locations, and prevented unexempted Africans from living outside them, though their right to buy property outside locations remained until 1937. Restrictions were imposed on African residence in peri-urban areas, but these were difficult to implement. Municipalities were required to keep separate Native revenue accounts, and the revenue accruing to them from rents, fines and beer hall profits had to be spent on the welfare of the location, which had not always been the case hitherto. The Act also provided for an embryonic form of consultation through advisory boards, and brought location brewing and trading under a system of control, which was for the local authorities to use or abuse.

Adoption of the Act was optional. Some municipalities, especially larger ones such as Bloemfontein and Johannesburg, adopted it without delay. There was some reluctance among smaller municipalities, which feared that adoption of the Act might involve them in excessive financial responsibilities, but by 1937 most urban locations had been registered. Few local authorities, however, were prepared to subsidise African housing from general revenue in the inter-war years; by 1942, only 41 out of 472 urban councils had secured loans for urban housing.[17]

Machinery providing for systematic control over the African influx to the towns was introduced only in the Native Laws Amendment Act of 1937. The urban African population had risen from 587,000 in 1921 to 1,150,000 in 1936, and was increasing steadily in response to the demands of expanding industry. Under the new Act, Africans coming to the towns were allowed fourteen days to find work (only seventy-two hours are permitted today), and individual Africans might be 'rusticated' if the municipal returns showed a labour surplus in the area. The government was also anxious to curb the growth of female urbanisation, but shrank from making women carry passes, without which the policy was probably unenforceable, on account of the unrest which had developed in the Free State over this issue in 1913.[18] When passes for African women came back in the late 1950s serious unrest broke out again.

Whilst segregation was accepted by both main parliamentary parties, the Nationalist Opposition continually criticised the United Party government after 1933 for failing to implement the policy with sufficient rigour, thereby allegedly allowing 'surplus' Africans to accumulate in the towns and depriving farmers of labour. Between 1942 and 1948, when industrialists began to stress the value of semi-skilled Africans in manufacturing employment, the government appeared slowly to be recognising the need for reform of urban African policy. Industry expanded rapidly during the war and the demand for labour increased dramatically. At the same time several official voices urged reform. The Van Eck Commission considered a further townward movement of Africans to be an economic necessity if rural African incomes were to rise to a level comparable with urban ones.[19] In 1942 the Smit Committee[20] and in 1946 the Social and Economic Planning

Council[21] condemned the migrant labour system. The latter emphasised the need for the development of a permanent urban labour force, and would have rejected the continuation of migrant labour on the goldmines 'were it not convinced that the mines are a disappearing asset.' Smuts himself viewed African urbanisation realistically, observing:

> Segregation tried to stop it. It has, however, not stopped it in the least. The process has been accelerated. You might as well try to sweep the ocean back with a broom.[22]

His government was, nevertheless, responsible for the Natives (Urban Areas) Consolidation Act of 1945, which further restricted African rights in urban areas. Under Section 10 of the Act, which remains in force (as amended) today, an African may claim permanent residence in an urban area only if he has resided there continuously since birth, has lawfully resided there continuously for fifteen years, or has worked there for the same employer for ten years. Dependants of those who qualify under Section 10 were also entitled to permanent residence in the same area, but since 1964 women have been refused entry unless they qualified independently of their husbands. This, together with the removal of women from urban areas, is eroding the number who can qualify under the birth or continuous residence clauses.

During the Second World War, manpower and materials were concentrated on wartime needs and housing lagged badly behind. The situation worsened in the early post-war years of further rapid industrial growth as squatter settlements and shanty towns mushroomed around South African cities. Most cities made some attempt to catch up on the backlog of housing, but several factors combined to prevent any large scale effort in this direction, including the sheer immensity of the task, reluctance to increase the rates unduly, and doubts about the permanency of the urban African population. Meanwhile the growth of the squatter settlements produced fresh outbursts of political bitterness and a more radical cadre of African, Indian and Coloured leaders. Under such conditions, further strong criticism of the migrant labour system and the inhumanity of the pass laws by the Fagan Commission[23] had little political significance, whereas the usual 'swart gevaar' (black danger) element in the 1948 general election was strengthened and contributed to the Nationalist victory.

The Group Areas Act and supporting legislation

The Group Areas Act (No. 41 of 1950, amended and consolidated in No. 77 of 1957) has had more far-reaching effects than any previous

72

legislation on racial segregation. It provides for the extension throughout South Africa, and to all races, of the land apportionment principle long existing in the African reserves. The operation of the Act is essentially in the towns, as many of its provisions effectively applied elsewhere already. It imposes control of interracial property transactions and interracial changes in occupation of property, which are made subject to permit. No less than ten different kinds of area are defined, but the ultimate goal of the Act is the establishment of group areas for the exclusive occupation of each racial group, though it has sometimes been thought necessary in particular circumstances to pass through a number of intermediate stages first. Group areas may be proclaimed in respect of either ownership (with controlled occupation) or occupation (with controlled ownership), but the proclamation applies to both ownership and occupation in the final form, the full group area. 'Border strips' may be designated to act as barriers between different group areas to ensure that no 'undesirable contiguity' occurs. 'Future group areas' may also be proclaimed if an area is considered suitable for proclamation but is not immediately required: a certain amount of control is then exercised over the use and development of the area, which is intended to facilitate its eventual proclamation as a group area. 'Future border strips' may likewise be set aside with the needs of future group areas in mind. Control over occupation may be temporarily withdrawn at any time by special proclamation. Areas so affected have come to be known as 'open areas', although they are not given a name in the Act. The possibility of establishing open areas was the cause of much controversy between several local authorities and the Group Areas Board, especially where it was decided to retain a non-White (usually Indian) commercial district in what had been proclaimed a White group area (chapter 6).

Implementation of the Act is the responsibility of the Group Areas Board and, subsequently, the Community Development Board. The former, in order to provide effective recommendations, must have the assistance of experienced surveyors, engineers and planners. Such assistance can only be provided by the local authorities, whose co-operation is therefore necessary. Should a local authority refuse to co-operate, however, it risks the imposition of a completely arbitrary and probably unsuitable zoning plan. When, after opportunity for objection and inquiry, the government finally approves any recommendations of the Group Areas Board, their implementation becomes the responsibility of the Community Development Board. The latter has to deal with housing, the development of group areas, the resettlement of dislocated persons, slum clearance and urban renewal.

The Act radically extends control over private property. The Group Areas Development Act (1955) provides machinery for compensation, but makes further inroads into the rights of ownership, by procedures for regulating the sale price of property in the open market, and by expropriation of properties under a system of public acquisition for the development of group areas. White acceptance of such revolutionary changes in traditionally sacred rights would have been most unlikely, had Whites themselves suffered greatly as a result. In practice zoning has benefited the Whites, who are alone represented on city and town councils and are in other ways far better able to defend their interests at the expense of other groups.

The availability of other accommodation must be taken into consideration when group areas are proclaimed, but there is no compulsion to increase the availability of such accommodation in any way. Kuper et al. state that in Durban the phrase 'alternative accommodation' appears to be interpreted as an area where accommodation could be built, not as actual accommodation.[24] In a more recent study of Port Elizabeth, however, W.J. Davies notes that the shortage of funds from the National Housing Commission has seriously retarded the progress of the Community Development Board's activities, 'since it remains basic policy that no group should be moved before alternate adequate accommodation has been provided.'[25]

Effects of the Group Areas Act

It is undeniable that far greater financial resources have been allocated to non-White housing since the implementation of the Group Areas Act than hitherto, and that squatting has not assumed the dimensions which seemed likely in the 1940s. In part this reflects the enforcement of influx control, together with the Prevention of Illegal Squatting Act (1951), which specifies that no one may enter any African location or village, nor erect any buildings in such areas, without permission. Nevertheless, the energy and resources expended upon housing have been considerable by any standards; it is only regrettable that they have been primarily directed to the fulfilment of an ideological commitment, at no small cost to what might have been achieved by devoting the same resources to the solving of housing problems *per se*.

Implementation of the Act has achieved indices of segregation approaching 100 per cent: domestic servants living with their employers, mainly White but including some Indian and Coloured, constitute the major exception. This must be viewed in relation to the substantial degree of segregation which existed prior to implementation. In Durban, indices of segregation for 1951 included the following: Indian/White 0·91, Indian/African 0·81, Coloured/White 0·84, African/White 0·81.[26] Only Coloureds and Indians lived in the same area to an appreciable extent, whilst African/White segregation would have been almost total if domestic servants had been excluded. Similarly, in Port Elizabeth, also in 1951, the segregation index was 0·89 between Whites and other groups, 0·80 between Coloureds and Africans, but only 0·35 between Coloureds and Asians (Indians and Chinese).[27] Both cities would have ranked as more highly segregated than most of the sixty large American cities studied by Duncan and Davis in 1953.[28] The Group Areas Act could thus increase segregation substantially only in the case of Coloureds and Indians, yet it has entailed extensive re-zoning and wholesale movement, mainly of non-Whites. This implies that something more than mere segregation is intended.

This is indeed the case. Residential segregation is intended to be sufficiently effective not only to avoid contact between races within each zone, but also to discourage movement of people of one race into the zone of another. Thus the Group Areas Board rejected Coloured 'islands' at Fairview and South End in Port Elizabeth.[29] 'Natural' border areas such as rivers, steep valleys, cliffs and hill tops are preferred: as these are not common in urban areas, industrial or commercial belts may be used instead, but vacant land is avoided where possible as it might become a communal park. The requirement that one race should not be routed through the residential area of another to reach its workplace also profoundly affects the town plan. In Durban, for instance, this is achieved by means of a long north–south industrial and commercial area, from which racial zones radiate, whilst in Port Elizabeth the industrial areas are centrally placed in relation to all group areas (see Fig. 4.2).

The intention, implicit in the Act, to provide for *future* expansion of the group areas whilst preserving the above conditions has further contributed to the need for fundamental rearrangement of the pre-existing residential patterns, despite the fact that these already displayed a high degree of segregation.

Implementation of the Act has resulted in non-Whites being settled, even more than previously, in peripheral areas. Port Elizabeth is relatively fortunate in this respect, since the maximum straight line distance involved from Coloured and African group areas to the main employment areas is ten kilometres; Soweto is almost twice as far from similar employment areas in Johannesburg. Thus the poor live at higher densities,

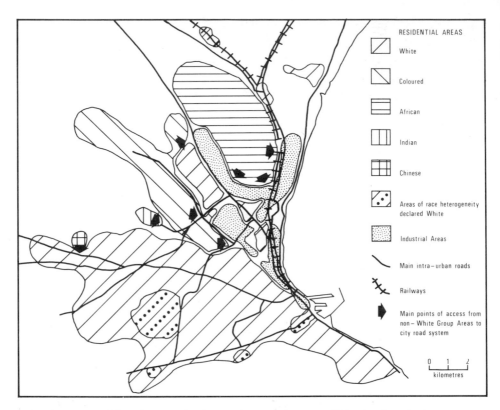

RESIDENTIAL AREAS

White

Coloured

African

Indian

Chinese

Areas of race heterogeneity declared White

Industrial Areas

Main intra-urban roads

Railways

Main points of access from non-White Group Areas to city road system

0   1   2
kilometres

Fig. 4.2   Residential and industrial areas in Port Elizabeth, 1970
Source: W.J. Davies (1970), *Patterns of Non-White Population Distribution in Port Elizabeth with special reference to the application of the Group Areas Act.*

but further from the city, than do Whites. This is the reverse of the income gradient normally associated with Western European cities, which also applies within the White sectors of South African cities. For non-Whites this situation is mitigated in most cases by the siting of their group areas close to cheap rail transport, as in the case of Umlazi (Durban) and Soweto. Construction of new rail links has been subsidised from a 'transport services levy' on employers, which has subsequently been used to subsidise bus and train services for African workers. In addition, the government subsidised railway services carrying Black commuters to the tune of R22·1 million in the fiscal year 1975–76.[30] For those not living near railways, however, the journey to work may be long, tiring, and, despite subsidies, expensive. Africans in Soweto, and more recently (1975) in Madadeni near Newcastle (Natal) and Mdantsane near

76

East London, have successfully boycotted buses in the face of excessive fare increases. Such instances of successful organised action by urban Africans are as yet rare, and there is little or no evidence of African ability to translate such capacity for protest about localised economic issues into effective widespread *political* action.

The African population in 'White' urban areas

Industrial and mining development stimulated further large scale African urbanisation after 1945. In 1951 Africans outnumbered Whites in urban areas for the first time. By 1970 there were 4,405,000 Africans and 3,244,000 Whites in urban areas, a ratio of 1·36 to 1. Despite the retarding effect of a stricter application of influx control after 1948, large increases in the African population still occurred, especially in the four major urban areas and East London. In the 1960s the urban African population appears to have increased more slowly, by 29 per cent, whereas the total African population increased by 37·5 per cent. This lower rate of increase is partly due to the decentralisation programme, the Physical Planning Act (1967), stricter control measures, and the erection of towns in homelands close to big metropolitan centres. The 1970 figures do, however, exclude the 300,000 or so people living in urban townships simply 'reclassified' as part of adjacent homelands during the 1960s.[31] By early 1975 there were over five million Africans in 'White' urban areas, representing a further 15 per cent increase on the 1970 figure, despite further reclassification of townships. Official figures also omit, of necessity, the very large number of Africans illegally resident in urban areas. In the year 1973–74, 511,000 Africans were prosecuted for breaches of influx control measures – and these were only the ones who were caught.[32] A study of Mdantsane (pop. 71,000 in 1970) has estimated that the real population is 30 per cent higher than the official figure.[33] In Soweto the actual number of schoolchildren aged between five and fourteen represented 111·7 per cent of the official number of children of this age living there in 1973.[34] The population of Umlazi in 1973, officially 120,000, was unofficially estimated at 200,000.[35] For the authorities, the number of 'illegal' Africans is a growing problem. For the Africans themselves, illegal status is a source of insecurity, with the constant threat of being 'endorsed out' by the authorities if discovered. For employers, this sizeable addition to the urban labour force is welcome both in itself, and because it contributes to the economically desirable stabilisation of urban labour.

More than two-thirds of all urban Africans live in the PWV, Durban–Pinetown, Cape Town, East London and Port Elizabeth–Uitenhage metropolitan areas. The first two appear to have experienced a large exodus of Africans in the 1960s, owing to reclassification of townships and the development of dormitory towns in the homelands.[36] Towns in the Free State and Western Transvaal goldfields and on the Natal coalfields, which experienced great increases in African population in the 1950s, have now reached saturation point, mainly because of mechanisation in the mining industry. In Cape Town the African growth rate has been increasing since 1960, although surrounding urban areas have experienced a net exodus, chiefly due to stricter influx control regulations to protect Coloured labour. As the process of reclassifying urban townships comes to an end, rates of increase in the African population of 'White' towns will depend chiefly on the speed at which decentralisation of industries progresses, the provision of housing in adjacent homelands, and the provision of express transport for African commuters.

In the 1940s and 1950s the influx of African women to urban areas increased strongly whilst the influx of men was limited. Sex ratios have thus become more normal: although there were still 135 African men for every 100 women in urban areas in 1970, the male:female ratio in the 15–49 age group is more even, owing to the predominance of women in their reproductive years amongst those migrating to the towns. As a result, increases in the urban African population are no longer dependent on migration from the homelands; the population can now grow more rapidly than the White urban population without further influx. As Africans born in White towns will automatically enjoy 'Section 10 rights', it is difficult to see how the continuance of those rights is compatible with the official aim of a stable or declining number of Africans in urban areas.

The rights of urban Africans

Urban Africans are denied normal citizenship rights in White areas on the ground that they may exercise such rights in their 'home' areas. Homeland leaders have, however, repeatedly pressed for other rights than mere residence for Africans who are legally and permanently resident in urban areas, and in May 1975 the government announced some significant concessions. Restrictions imposed in 1968 on home ownership by Africans in urban townships are to be removed. Africans will still not be granted freehold title to land, but will again be able to buy houses situated on land belonging to Bantu Administration Boards. Many still own houses acquired under the old system: these owners, together with new ones, will be permitted to sell or bequeath their houses to Africans qualified to live in the areas concerned. Qualified Africans may also buy houses from the Administration Boards or lease vacant plots and build their own homes (payment for which may be made in a lump sum or over a period). Those wishing to own houses must become citizens of a homeland first; they will then qualify for thirty-year leasehold occupation of the land, renewable for up to another thirty years. Restrictions imposed in 1969 on the ownership of consulting rooms and offices by African doctors and other professional men in urban townships are also to be abolished.

The activities of African traders in urban areas have been restricted in various ways since 1963. A ceiling to African commercial expansion was imposed, and the more successful African traders were directed to invest in the homelands. Thus African consumer demand in the towns was channelled to White commercial interests, a course advocated by some Afrikaner spokesmen 'who claimed that their nation should now be compensated because other groups [the English] had been entrenching themselves in commerce and industry while the Afrikaners were opening up the country and making it safe for White civilisation',[37] an argument which displays characteristic Afrikaner consciousness of, and preoccupation with, history. In 1975, however, it was announced that restrictions on African traders were to be removed. The procedure for renewal of licences will, as far as possible, be brought into line with that applying to White traders, and Africans will again be allowed to own and start their own businesses, to trade in an increasing range of commodities, to establish more than one type of business on the same premises, and to enter partnerships.

Cultural adjustment

Considerable problems of adaptation and cultural adjustment face Africans in urban environments, particularly if they have relatively recent experience of tribal life in the homelands. Acculturation does not necessarily lead to total 'Europeanisation'. Tribal tradition, heritage and customs are so strong that they are retained but adjusted where necessary to the new environment. Holzner notes that of the twelve most significant tribal customs practised among all Bantu nations of Southern Africa, only four seem to disappear in urban society: prescribed marriage, polygamy, initiation rites, and consulting witchdoctors before medical doctors.[38] Degrees of acculturation vary more than this generalisation suggests, however. Mayer[39] distinguishes between 'Red' and 'school' migrants to East London, the latter favouring the adoption of 'White man's ways' but the former insisting that traditional Xhosa ways are best: in this instance, attitudes formed in rural areas significantly affect subsequent behaviour in the town. Important differences also exist between urban areas where migrants are mainly from one tribal group, such as the Xhosa in East London and the Zulu in Durban or Pietermaritzburg, and others such as Soweto where migrant workers come from many parts of southern Africa and form a 'melting pot' of varying tribal backgrounds, and various stages of education and Westernisation. Government policy is to separate the various tribes as far as possible, both residentially and educationally, in conformity with its 'multinational' view of South Africa (chapter 5), but such segregation is by no means fully implemented, nor can it be in practice.

Welfare services and social amenities

In any rapidly growing city with a majority of its population living near the poverty line, problems of service provision (and housing) are very great. In South Africa they have been accentuated by apartheid, and particularly by the implementation of the Group Areas Act. Pirie[40] finds that 64 per cent of all health and social services in Greater Johannesburg are located in White areas. The overall population–service ratios were: 1,464:1 for Whites; 3,303:1 for Coloureds; 6,507:1 for Indians; and 7,727:1 for Africans. Such disparities are an almost inevitable consequence of the nature and evolution of South African urban society. The concept of towns as essentially created by and for Whites has not encouraged the provision of services for other groups, and even today the official view that African residential areas in the towns must not be made too attractive is strong: this, it is argued, would alienate the African from what is his own, i.e. the homeland environment. Under the Reservation of Separate Amenities Act (1953) facilities may be reserved for persons of one race without provision being made for other races, whether equal or otherwise.

Resource availability is part of the problem, particularly in the face of ideological commitment to the provision of racially separate facilities, both in residential group areas and in commercial areas where all races mix during working hours. To open up existing facilities to all races would, in the face of existing residential separation, still leave non-Whites at a severe disadvantage in terms of access to such facilities. As it is, the need to provide separate facilities not only results in some wasteful duplication but also means that many non-White areas must start from virtually nothing. Groups experiencing the most resettlement are clearly at a disadvantage, owing to the inevitable time lag between residential and service provision in new housing areas. By the end of 1974 the numbers of *families* resettled in group areas throughout South Africa was as follows:[41]

| White | 1,579 | Indian | 29,969 |
| Chinese | 91 | Coloured | 53,203 |

The African figure is not known, but it is thought to exceed one million *individuals*. To this financial problem of service provision for resettled populations (whose low income constitutes a poor tax base) must be added the further burdens imposed by immigration and the natural increase of population. Small wonder that the available resources have been expended upon attempts to keep up with housing needs with repeated postponement of social and welfare provisions as an inevitable consequence.

The greatest problems of access to amenities are suffered by non-Whites living in White areas, who 'constitute a largely ignored category of "non-people" whose existence is socially ignored both in planning and in the day-to-day community life of these White areas.'[42] In Greater Johannesburg such groups included 141,000 Africans, 73,167 Coloureds and 38,405 Indians.[43] They include those living in hostels and compounds run by private organisations and by municipal, provincial and governmental bodies, together with large numbers of domestic servants living on their employers' premises: in Durban alone the latter group numbers between 30,000 and 55,000.[44] Certain mobile health services such as family planning clinics cater for non-Whites in White areas, and small scale private facilities are sometimes available. In Johannesburg, for instance, eleven 'centres of concern' open weekly in White suburbs to teach domestic servants such skills as cooking, sewing, literacy and crafts.[45] Generally speaking, however, religious and social facilities for non-Whites in White areas have decreased, as all but a few of the churches, halls and social centres which once existed to serve Africans in central city areas have been closed or moved to the townships, where all new recreational facilities must be established. Shops and new commercial undertakings intended to serve Africans are increasingly discouraged or restricted in the central areas, a factor which affects those who work in White areas as well as those who live there. Suburban Whites have begun to recognise the problems faced by their servants, and show some acceptance of the need to provide a minimum of facilities locally, but invariably the reaction is 'Yes, but not here.' Meanwhile Africans must either travel considerable distances to use facilities in the townships, or be restricted to gathering in small groups in the street or in their 'kias' (servants' rooms, usually in the garden or adjoining the garage) when not on duty. Servants living out, on the other hand, face long and difficult journeys from townships to White suburb, necessitating an extremely early departure in the morning and leaving little leisure time.

Crime

Overcrowded housing conditions and inadequate social and recreational amenities help to explain the high incidence of crime in African townships. The loss of community life following resettlement is another factor, which is in turn accentuated by the impersonal, characterless urban environments of most townships. Those not long resident in the townships experience frustrations arising from the unfamiliarity of the urban environment. The absence of wife and family, and the unbalanced sex ratios still found in some urban areas, are clearly associated with high rates of sexual crimes. The absence of both parents at work long after the school day finishes contributes to juvenile delinquency.

Most of these conditions are nowhere better exemplified than in Soweto, the *de facto* population of which may well exceed one million. The large increase in the number of crimes there (see Table 4.3) has no more than kept pace with population increase, although the increase in violent crimes alone is more disturbing, as is the decreasing rate of detection. Some Africans have formed a 'makgotla' movement which operates makeshift courts at weekends. These deal with juvenile delinquency, minor crimes and family disputes. In some areas offenders are handed over to the police, but some courts still illegally administer floggings. The operation of such courts is clearly a reaction to the insecurity of life in an urban community where crime is commonplace, and where the police are so fully stretched in dealing with major crimes that minor criminals can often thrive undetected.

Insiders and outsiders in the townships

Continuing emphasis on the migrant labour system means that in most

Table 4.3
Crime in Soweto, 1962 and 1973

	1962		1973		Percentage change
	Number	Percentage unsolved	Number	Percentage unsolved	
Assaults	4,467	14·6	9,111	16·9	+ 104
Rapes	446	17·5	1,138	32·6	+ 155
Murders	423	27·2	952	32·4	+ 125
Thefts	2,266	39·9	3,856	49·1	+ 70
Total	7,602	23·5	15,057	27·6	+ 98

Source: M. Horrell (1975), *A Survey of Race Relations in South Africa 1974,* SAIRR, p. 88.

industrial areas there are substantial numbers of migrant workers housed as single men in the townships. Proportions vary considerably, from an estimated 20 per cent of economically active men in Port Elizabeth to 85 per cent in Cape Town; on most of the Witwatersrand, including Pretoria, and in Durban, the proportion appears to be about 50 per cent.[46] Wilson labels these men 'urban outsiders' in contrast to the 'urban insiders' who live with their families within daily commuting distance of work. A policy is emerging of reserving the more skilled African jobs for urban insiders by making it impossible for outsiders, or migrants, to accept any but tough, unattractive low paid jobs. This makes economic sense, in that skilled jobs require more training and a stabilised labour force: such a policy of discrimination between 'insiders' and 'outsiders' may thus be represented as an attempt to reconcile economic logic and the continuance of the migrant labour system.[47] The 'call-in card' system, whereby firms are able to increase the probability that contract workers will return to the same employer after a spell in the homelands, is another means to this end.

Tensions already exist between insiders and outsiders. Parents fear for their daughters and husbands for their wives when large numbers of migrant labourers are housed in the same townships as the insiders themselves. Job discrimination between the two groups, leading to differences in income and lifestyle, may well increase tensions between them. Such income differences may grow since the insiders, occupying relatively skilled occupations and therefore being more indispensable, have the power to increase their wages by effective strike action, as

83

demonstrated by the Putco bus drivers' strike in Johannesburg in June 1972.[48] Similar action is far more difficult for 'outsiders', particularly where, as on the Witwatersrand, they come from diverse tribal backgrounds. An increasing division of interest seems likely; already it is said that urban insiders are against the abolition of influx control because they see such a step leading to the lowering of their own living standards. The wider implications of such emergent attitudes will be explored in chapter 12.

References

[1] E.W.N. Mallows (1968), 'Some comments on urbanization in Southern Africa', *SAGJ* 50, p. 12.
[2] T.J.D. Fair (1965), 'The core–periphery concept and population growth in South Africa, 1911–1960', *SAGJ* 47, p. 65.
[3] C. Board (1973), 'Population concentration in South Africa 1960–1970: a shift and share analysis,' *Standard Bank Review,* supplement (September), pp. 5–13.
[4] Republic of South Africa (1975), *National Physical Development Plan,* Department of Planning and the Environment, p. 1.
[5] Ibid., p. 14.
[6] Ibid.
[7] T.J.D. Fair (1975), 'The National Physical Development Plan (NPDP): a summary and a review', *SAGJ* 57, p. 130.
[8] Ibid.
[9] L. Holzner (1970), 'Urbanism in Southern Africa', *Geoforum* 4, p.85.
[10] I.J. van der Merwe (1973), 'Differential urbanization in South Africa', *Geography* 58, p. 337.
[11] L. Kuper, H. Watts and R. Davies (1958), *Durban: a study in racial ecology,* Jonathan Cape, London, p. 30.
[12] T.R.H. Davenport (1971), *The beginnings of urban segregation in South Africa: the Natives (Urban Areas) Act of 1923 and its background,* Institute of Social and Economic Research, Rhodes University (Grahamstown), Occasional Paper No. 15, p. 6.
[13] Ibid.
[14] P.R.B. Lewis (1966), 'A "city" within a city – the creation of Soweto', *SAGJ* 48, p. 46.
[15] *Report of the Transvaal Local Government Commission.* TP1/1922, para. 42.
[16] T.R.H. Davenport (1969), 'African townsmen? South African

Natives (urban areas) legislation through the years', *Afn Aff.* 68, p. 99.

[17] F. Meer (1976), 'Domination through separation: a résumé of the major laws enacting and preserving racial segregation', in D.M. Smith (ed.), *Separation in South Africa: peoples and policies,* Queen Mary College, London, Department of Geography Occasional Paper No.6, p.20.

[18] T.R.H. Davenport (1969), op. cit., p. 102.

[19] Union of South Africa (1941), *Third Interim Report of the Industrial and Agricultural Requirements Commission,* UG40/1941, p. 248.

[20] Union of South Africa (1942), *Report of the Interdepartmental Committee on the Social, Health and Economic Conditions of Urban Natives,* Annexure 47/1943, para. 8.

[21] Union of South Africa (1946), *The Native Reserves and Their Place in the Economy of the Union of South Africa,* Social and Economic Planning Council, UG32/1946, para. 11.

[22] J.C. Smuts (1942), *The Basis of Trusteeship,* New Africa Pamphlet No. 2, SAIRR, Johannesburg, p. 10.

[23] Union of South Africa (1948), *Report of the Native Laws Commission, 1946–1948,* UG28/1948.

[24] L. Kuper, H. Watts and R. Davies, op. cit., p. 160.

[25] W.J. Davies (1971), *Patterns of Non-White Population Distribution in Port Elizabeth with special reference to the application of the Group Areas Act,* Institute of Planning Research, University of Port Elizabeth, p. 27.

[26] L. Kuper, H. Watts and R. Davies, op. cit., pp. 154, 156–7.

[27] W.J. Davies, op. cit., p. 148.

[28] O.D. Duncan and B. Davis (1953), *The Chicago Urban Analysis Project,* University of Chicago.

[29] W.J. Davies, op. cit., p. 233.

[30] M. Horrell and T. Hodgson (1976), *A Survey of Race Relations in South Africa 1975,* SAIRR, Johannesburg, p. 87.

[31] M. Lipton (1972), 'The South African census and the Bantustan policy', *The World Today* 28, p. 260.

[32] M. Horrell and T. Hodgson, op. cit., p. 99.

[33] P. Mayer (1971), *Townsmen and Tribesmen,* Oxford University Press, London, p. 295.

[34] S.F. Ronaldson (1976), 'Residential patterns in Soweto, Johannesburg', unpublished BA dissertation, University of Oxford, p. 25.

[35] Personal communication.

[36] This and the following paragraph draw upon the analysis made by P. Smit in 'The Black population' in *Separation in South Africa: peoples and policies* (see ref. 17).

[37] M. Banton (1967), *Race Relations,* Tavistock Publications, London, p. 179.

[38] L. Holzner, op. cit., p. 86.

[39] P. Mayer, op. cit.

[40] G.H. Pirie (1976), 'Apartheid, health and social services in Greater Johannesburg', part of a Queen Mary College, London, Department of Geography Occasional Paper.

[41] M. Horrell and T. Hodgson, op. cit., p. 69.

[42] E. Preston-Whyte (1976), 'Segregation and inter-personal relationships: a case study', unpublished paper, p. 1.

[43] G.H. Pirie, op. cit., p. 8.

[44] G. Maasdorp and A.S.B. Humphreys (1975), *From Shantytown to Township,* Juta, Cape Town, p. 71.

[45] G.H. Pirie, op. cit., p. 8.

[46] F. Wilson (1975), 'The political implications for Blacks of economic changes now taking place in Southern Africa', in L. Thompson and J. Butler (eds), *Change in Contemporary South Africa,* University of California Press, Berkeley, p. 173.

[47] Ibid., pp. 182–3.

[48] Ibid., p. 189.

5 Political attitudes and voting behaviour*

The logic of separate development: South African attitudes

To attempt a brief outline review, let alone an objective assessment, of this subject is no easy task when dealing with a country which is a mosaic of different people living within a very complex, highly artificial and often incomprehensible social structure.[1] South Africans tend to regard themselves not as a single community, but as four distinct and different groups which in local usage are referred to as Europeans or Whites, Coloureds, Indians or Asians or Asiatics, and Bantu or Africans (or in recent years Blacks). The distinction is rendered more complex by the fact that none of the groups is homogeneous, especially as regards its origins and culture (chapter 1). The critical distinction, obviously reflecting the White standpoint, is between European and non-European, or White and non-White, or today sometimes between White and Black. Between these two groups, and particularly between Whites and Africans, lies a profound social gulf evident in such diverse aspects as geographical distribution, status, levels of skill and advancement, job opportunities and wage rates, housing and public facilities, voting rights, and indeed life expectancy. The groups live in two different worlds, coexistent, but in general separate. Such a situation, a recognition of difference, is not new; its roots lie in the occupation of the country by early White settlers and it has traditionally been accepted over the years. The coming to power of the Nationalist Party in 1948 simply set in motion a process of confirmation and regularisation, formulated through an explicit and defined policy blueprinted in the Tomlinson Report[2] (but flexible enough to permit modification and improvisation as circumstances warrant) and systematically implemented so as to ensure its continuance.

This then is a plural and multi-racial society, the world in microcosm, with a broad spectrum of race, colour, language, creed and culture within a single country. Such a society is inevitably subject to problems engendered by such differences, whilst confrontations must be avoided.

---

* This chapter has been contributed by Owen Williams.

The essential problem facing the Whites is to what extent, by what methods, for how long, whether left to themselves or influenced by the rest of the world, can or should they retain control in the face of a White:non-White ratio of some 5:1 and a White:African ratio of some 4:1, with the gap widening each year (chapter 8).[3] The decision by most, but not all, Whites, supported by a minority of non-Whites, is that they should retain control, and that they should do so through the policy of apartheid or separate development.

This policy has been pursued since 1948 by a strong and single-minded government which has been preoccupied and indeed obsessed by it; it has been implemented by legislation so that it now affects everyone in the country. The reasons are many and complex. The Whites have always possessed a superior material culture and have generally regarded other groups, particularly Africans, as social inferiors. Associated with this is a long tradition of separation, discrimination and an awareness of colour which is virtually inbred. But perhaps the ultimate reason is self-interest, and indeed self-preservation and survival; any relaxation in the policy is seen as ultimately implying loss of White identity through miscegenation, and loss of economic privilege through African majority rule. Such views have been confirmed locally both by the conflicts so evident in many countries with racially, linguistically or religiously diverse populations (e.g. USA, Northern Ireland, Lebanon), and by the record of the African states to the north since independence.

The solution is thus seen as separate development. This has negative connotations of separation, segregation and partition, but goes beyond this to parallel and separate development (whereby White and other nationalisms are diverted into parallel channels), and indeed to self-determination which maintains and protects the identity and cultural heritage of each group. It aims at minimising confrontation, conflict and indeed contact, envisaging a situation whereby each group develops in its own way, in its own areas with its own facilities, and where each person belongs to his own people. Spatial and residential separation has reinforced natural tendencies of social separation, although social barriers are today being crossed in some contexts. Economic separation, however, seems almost unattainable, as efforts to move towards it are overtaken by events in the White urban and industrial areas.

Separation occurs on two scales. In the urban centres, which were founded by Whites, all sections of the population have their own defined residential areas (chapter 4), whilst using the same commercial facilities in the White Central Business District (CBD). Today the towns contain all ethnic groups and hardly any of them has a White majority. Three of the groups are already heavily urbanised and only the Africans still have the capacity for further massive progress in this direction. Influx control is thus seen to be critical; so too is the development of the African homelands in order to reduce the attraction of the towns,[4] although as the urban way of life continues to erode rural traditions this tends to weaken attachment to the homelands. The latter constitute the macro-scale separation, with just under 14 per cent of the total area of South Africa set aside for them (no provision exists, however, for Asian or Coloured homelands). Each African homeland has its own ethnic identity and an increasing degree of self-government, with the prospect of ultimate and early independence. This process is seen as leading to equal status with White South Africa, and thus the presence of a group of independent states linked by common interests: separation is to be followed by co-operation. The process is regarded as a classic policy of de-colonisation which will satisfy national aspirations. The homelands are viewed as the homes of the African peoples, the place where they belong and hold citizenship. Those who live and work outside them in White South Africa are regarded essentially as temporary sojourners regardless of the length of time they may have spent there either permanently engaged in its economic activities or as migrant workers returning periodically to the homelands. Despite very considerable expenditure incurred in their development, however, the homelands remain poor, overpopulated, lacking in resources, and unable to provide the range and wealth of economic opportunities available outside their borders (chapters 8–10). It is questionable whether they are capable of becoming viable economic or political units and thus genuinely independent states (chapter 11).

The precise degree to which separate development enjoys the support of South Africans is impossible to assess; only some generalisations can be suggested, and there are naturally exceptions in all cases. White attitudes may have been more important in the past, but the views of other groups are becoming increasingly relevant. Attitudes are usually more a matter of feeling than of thinking, and few converts are made from those who approve or disapprove of apartheid. It is also important to appreciate that the policy exists, and that those who live in South Africa are obliged to live as best they can within its constraints, and with the personal moral issues involved. A large number of Whites do so complacently, but others are seriously concerned and anxious about the implications of apartheid; some actively oppose it, whilst others fear the consequences, real or imagined, of so doing.

In terms of White political parties and their supporters approval clearly decreases from the right to the left of the spectrum, from the Herstigte Nasionale Partie ('Purified' Nationalist Party) to the Progressive Reform Party, for party loyalties reflect attitudes to separate development more than anything else. But among these, and indeed all groups, support is a matter of degree. Amongst the Nationalists, for example, differences exist between the 'verligte' ('enlightened' or liberal) and 'verkrampte' (conservative) elements; between their more liberal western Cape supporters and the more conservative elements in the Orange Free State and the Transvaal; and between their intellectual leaders and those who follow. Similarly, Afrikaners generally support apartheid whilst people of English stock evince less enthusiasm, although many of them may be happy with a more lenient version of it.[5] The Afrikaners are generally more politically aware and active, the English less so. Amongst all Whites there is a clear awareness of the immense cost of separate development, and indeed some opposition from its supporters to the scale of expenditure on homeland development. Many people feel a more satisfactory result could be achieved if these efforts were put into some sort of alternative multi-racial policy, especially since economic integration is so clearly taking place, but to most Whites group self-interest and the perpetuation of an affluent society protected from competition suggests in general a tacit (if not always positive) support. The strongest support for the negative aspects of the *status quo* comes from those who can least afford to oppose it on grounds of wealth, social status and education: lower income Whites feel themselves most immediately threatened by other groups.

Amongst the non-White groups there is little doubt that the majority oppose the policy, but they, like the Whites, have to recognise it as a current fact of life. By accepting what apartheid offers them they secure certain advantages, including self-government and independence for the African homelands, and for Indians and Coloureds some tangible advantages over the African majority (chapters 6 and 7). These advantages, which include increasing and more clearly defined powers, are already enabling non-Whites to bargain from improving positions of strength.

The general overall reactions to separate development are well-known. Outside the country they represent reactions to the country itself which is equated with its policies. The result is condemnation by much of the world and the isolation of South Africa in many spheres (chapter 13). Against this is the desire of those who support the policy to be left alone to solve their problems without outside interference. Within the country their attempts have resulted in the further deliberate division of an already divided people; a division into separate groups and the breaking down of contacts between them in everyday life. But always this is accompanied by the protests of those opposed to separate development, who hope either for a change of heart and a policy reappraisal by the government in power, or for a change in that government (chapter 12).

The White voter: a spatial analysis of voting patterns in general elections, 1943–74

The legislative power of the Republic is vested in its Parliament which consists of the State President, a Senate and a House of Assembly. To the Senate, the Upper House, are appointed Senators. To the House of Assembly, the Lower House, are elected Members of Parliament at general elections normally held every five years; at present it has 171 members representing 165 electoral divisions in the Republic and 6 in South-West Africa. The Senate has fifty-five members and its party composition is essentially determined by the composition of the House of Assembly, so that the ultimate level of voting is that of the general election. The franchise is limited to White citizens over eighteen years of age, and thus excludes all other groups who together constitute some 82 per cent of the country's population: for them, separate or parallel political institutions are being developed.

Three parties were represented in Parliament after the 1974 election – Nationalist, United and Progressive. The political spectrum ended with the Progressives: there have been no parties further to the left since the dissolution of the Liberal Party in 1968 following the prohibition of multi-racial political parties. On occasions over the years all three parties have changed their names, absorbed or lost splinter groups, or amalgamated.[6] Progressive and United Party alternatives to separate development will be examined in chapter 12.

The Nationalist Party was founded in 1912, its early aims being the survival and consolidation of Afrikanerdom after the Anglo-Boer War, and ultimately the establishment of a Republic in South Africa. Its first election was fought in 1915; it first came to power in 1948 and has stayed there ever since. During this time it has developed powerful and positive aims, particularly those implied by separate development. The cornerstone of its power comes from Afrikaners (some 58 per cent of the White population), and together with some English-speaking support this ensures its majority. In 1969 its extreme right-wing element broke away to contest the 1970 and 1974 elections as the Herstigte Nasionale Partie mentioned above.

The United Party was first founded as the South African Party in 1910, and contested its first election as the United Party in 1938. It lost the 1948 election in the face of growing support for the Nationalist Party, and has since been in opposition. It is more broadly based than the Nationalist Party, with a very wide range of opinion between its relatively liberal and conservative elements. In order to survive as a sizeable party, it cannot afford to lose support from either end of its spectrum, for if it does it may forfeit its chances in future elections. The party relies heavily on English votes, many of them cast for nationalistic reasons rather than in support of United Party policies, which have tended to be vague. Because it attracts few Afrikaner votes, the United Party is unlikely to gain power, yet it remains too large to allow the Nationalist Party the luxury of splitting into two.[7]

The Progressive Party founded in 1959 has been supported by the most liberal sections of the electorate. It has represented a potential threat not only to the Nationalist Party but also to the United Party, in that it contributes to polarisation in the political arena and tends to split the opposition vote; these attitudes were clearly evident in the political events of 1974 and 1975.

Constituencies, voters and seats

A Delimitation Commission[8] whose members are nominated by the State President determines the precise boundaries of each electoral division on the basis of the number of registered voters in various parts of the country. The total number of the country's voters is divided by the number of seats in the House of Assembly. Each electoral division would thus have a quota (12,978 in the 1974 election) of voters, which would be adhered to as closely as possible in the delimitation. South-West Africa has its own quota (7,784 in the 1974 election) determined in a similar manner. The Commission is, however, required to give due consideration to community or diversity of interests, the boundaries of existing local authorities, magisterial districts and electoral divisions, means of communication, physical features, sparsity or density of population and the probability of an increase or decrease in the population; where deemed necessary in these respects it may 'load' or 'unload' the quota by a maximum of 15 per cent. The effect would be that a Member might be elected in one constituency having up to 35 per cent more voters than another (115:85). Furthermore, within the Republic, in an electoral division with an area of 25,000 square kilometres or more, the number of voters may be as little as 70 per cent of the quota. In such a case the voters in two constituencies might have a 64 per cent difference in numbers (115:70), although there are only seventeen such large divisions. Population changes beyond those anticipated by the Delimitation Commission may further accentuate these differences. The result of such differentials was that in 1974 the largest electorate was Boksburg (Transvaal) with 16,205 voters, and the smallest Fauresmith (Orange Free State) with 9,028, whilst the numbers of voters in South-West African constituencies averaged 7,867. The reasons for differential loading are largely historical. In earlier days communications were poor and physical obstacles more formidable; many voters were not able to reach polling stations, and candidates faced the same problems in their electioneering campaigns. Thus size of constituencies together with their population numbers and degree of rurality is important; large rural constituencies with small populations have in practice better representation in Parliament than small highly populated urban divisions. Uncontested seats are also relevant; these exhibit so clear a preference that no contest takes place and no votes are cast, although a Member is returned to Parliament. A number of potential voters are thus eliminated from the final total.

Differential loading and uncontested seats heighten the discrepancy between seats and votes which would anyway be likely to occur in a 'first past the post' electoral system.[9] The beneficiary in all elections since 1943 has clearly been the Nationalist Party, as Table 5.1 demonstrates.

Table 5.1
Electoral performance of the Nationalist Party, 1943–74

General election	% of seats	% of votes
1943	43	36
1948	53	32
1953	62	39
1958	66	55
1961	67	46
1966	76	59
1970	71	54
1974	72	51

Source: *Stats* (Johannesburg), 30 June 1965, 31 March 1966, 30 April 1970; *Africa Institute Bulletin* 12, no. 4 (1974).

The spatial pattern of general election results

This may be examined by tracing changes in party representation (Tables 5.1 and 5.2, and Figs. 5.1 to 5.3). In Figs. 5.1 and 5.2 the successes of minor parties in the general elections of 1943 and 1948 respectively are plotted according to their alliances with the Nationalist and United Parties, thus reflecting the relative overall strength of government and opposition. The figures inevitably emphasise the *areal* extent of political representation, but it should be borne in mind (see Table 5.2) that most of the country consists of large, lightly populated rural constituencies (eighty-nine in 1974). Special note should therefore be taken of the urban constituencies (eighty-two in 1974), limited in area, but representing the major concentrations of population as well as of economic, and indeed political, activity.

In 1943 the United Party (with its associates) was at the pinnacle of its power (see Fig. 5.1). It held large areas of the country, and virtually every urban constituency. The Nationalist Party secured only its traditional Platteland constituencies in the Orange Free State, the north and western Transvaal, and the Cape interior; it gained 43 per cent of the country's seats but only 36 per cent of its votes.

The critical election was that of 1948 (Fig. 5.2), when for the first time the Nationalist Party came into that power which it has retained ever since. It acquired 53 per cent of the seats, though only 32 per cent of the votes, an even smaller proportion than in 1943. The result was a surprise to much of the electorate.[10] The number of seats won by the Nationalists may have been due to a reaction against wartime controls, to a feeling that change was desirable after many years of United Party control, or to the attraction of segregation to many voters; however, efficient Nationalist campaigning cannot be discounted nor should the loaded value of the rural constituencies be overlooked. The Nationalist Party gained control of most of rural South Africa; the United Party retained only coastal and southern Natal – the northern interior of the province with its historical links with the Transvaal was lost together with the adjacent Eastern Province and Border area of the Cape, and one constituency in the south-west Cape. Equally significant were the Nationalist successes in urban constituencies; for the first time dominance was secured in Pretoria, and in particular a clear foothold was established in the Witwatersrand.

By 1953 it was clear that the 1948 victory had been no accident. Further gains were made in urban areas, and the six Nationalist seats won in South-West Africa, which was thus represented in Parliament for the first time,

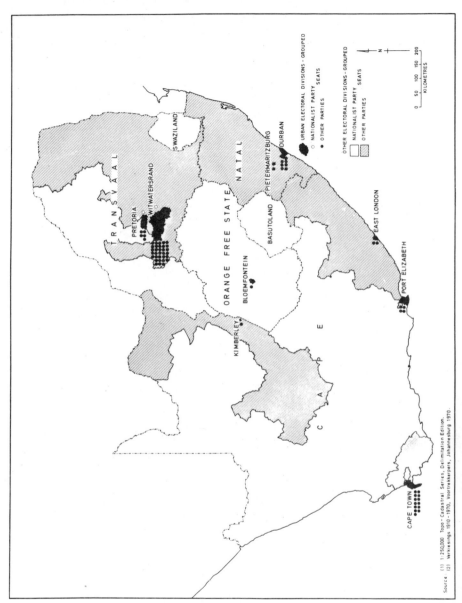

Fig. 5.1 General election results 1943

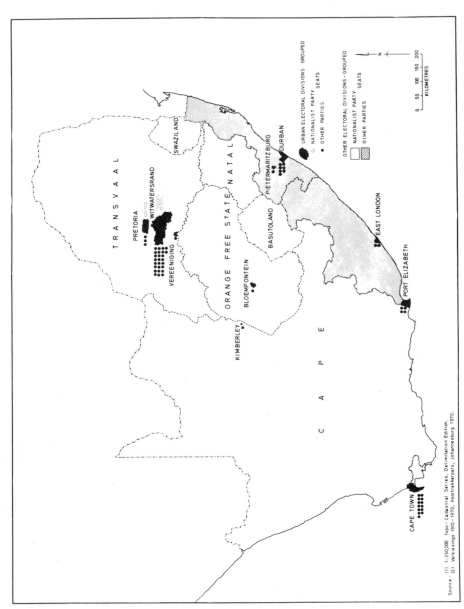

Fig. 5.2 General election results 1948

Source: (1) 1:250,000 Topo - Cadastral Series, Delimitation Edition.
(2) Verkiesings 1910 - 1970, Voortrekkerpers, Johannesburg 1970.

96

were of particular significance on the rural scene. In 1958 the Nationalist hold on the urban divisions was further strengthened, reflecting the growing urbanisation of Afrikaners; the lowering of the voting age to eighteen had also increased the proportion of Afrikaner votes in urban areas. For the first time the government secured a clear majority of both seats and votes (see Table 5.1). Its strength was further demonstrated by the results of the 1960 Referendum, where by a 4·6 per cent majority of White votes[11] South Africa declared herself a Republic (she subsequently left the Commonwealth in 1961).

The 1961 election represented a vote of confidence in the government and without doubt was influenced by the need for internal unity – a closing of the ranks – to ensure the success of the new Republic, especially in view of its evident isolation. The election was also notable for the emergence of the Progressive Party, which secured one seat at Houghton (on the Witwatersrand) which it has retained ever since. The 1966 election represents the maximum extent of Nationalist power to date. The result was perhaps influenced, *inter alia,* by the emergence of independent states to the north and subsequent unrest in the Congo and elsewhere; the presence of a strong government was reassuring to the country's voters. In 1970 the Nationalist Party lost ground (to the extent of eight constituencies) for the first time since 1948.[12] The Progressive Party again retained its single seat, and a feature of considerable significance at the other end of the spectrum was the elimination at birth from the parliamentary scene of the newly formed Herstigte Nasionale Partie. Despite this, the Nationalist leadership displays constant and seemingly exaggerated fears of a rightwing backlash within its own ranks, which have acted as a brake on progress towards more 'verligte' policies.

For the 1974 election a new thirteenth delimitation was introduced to take account of changing population distributions since the previous one of 1965.[13] As in the past, this was inevitably linked with the demarcation and relative voting values of rural and urban constituencies. Three additional constituencies were created in the Transvaal, two in Natal and one in the Cape, in most cases in the larger urban centres or their growing fringes, whilst the Orange Free State lost a seat.

The main features of the 1974 election are summarised in Fig. 5.3 and Table 5.2. The Nationalist Party (with 51 per cent of votes cast) retained its dominance and the United Party (29 per cent) suffered its worst setback since 1948, losing seats both to its right and left. To the Nationalist Party it lost seats on the Witwatersrand and in Natal, but even more significant was the erosion of its strength by the Progressive Party which captured six of its seats (one after a by-election). Three were

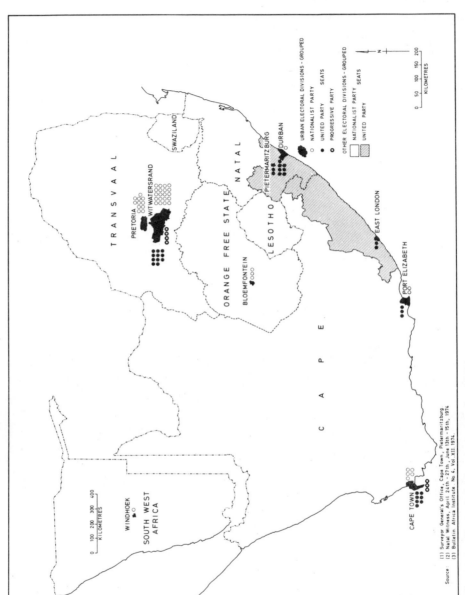

Fig. 5.3 General election results 1974

Source (1) Surveyor General's Office, Cape Town, Pietermaritzburg
(2) Natal Witness, April 24th–27th, June 13th–15th, 1974
(3) Bulletin Africa Institute No 4, Vol XII 1974

Table 5.2
1974 general election results

	Seats		
	Total	Urban	Rural
South Africa			
Nationalist	123	43	80
United	41	32	9
Progressive	7	7	0
	171	82	89
Provinces and S. W. Africa			
Cape:			
NP	37	7	30
UP	15	12	3
PP	3	3	0
	55	22	33
Transvaal:			
NP	61	31	30
UP	11	11	0
PP	4	4	0
	76	46	30
Orange Free State:			
NP	14	3	11
UP	0	0	0
PP	0	0	0
	14	3	11
Natal:			
NP	5	1	4
UP	15	9	6
PP	0	0	0
	20	10	10
South-West Africa:			
NP	6	1	5
UP	0	0	0
PP	0	0	0
	6	1	5

Source: *Africa Institute Bulletin* 12, no. 4 (1974); *Government Gazette,*
17 and 24 May, and 21 June 1974.

wealthy White suburban constituencies in the Witwatersrand, which include large Jewish populations, whilst the other three were in relatively well-to-do suburbs of Cape Town in an area where the old liberal elements in the Cape are still significant. The distribution of Progressive victories thus underlines the restricted electoral base of the party, but the Progressives nevertheless emerged as a larger and more influential party in Parliament, with an impressive team of MPs, although they attracted only 6 per cent of total votes cast.[14] In May 1976 the Progressive Reform Party defeated the United Party in a by-election at Durban North, thereby winning its first seat in Natal.

The weakening of the United Party, the central and major opposition, has subsequently resulted in the emergence of a different and more effective opposition which may play a more prominent rôle in future. This has arisen since the 1974 elections as a result of a combination of internal dissension within the United Party and the effective contribution of the Progressive Party towards political polarisation. The process to date includes two significant features. The first was the formation in February 1975 of a new party, the Reform Party, by four of the more 'verligte' United Party members holding Johannesburg seats. The second was its merger with the Progressive Party in July 1975 to form the Progressive Reform Party.[15] The full implications of these events, and their effects upon the United Party, are not yet clear. But a significant realignment in the opposition ranks has taken place, and a small but effective new party with relatively liberal views has emerged, holding eleven seats in the most strategically significant urban centres of the country – eight on the Witwatersrand and three in Cape Town. Nevertheless, in present circumstances it is difficult to foresee any significant change in the existing pattern of political control. The Nationalist Party has been in power for twenty-eight years (young people have known no other government), and its views have the tacit support of most Whites to varying degrees.

Expressed in spatial terms (Figs. 5.1–5.3), the above story is a simple one – the expansion of Nationalist power in two arenas. In the rural setting the spread from its heartland areas of the Orange Free State, the northern and western Transvaal and the Cape interior is evident. Even more significant have been its successes in the urban constituencies, particularly on the Witwatersrand. The strength of the United Party has been correspondingly reduced; it now holds only the traditional core areas of early British settlement in parts of the eastern Cape and Natal, including their major urban centres, and its representation in other major urban areas has diminished.

References

[1] N. Hurwitz and O. Williams (1962), *The Economic Framework of South Africa,* Shuter and Shooter, Pietermaritzburg.

[2] Union of South Africa (1955), *Report of the Tomlinson Commission on the Socio-Economic Development of the Bantu Areas,* UG 61/1955.

[3] O. Williams (1973), 'South Africa: land, people, policies', *Proceedings of the Rhodesian Geographical Association* 6, pp. 38–45.

[4] H.C. Brookfield (1957), 'Some geographical implications of the apartheid and racial partnership policies in Southern Africa', *IBG* 23, pp. 225–47.

[5] A. Nel (1962), 'Geographical aspects of apartheid in South Africa', *Tijdschrift voor Economische en Sociale Geografie* 53 (October).

[6] *Sunday Tribune* (Durban), 26 April 1970 and 25 May 1975; *Comment and Opinion* (Pretoria), 30 May and 1 August 1975.

[7] K.A. Heard (1965), 'Voting trends in South Africa as revealed in recent elections and the 1960 referendum, and their implications for the theory of representation', unpublished PhD thesis, University of Natal.

[8] Republic of South Africa (1974), *Report of the Thirteenth Delimitation Commission,* Pretoria; *Government Gazette,* 8 February 1974; (for South-West Africa) *Official Gazette Extraordinary,* 8 February 1974.

[9] *Stats* (Johannesburg), 30 June 1965, 31 March 1966, 30 April 1970; *Africa Institute Bulletin* 12, no. 4 (1974).

[10] *Natal Witness,* 26 May 1948.

[11] Union of South Africa (1960), *Official Yearbook,* no. 30, Pretoria.

[12] A. Keppel-Jones in the *Sunday Tribune* (Durban), 26 April 1970.

[13] *Report of the Thirteenth Delimitation Commission,* op. cit.

[14] *Africa Institute Bulletin* 12, no. 4.

[15] *Comment and Opinion,* 30 May and 1 August 1975; *Sunday Tribune,* 25 May 1975.

PART III

INDIANS AND COLOUREDS: AN UNRESOLVED PROBLEM

6 The Indian community

Indentured and 'passenger' immigrants

Indentured Indians originally came from areas of rural poverty and unemployment in the south and central provinces of India. They constituted a heterogeneous community in terms of language and religion, although some 60 per cent were Hindus of various sects. Most came as isolated persons, or with a few kin or friends. Women were recruited in the ratio 30:100 and later 50:100. Initially recruited for work on sugar plantations, the Indians quickly became an essential element in almost every sector of the Natal economy, but the conditions of their service contracts restricted their freedom of movement and forbade them to associate as equals with Europeans. They were indentured for periods of three and later five years, at the end of which they could remain as free citizens or receive a free return passage to India. Many were offered land as an inducement to re-indenture, but as their numbers increased the earlier promise of citizenship was not fulfilled, and after a few years the offer of land was also withdrawn. Nearly all Indians nevertheless remained in South Africa, where their prospects were brighter than in India. They turned mostly to market gardening and trading in peri-urban and urban areas, where they established more permanent roots, whilst some were attracted to the coalmines of northern Natal.

When Zulu political and economic independence had been broken, the Zulu were brought into competition with indentured Indians as unskilled manual workers. Zulu wages were lower than those of Indians, this being based on the assumption that the workers were unmarried or that their families were supporting themselves in the reserves; their period of service was limited to approximately nine months. There was little communication and considerable latent hostility between indentured Indians and these migrant Africans. The former, whilst many of them were illiterate peasants of lower castes, were aware of a great literate tradition, and of the existence of many non-agricultural occupations and a money economy. Although the Indian caste hierarchy broke down on the estates, Indians remained a distinctive and isolated enclave largely through their particular type of kinship network, in which the ideal of the extended joint family played a central role.[1] They tried to arrange marriages within narrow religious and linguistic boundaries, and were opposed to marriage with Africans on cultural grounds. Africans resented this and the close supervision exercised by Indians over their women. Antagonism is said to have been intensified by the fact that the few cases of miscegenation which occurred were between Indian (Muslim) men and African women.[2] Africans also despised Indians as servile and of poor physique.

Some 10 per cent of all Indian immigrants were 'passengers' who had entered South Africa at their own expense to trade and work in commerce in the 1880s and 1890s. Initially they opened shops not only on the plantations, but also in African tribal areas and European towns. After 1896, when riots attended the arrival of ships carrying 'free' Indians at Durban, passenger immigration was restricted. Most passenger immigrants were Gujerati- and Urdu-speaking Muslims who had embarked from Bombay. Once in South Africa they managed to retain basic relations with kin outside Africa, and contracted correct marriages in India. 'Passengers' thus constituted a more cohesive group than indentured immigrants, whom they excluded at first from their organisations. This economic cleavage, reinforced by cultural divisions, was narrowed under the leadership of Mahatma Gandhi, who first entered South Africa in 1893 to represent the legal interests of Gujerati businessmen.

Of the present South African Indian population of 620,000 (1970 figures), over 70 per cent are descended from indentured immigrants: that the figure is not higher reflects the unbalanced sex structure of indentured as compared with passenger immigrants. The male:female ratio of the Indian population as a whole dropped from 171·5:100 in 1911 to 121·8:100 in 1936 and a more normal 99·4:100 in 1970. By 1960, a mere 5·5 per cent of Indians had been born outside South Africa.[3] Immigration has been limited to dependants of existing residents since the Immigrants Regulation Act of 1913, which was aimed primarily at Indians. A law which came into operation in 1956 effectively inhibits Indians from marrying women in the Indian subcontinent and thus acquiring the necessary immigration qualifications for them. Between 1936 and 1960 total net immigration amounted to only 9,100, although some assisted emigration was still occurring during this period under the Cape Town Agreement of 1927, with the consent of the Indian government.

Indians appear to have reached a relatively advanced phase of the demographic cycle. Their rate of natural increase has dropped from a peak of 3·39 per cent per annum in 1946–51 to only 2·6 per cent in

106

1966–70. A gradual increase in the average age of marriage, which was only 18·7 years in 1921, is a major factor in this change.

European attitudes: restrictions and repatriation

Anti-Asian propaganda and legislation began in Natal as early as the 1880s. The major cause was the number of Indian traders, known inaccurately as 'Arabs'. These early years of European hostility mark the beginning of an ambivalence and hesitancy, arising almost entirely out of European economic interests, which ran through the history of racial attitudes in Natal for the next seventy years: employers found Indians useful for their labour, but traders and businessmen feared competition. As late as 1944 the Natal Post-war Works and Reconstruction Commission in its report to the Provincial Council stated that, although the Indian of the labouring classes served a useful purpose, the affluent Indian was a menace to European civilisation in Natal:[4] this is a direct echo from the 1880s.

Such attitudes were by no means confined to Natal. Since 1891 Indians have been excluded altogether from the Orange Free State. The Transvaal would probably have preferred to act likewise, but was bound by a convention with Britain. However, by a law of 1885, Indians were prevented from owning property there except in limited areas assigned for their residence. In 1908 they were specifically excluded from mining or acquiring land in mining areas. These restrictions were never fully enforced, however, and Indians formed themselves into companies to buy property where they wished. They also circumvented the immigration restrictions imposed in 1907, soon after the granting of responsible government to the Transvaal. In the Cape the approach was more permissive: the Coloured community had a recognised place in the social design of the Colony, into which Indians could easily fit. Like the Coloureds, Indians with appropriate qualifications were eligible to vote. The Cape was, however, out of the way for Natal Indians, and attracted relatively few, whilst an Act of 1906 prohibited the entry of male Asians of sixteen years and over from overseas.

The concentration of the Indian population in Natal was maintained after the Act of Union by continued restriction on interprovincial movement. Indians are still excluded from the Orange Free State, together with certain areas of northern Natal where exclusion of those not already resident there was imposed in 1927.[5] Other restrictions on movement and settlement of Indians were abolished in 1975, which means that all

Indians may now move freely from one province to another, and may settle without permission in any province except the Free State. It remains to be seen whether this leads to a significant change in the distribution of the Indian population, over four-fifths of which is currently in Natal, and two-thirds of the remainder in the Transvaal. Had it not been for past restrictions, a larger number of Indian businessmen and traders would almost certainly be found in the towns of the Transvaal and the Orange Free State today.

European ambivalence is nowhere better reflected than in the continued encouragement of voluntary 'repatriation', first under the 1914 Indians Relief Act, which in other respects went some way to recognising Indians as part of the population, and later as part of the Cape Town Agreement. Some 47,000 Indians emigrated up to 1933, an average of only 2,500 per annum. By that time more than 80 per cent of Indians were South African-born and emigration, much reduced, was exceeded by immigration. The time had clearly come for South Africa to recognise Indians as a permanent part of her population; remarkably, she refrained from doing so formally until 1961. Assisted emigration was finally terminated only in 1975, although the last Indian to take advantage of the scheme did so in 1970.[6]

Europeans found a new cause for grievance in the late 1930s as Indians began to 'infiltrate' into predominantly White areas, especially in Durban. In 1940 the government appointed an Indian Penetration Commission, which found the number of cases to be 512 in Durban, 328 elsewhere in Natal, and 339 in the Transvaal. Whereas 73 per cent of cases in the Transvaal concerned trading sites, in Natal residential sites were the main ones affected: more than 70 per cent of them were not occupied by Indians, but merely bought as investments. The White reaction seemed wholly disproportionate to the scale and nature of penetration. Nevertheless, when a second Commission reported increased penetration in 1943, temporary restrictions on Indian acquisition of property in White areas of Durban were incorportated into the 'pegging' Act of 1943. Three years later the Asiatic Land Tenure and Indian Representation Act, unofficially known as the 'Ghetto Act', restricted the occupation and ownership of property by Indians in the Transvaal and Natal to 'exempted' areas. This Act was itself superseded by the Group Areas Act (1950), whereby Indians are confined to their own group areas throughout the country.

The question of assimilation

The strength of White reactions to penetration, together with official reluctance to abandon repatriation and recognise Indian citizenship, reflects the underlying conviction that Indians are 'alien' and 'unassimilable'. A relatively sympathetic expression of this view is that of Keppel-Jones who says of the Indians that:

> Like the Coloured people, they are civilised; but in its roots their civilisation is different from the West. They therefore are not allied to us in the way Coloured people are . . . Their place in South African society is more difficult to establish on lines satisfactory to themselves and others than that of any other group.[7]

Such a view is based largely on visible symbols of cultural pluralism such as religion, food and dress. In practice, cultural differences cut through and across such categories, and the Natal Indian community, although certainly distinctive, is more westernised than any other overseas Indian community.[8] European dress has become the norm, and more European food is eaten. Wage labour has done much to break down the joint family system: research carried out by the Department of Economics at the University of Natal shows that only about one-fifth of all Indian households still contain joint families, although kinship bonds still appear to be very strong in Indian life. Conservative attitudes to the employment of women are gradually breaking down. Educated Indians are pursuing European arts and literature, whilst almost all Indians now speak English, many of them using it as the first language in the home.

Indians are themselves culturally diverse – a fact seldom recognised by Whites – and nowhere is this more true than in terms of religion. Hinduism is dominant in Natal, whilst Moslems outnumber Hindus in the Transvaal and the Cape, but these are merely umbrella terms which conceal great complexity. Less than 10 per cent of Indians are Christians, although there are notable Roman Catholic minorities in Kimberley and Port Elizabeth. But religion is not necessarily so significant a barrier to assimilation as it seems at first. Hinduism is singularly eclectic, and Western influences are particularly noticeable in the Arya Samaj (reform movement), in such features as the structure of the temple and the 'middle class decorum' preserved by worshippers. Religion is in any case a personal, private affair for both Hindus and Moslems, and as such it need impinge relatively little on everyday social relationships.

The Indian place in South African society as traditionally viewed by the European exemplifies Furnivall's characterisation of a plural society as a 'business partnership rather than a family concern' in which 'the social will linking the sections does not extend beyond the common business interests.'[9] But for Indians the spontaneous expression of that social will is difficult if not impossible to measure, as it is restricted by both White laws and White attitudes.

The Indian occupational rôle

Indentured immigration from India ceased in 1913. Thereafter a slow but steady growth of educational opportunities, culminating in the provision of university education in 1938, opened the door to the teaching profession, whilst some Indians received medical and legal training abroad. Agriculture declined as a source of employment in favour of manufacturing, commerce and services (see Table 6.1). These trends, which have continued since 1945, have been accompanied by increasing urbanisation: the percentage of Indians residing in urban areas has increased from 62 in 1936 to 74 in 1951, 81 in 1960, and 84 in 1970.

Indian smallholders and market gardeners were the major suppliers of fruit and vegetables to the European population of Durban as long ago as the 1870s and 1880s.[10] Whilst they remain important in the Durban

Table 6.1
Percentage distribution of Indian workers by industry division in Natal, 1936–70

Industry division	1936	1951	1960	1970
Agriculture	37·8	20·3	12·0	4·8
Mining	1·4	0·8	0·6	0·4
Manufacturing	19·1	31·4	37·7	41·9
Construction	2·0	3·4	2·4	6·8
Commerce	16·1	18·1	18·1	24·0
Transport	3·1	3·6	4·7	5·1
Services	20·4	22·4	24·2	15·3
Other	–	–	0·3	1·5
Total	47,000	63,000	79,000	134,000

Source: G. Maasdorp and N. Pillay, 'Occupational mobility among the Indian people of Natal', paper presented at the fifth Workshop on Mobility and Social Change in South Africa, Centre for Intergroup Studies, University of Cape Town, June 1975.

and Pinetown districts, their numbers are declining due to the spread of urbanisation, rising costs, insufficient capital and the inadequacy of their land; smallholders have been displaced from areas such as the Bayhead, Springfield Flats and Chatsworth without the provision of any alternative agricultural land. In the coastal districts of Lower Tugela and Inanda north of Durban, and Umzinto and Port Shepstone to the south most Indian farmers grow sugar cane. They hold 9·5 per cent of all registered quota land, but account for only 7 per cent of production:[11] this is because of the steepness of most of their land (much of which would be rejected by White farmers), lack of expertise and capital, and the small size of individual holdings which precludes scale economies. Many farmers rely on income from non-farming activities because of the low incomes afforded by their holdings. These problems have been accentuated by widespread fragmentation, as no additional land is available for Indian agriculture, although some former cane growers now work in the sugar mills instead.

Indian agricultural potential is undoubtedly an under-utilised resource. Production could be greatly increased given training facilities, easier capital availability, and more land. The achievement of scale economies clearly demands the establishment of co-operative arrangements whereby farmers can share in a common pool of machinery and equipment. The possibility of an irrigation scheme on one of the north coast rivers of Natal has been suggested,[12] but there has been no official reponse as yet.

The major manufacturing industries employing Indians are, in order of importance, clothing, food and drink, footwear, textiles, wool and furniture, and paper and printing. These are sectors which Indians penetrated in large numbers in the 1940s, when large numbers of Whites were in the armed forces, and in which there has been a consistent qualitative improvement in the work done. In recent years Indians have made important advances as mechanics in the motor industry, whilst perhaps their most significant industrial breakthrough has been in the iron and steel industry, where 1,000 are already employed in the third ISCOR works at Newcastle. The number of Indian artisans and apprentices in manufacturing industry increased from 4,100 in 1969 to 6,500 in 1973; the majority have higher academic qualifications than their White counterparts.[13]

The creation of the Department of Indian Affairs in 1961, the government takeover of Indian education from the provinces, and the extension of local government to Indian towns and townships have created wider job opportunities for Indians, although they would undoubtedly have entered administrative employment much earlier if competition had been unrestricted. The scope for Indian workers in commerce has also widened, with a continued increase in the employment of Indian clerks and sales representatives by White firms and, in the last decade, the opening of branches of banks, building societies and insurance societies staffed entirely by Indians in Indian areas. In transport Indians have advanced both on the driving and maintenance sides.

An increasingly wide range of professions is now open to Indians, including those such as engineering, architecture and accountancy where the lack of training facilities available has been a limiting factor hitherto. Proportionately nearly five times as many Indians as Coloureds are enrolled at universities: in 1974 the Indian figure was 4,863, compared with only 3,142 Coloureds in a population three times as large.[14] The Indian total included 1,946 students registered for correspondence degree courses with the University of South Africa (UNISA), 347 studying at Natal University's non-White medical faculty in Durban, and 228 permitted to study at other White universities owing to the absence of suitable facilities at the Indian University itself in Durban–Westville.

Indian women are increasingly entering the labour force. The range of opportunities open to them is generally wider in Durban and Pietermaritzburg than in small country towns. They work as secretaries, typists, receptionists and sales assistants in White firms, whilst Indian firms are replacing men with women in similar jobs. Considerable numbers of women are working in industry, especially as operatives in the clothing industry, and in the professions as teachers, nurses, and social workers, with a smaller number as doctors and lawyers. In addition to the social and cultural factors mentioned above, economic circumstances have virtually forced the Indian community to accept female employment. In the 1950s and early 1960s Indian unemployment in Natal was a major problem, reaching 16–20 per cent in Durban according to two 1963 studies, one of which also found that 63·7 per cent of Indians were living below the Poverty Datum Line (PDL), and a further 28·3 per cent not far above it.[15] During such periods it was realised that the low activity rate and earning capacity of Indian women (owing to lack of education or qualifications) were important contributory reasons for poverty amongst Indians. With the rapid economic growth of Natal since the mid-1960s unemployment is no longer a problem. The Indian labour force is, however, a rapidly growing one, and with the increasing participation of women the rate of growth will be greater still: absorption of this labour force depends upon a continuing rapid rate of economic growth together with the further opening up of skilled and professional jobs to Indians.

Indian industrialists

Indian cottage industries existed as long ago as the 1880s: the many small jewellery firms which still exist today, and which both manufacture and retail their own products, are a good example of their development. A few Indian traders and merchants diversified into manufacturing proper in the 1890s, but for the most part the emergence of an Indian industrial group was delayed until the 1950s, when several of the wealthier Indian trading families acquired manufacturing interests. The most rapid growth has occurred only since 1961, encouraged partly by the Department of Indian Affairs, which hoped that industrial opportunities might compensate for the negative effects of the Group Areas Act of Indian traders. The latter certainly encouraged those Indians with capital and know-how – a very small proportion of all traders – to diversify into manufacturing. The tendency for Indian wholesalers to suffer from changing trade patterns whereby department stores and supermarkets deal directly with manufacturers has similarly stimulated Indian industrial investment. The overall number of Indian industrial concerns, including laundry and dry-cleaning businesses, has increased from 181 in 1961 to over 600 today in South Africa as a whole.[16] Although the number of large enterprises run on modern business lines is increasing, most are still small scale concerns employing only a few people. Clothing continues to be the most popular field, with textiles, footwear, furniture, food processing, printing, servicing and repair establishments also important. Indians also figure prominently in the building industry where they compete for government contracts; they have also received a considerable boost from the development of private townships for Indians.

In 1965 the government announced the designation of industrial development areas for Indians in Stanger, Tongaat and Verulam on the north coast of Natal (see Fig. 3.2), as well as in Pietermaritzburg. A number of industrial sites have also been designated for Indians in and around Durban. The Industrial Development Corporation began to assist Indian firms in the 1960s, although the number of beneficiaries is still small: in 1974 three Indians were assisted in establishing small factories at Rustenburg and Pietersburg in the Transvaal.[17] The IDC has reportedly embarked on a programme costing over R3 million to develop fifteen industrial sites at Chatsworth (Durban) and others at Stanger and Tongaat; similar developments are expected to follow in the Transvaal and the Cape.

These developments are not wholly advantageous to Indian industrialists. They are discouraged or restricted from establishing industry in 'open' industrial zones, not to mention African homelands. This effectively continues the discriminatory application of licensing laws of earlier years. The relatively small areas of land now allocated specifically for Indian use means that prices are high – in the Durban area they are generally 10–20 per cent higher than those asked for 'White' land at similar distances from central Durban. This has resulted in some vertical development and 'flatted' factories for Indian tenants in heavy demand areas.[18] Some Indian industrialists have found themselves in areas proclaimed White, or non-Indian, under the Group Areas Act, which has restricted their further expansion and prompted them to search for new sites where practicable. Others have suffered from uncertainty, in areas such as Clairwood at the head of Durban Bay and Durban's Grey Street complex. When the latter was finally proclaimed an area for Indian-owned commercial and industrial activities in 1973, after twelve years' uncertainty, several clothing manufacturers were particularly relieved, although rising rents and distance from their labour supply may yet induce them to move.

The overall impact of apartheid upon Indian entrepreneurial achievement is difficult to assess. The general reaction of Indian industrialists has been characteristic: to accept the inevitable, and work within the framework of separate development.

Indian traders and the Group Areas Act

Owing to the extent of their commercial involvement, Indians have suffered disproportionately as a result of the Group Areas Act. Many Afrikaner Nationalists have rejected Indians as non-productive and parasitical due to their association with commerce, and it is therefore understandable that a prominent South African Indian, Fatima Meer, should assert that:

> There is little doubt that one of the prime purposes of the Group Areas Act is to eliminate, or at least reduce to a minimum, Indian commerce, and it is succeeding in doing so.[19]

Whether the intentions behind the Act are as blatantly anti-Indian as this seems doubtful, but the effects are undeniable. By the middle of 1974, 5,058 Indian traders had become disqualified to remain in their existing premises: out of these 984 had been resettled. In addition 620 Chinese traders had become affected, of whom one had been resettled (there are proclaimed Group Areas for Chinese only at Port Elizabeth and

Table 6.2

Asian traders and the Group Areas Act

(a) Distribution of Indian traders

	Number affected	Resettled	Not yet resettled
Natal	1,022	326	696
Transvaal	3,000	566	2,434
Cape	1,036	92	944
	5,058	984	4,074

(b) Distribution of those not yet resettled

	Indians	Chinese
Municipal areas of:		
Cape Town	428	7
Port Elizabeth	125	183
Durban	401	10
Johannesburg	930	139
Pretoria	119	41
Rest of Cape Province	391	116
Natal	295	–
Transvaal	1,385	123
	4,074	619

Source: M. Horrell and T. Hodgson (1976), *A Survey of Race Relations in South Africa 1975,* SAIRR, p. 74.

Uitenhage).[20] More detailed figures are given in Table 6.2. It is evident from these figures that dislocation has been particularly great in the Transvaal and the Cape, where absolute numbers of Indians are relatively small but the proportion dependent on commerce is high – as many as 87·6 per cent of Transvaal Indians in 1963, according to the Transvaal Indian Congress.[21] By 1966, only 7·5 per cent of Transvaal Indians remained unaffected by proclamations of group areas. In Johannesburg the vast majority of traders have been evicted and only a relatively small minority have succeeded in re-establishing themselves in commerce. In

Pretoria, the proclamation of group areas in 1958 left nearly one-third of the Indian traders unaffected, but since the African and Coloured populations living in close proximity to the Asiatic bazaar area were required to move, loss of business was inevitable.

Indian traders in the small towns of Natal and the Transvaal have escaped no more lightly. Indeed their plight may be even worse, for in such towns distances are short and there is no scope for suburban shopping centres. Two good examples of the kind of fate which has befallen Indian traders are the proposed removal of traders from Retief Street in the centre of Piet Retief (Transvaal) to a shopping centre at Kempville, 1·5 kilometres from the outskirts of the town, and from Kerk Street in the centre of Bethal (Transvaal) to a shopping centre at Milan Park, three kilometres away.[22] Indians have been established in Bethal since 1885 and in Piet Retief since 1904 and have operated from their present trading areas from the beginning, making an important contribution to the economic growth of both communities and assisting the farming community during the depression years of the 1930s. Of the annual turnover of these traders in 1973–74, Whites were responsible for 55·7 per cent at Piet Retief and 45·6 per cent at Bethal, and Africans for 35·8 and 30·8 per cent respectively. Virtually all this trade would be lost as a result of the proposed move, and it is quite obvious that neither the fifteen traders in Piet Retief nor the thirty in Bethal could hope to make a living from trading mainly with their own communities, which in each case number only around five hundred.

The trading potential of all but a few Indian group areas in other towns is similarly insufficient to enable the present generation of Indian traders to make a living. Provision has now been made in the Group Areas Act for the proclamation of group areas for a specific purpose or usage, such as trading, instead of for ownership or occupation by a specific group. Such areas have been declared in Pretoria, Port Elizabeth, Newcastle and Ladysmith, and it is to be hoped that this solution will be applied in smaller towns where Indians have not already been displaced.

The most important Indian trading area in South Africa is the Grey Street complex of Durban. The case for its retention in Indian hands has been powerfully argued by academics at the University of Natal.[23] The complex is an area of mixed residential, industrial, office, retailing and other units, 95 per cent of which is Indian-owned, with a probable market value exceeding R50 million. Over half Durban's Indian traders operate there, as well as some 200 industrialists. The complex has an invaluable function in generating profits for further Indian investment in industry, as the government envisages. It is also the only remaining business area for

Indians which is close to the hub of a major city. In addition it is a major centre of Indian employment, and has important cultural and residential functions, although the latter could be expected to decline in the face of commercial pressures. There is little evidence that the Grey Street complex is retarding or limiting the expansion of the White central area, whilst important activities in the latter, such as banking and wholesale trade, would probably suffer if Indian rights in the Grey Street area were curtailed. As a central area accessible to all parts of the widely dispersed Indian residential areas, it is the only area in which higher order services and shopping facilities for Indians can be suitably located: to proclaim the area White would have been tantamount to demanding that the Indian urban economy become completely decentralised.

Despite the strength of these and other arguments, a decision on the future of the area was made only in 1975. Meanwhile the difficulties experienced by prospective developers in obtaining permission, and the restrictions accompanying such permission when granted, discouraged development. The postponement of determinations and conflicting impressions of government intentions created a climate of insecurity, which made loans difficult to raise and deterred many owners from properly maintaining their premises. It was finally decided to proclaim the Grey Street area an Indian group area for trading and light industrial, but not residential, purposes. This means that some 12,000 people will have to move despite the existing shortage of Indian housing in Durban, whilst an important educational and cultural complex representing a large investment by the Indian community has been excluded from the proclaimed area.[24]

Indian CBDs have been identified and analysed by geographers in other South African urban areas, including Newcastle and Pietermaritzburg.[25] Indian traders in the latter are fortunate in that their CBD forms the apex of a 'wedge' of the city set aside by group area proclamations for Coloured and Indian residential use: thus there is no White residential belt between the CBD and residential areas.[26] Distinctive features of Indian CBDs include the absence of hotels and government buildings, and the very low proportion of both offices and vacant building space. Retailing occupies a correspondingly higher proportion of floorspace, but the more specialised shops are lacking. Many of these features are not directly attributable to apartheid legislation, and the present degree of development may well be a stage in the evolution towards a fully-fledged CBD.[27]

Residential resettlement

Indians, like Coloureds and Africans, have been required to move in large numbers to the group areas set aside for them. In many cases, as in Durban where the bulk of the Indian population has been re-housed in peripheral areas north and south of the path of White expansion, the Indian townships are more distant from the CBD and the Indians' places of work than are the White residential areas. Indian families required to move may either find their own accommodation in private developments such as those at Verulam, or apply through the Community Development Board for municipal housing in areas like Chatsworth. Those who owned their homes are compensated, but properties are usually valued long before families are required to move, with the result that the owners have to relinquish houses at well below their current market value. A disproportionately small amount of land has been set aside for Indians, which results in high prices. This is evidenced by the building of large and often ostentatious houses on relatively small plots in the few affluent Indian suburbs such as Mountain Rise in Pietermaritzburg. In the municipal housing schemes, very little land is available for private gardens, and any traditional attachment to land retained by resettled families must very soon be lost.

Implementation of the Group Areas Act is also responsible for a new phenomenon in Indian residential areas: the spatial expression of socio-economic differences. Traditionally, Indian stratification patterns have rested more on family origins than on achieved status or housing quality,[28] but sub-economic municipal housing schemes intended for poorer families effectively segregate these people from the middle classes. Since the latter have hitherto been the leaders of Indian opinion, such segregation may have political repercussions. A further effect of municipal housing is to discourage Indians from maintaining joint families, which are officially forbidden in municipal houses.

Indian political development

As a small and powerless minority in South Africa, Indians have largely relied on negotiations and deputations at both national and international level to represent their views. On four occasions, however, they have engaged in passive resistance campaigns, the first two under the leadership of Gandhi. These campaigns show a gradual broadening of Indian political concern. In the first (1903), the resistance came from traders who were adversely affected by new laws in the Transvaal. The second campaign, ending in 1913, was directed against wider issues, directly related to indentured Indians; it emancipated Indian politics from the personal interests of the traders and paved the way for the rise of a political élite drawn from all sections of the Indian community.[29] Passive resistance was not tried again until 1946, when it was specifically directed at the 'Ghetto' Act, although it had far wider associations. The leaders were young, educated radicals who formed themselves into a non-racial anti-segregation council and subsequently took control of the South African Indian Congress. A fourth resistance movement in 1952 expressed a further development of identification between Africans and Indians, and was aimed at laws affecting Africans more directly than Indians.

Such African–Indian co-operation was a remarkable achievement coming only three years after the Zulu–Indian riots in Durban, when fifty Indians were killed and 503 injured. The Indian Congress on that occasion showed 'a forbearance and political wisdom which was almost superhuman.'[30] Its leaders realised that the causes of the riots were deep-rooted, and that the hatred exhibited was due partly to frustration and partly to the fact that the privileges enjoyed by Indians, such as freedom from the pass laws, were greater than those accorded to Africans. As storekeepers and moneylenders Indians occupied something of the position of the Jews in Eastern Europe. However, despite the intermittent co-operation which has occurred between the two races since 1952, most South African Indians must be acutely aware of the fate of Ugandan Indians, and many would view the prospect of African majority rule in South Africa with considerable apprehension.

Since the early 1950s, Indians have been organised on the two distinct ideological grounds of protest and compromise. Interracial political action is represented by the policies of the South African Indian Congress, led by educated radicals seeking mass support and identification with Africans. The South African Indian Organisation, on the other hand, sees African nationalism as potentially threatening to the hard-won position of the traders and merchants whose interests it articulates. It stands for compromise and accommodation with the Whites, and in doing so probably reflects the attitudes of most Indians. Such attitudes presumably underlie Niddrie's statement that the Indian community 'has, with a few individual exceptions, readily accepted separate development.'[31] This is highly misleading, however, because it confuses accommodation with acceptance.

Indian constitutional development is somewhat behind that of the

Coloureds, but it is officially envisaged that the two communities will tread similar paths. The South African Indian Council became a statutory body in 1968, but only in 1974 was it reconstituted so that fifteen of the thirty members were elected by Indians already occupying elected positions in local government. An increase in the proportion of elected members and a wider franchise are unlikely to be long delayed, and should make the Council more representative than hitherto: for nominated councillors the prestige gained from high level contact with Whites has too often been seen as an end in itself.[32] The Council at present acts in a purely advisory capacity.

Indian progress in local government has been equally slow. Most townships have only nominated local officers, management and consultative committees. The Indian local authority of Isipingo, near Durban, was elevated to the status of a borough council in 1975, whilst town boards function at Verulam and Umzinto. The Durban City Council was reportedly considering obtaining provincial council permission to offer local authority autonomy to the Indians of Chatsworth.[33] A similar offer was rejected by the elected management committee of Lenasia in Johannesburg on the ground that suburban autonomy was impossible without industrial autonomy.[34] Such splintering of authority within what is a functional whole (the conurbation) is by no means unfamiliar in Britain and the United States, where its disadvantages have long been manifest.

Conclusions

Indians have shown themselves to be an enterprising and adaptable people. For Natal, where most of them live, they constitute a human resource of great potential significance in the future economic growth of the province. The realisation of this potential depends upon the elimination of statutory barriers to Indian advancement, but perhaps more importantly upon the erosion of *customary* barriers reflected in the attitudes of White employers and employees. South Africa's growing shortage of skilled and professional people must draw Indians even more irrevocably into the 'White' economy. In such circumstances it will be increasingly difficult to defend their perpetual exclusion from White political institutions on the dubious ground that Indians are culturally unassimilable.

References

[1]   H. Kuper (1960), *Indian People in Natal,* Natal University Press, Pietermaritzburg, chapter 6.

[2]   H. Kuper (1971), ' "Strangers" in plural societies: Asians in South Africa and Uganda', in L. Kuper and M.G. Smith (eds), *Pluralism in Africa,* University of California Press, Los Angeles, p. 258.

[3]   J.L. Sadie (1970), 'An evaluation of demographic data pertaining to the non-White population of South Africa', *SAJE* 38, p. 7.

[4]   Quoted in V. Wetherall (1946), *The Indian Question in South Africa,* privately published, p. 4.

[5]   'Inter-provincial movements of Indians', *Fiat Lux,* June–July 1975, pp. 2–3. (Statement by the Ministry of Indian Affairs.)

[6]   M. Horrell and T. Hodgson (1976), *A Survey of Race Relations in South Africa 1975,* SAIRR, Johannesburg, p. 24.

[7]   A. Keppel-Jones (undated), *Friends or Foes?,* Shuter and Shooter, Pietermaritzburg, p. 62.

[8]   H.C. Brookfield and M.A. Tatham (1957), 'The distribution of racial groups in Durban: the background of apartheid in a South African city,' *Geog. Rev.* 47, p. 50.

[9]   J.S. Furnivall (1948), *Colonial Policy and Practice,* Cambridge University Press, London, p. 308.

[10] L.P. McCrystal and G.G. Maasdorp (1966), 'The rôle of the Indian in Natal's economy', paper presented at an SAIRR conference (Natal region), Durban, October 1966, p. 1.

[11] Ibid., p. 8.

[12] Ibid., p. 9.

[13] G. Maasdorp and N. Pillay (1975), 'Occupational mobility among the Indian people of Natal', paper presented at the Fifth Workshop on Mobility and Social Change in South Africa, Centre for Intergroup Studies, University of Cape Town, June 1975, p. 9.

[14] M. Horrell (1975), *A Survey of Race Relations in South Africa 1974,* SAIRR, Johannesburg, p. 369.

[15] G.G. Maasdorp (1968), *A Natal Indian Community.* Natal Regional Survey, Additional Report No. 5, Department of Economics, University of Natal, Durban, p. 88.

[16] B.S. Young (1976), 'Indian-owned industries in the Durban region', part of a Queen Mary College, London, Department of Geography Occasional Paper.

[17] M. Horrell and T. Hodgson, op. cit., p. 74.

[18] B.S. Young, op. cit., p. 6.

[19] F. Meer (1971), 'Indian people: current trends and policies', in *South Africa's Minorities,* SPRO-CAS Publication No. 2, Johannesburg, p. 23.
[20] M. Horrell and T. Hodgson, op. cit., p. 73.
[21] Quoted by F. Meer, op. cit., p. 23.
[22] G.G. Maasdorp and P.N. Pillay (1975), 'Memorandum on behalf of the Indian traders of Bethal regarding their proposed removal to a shopping centre in Milan Park township' and 'Memorandum on behalf of the Indian traders of Piet Retief regarding their proposed removal to a shopping centre at Kempville township', Department of Economics, University of Natal, Durban (mimeograph). (The text of the ensuing paragraph is based on these memoranda.)
[23] H.L. Watts et. al. (1971), 'Group Areas and the "Grey Street" Complex, Durban', University of Natal, Durban (mimeograph).
[24] R.J. Davies et. al. (1973), 'The Grey Street Complex, Durban', University of Natal, Durban (mimeograph), p. 3.
[25] R.E. Schulze (1974), 'The business land use of central Newcastle: present and future', *S.Afn. Geographer* 4, pp. 308-19; T.M. Wills and R.E. Schulze (1976), 'Segregated business districts in a South African city', part of a Queen Mary College, London, Department of Geography Occasional Paper.
[26] Ibid., p. 13.
[27] R. Davies and D.S. Rajah (1965), 'The Durban CBD: boundary delimitation and racial dualism', *SAGJ* 47, pp. 45–58.
[28] L. Schlemmer (1966), 'The resettlement of Indian communities in Durban and some economic, social and cultural effects on the Indian community', paper presented at an *SAIRR* conference (Natal region), Durban, October 1966, p. 21.
[29] H. Kuper (1971), op. cit., p. 264.
[30] E.H. Brookes and C. de B. Webb (1965), *A History of Natal,* University of Natal Press, Pietermaritzburg, p. 292.
[31] D.L. Niddrie (1968), *South Africa: Nation or Nations?,* Van Nostrand, Princeton, p. 73.
[32] F. Meer, op. cit., p. 21.
[33] M. Horrell and T. Hodgson, op. cit., p. 79.
[34] Ibid., p. 80.

7 The Coloured people

The emergence of a rural proletariat

Ordinance 50 of 1828 put Hottentots and all other 'free people of colour' on an equal footing with Whites. One of the major effects of this change was the unrestricted movement of population, which led to considerable rural–urban migration. Emancipation in the years 1834–38 brought the same freedom to slaves, which contributed to their rapid integration with Hottentots into the emergent Coloured population: no clear cut dividing line can be drawn between Hottentot and Coloured in the late eighteenth and early nineteenth centuries.

The Hottentots in the western Cape had sunk into the position of a landless proletariat by 1795.[1] Many had been displaced as the Dutch East India Company gave farms to European colonists. The only ones to remain more or less independent of European farms lived in what were known as 'kraals', some of which subsequently became mission stations such as Zuurbraak and Ebenezer (see Fig. 7.1). In the eastern Cape there were even fewer traces of Hottentot independence left in 1795, following depredations by Bushmen, wars with the Xhosa, and internecine feuds. Missionary institutions were set up with the object of conversion, but unlike the mission stations they were quite unable to support their inhabitants. For White farmers they served as occasional reservoirs of labour.

The weak Griqua states on the Orange River failed to survive the onslaught of the Great Trek. Repeated references by missionaries clearly indicate that in return for wagons, oxen and possibly brandy, the unstable Griquas readily gave the encroaching Boers extensive rights to lease or occupy land.[2] For some years the Griquas who had trekked across the Drakensberg with Adam Kok in 1862–63 had their own self-governing 'Volksraad' (Parliament) in East Griqualand, but soon after the European government took over, Whites bought land and also did much harm by bringing liquor canteens to the area: by 1905 virtually no land remained in Griqua hands. Other groups of 'Bastards' attempted to retain a foothold south of the Orange in what is now the north-west Cape. They were essentially frontier societies, forming a curious intermediate class between Europeans and Coloured people. Like the Griquas and other

Coloured groups they were much influenced by their missionaries and clung pathetically to such European standards as they knew. They appeared to be unable to help themselves in a harsh environment and their hold on the soil was weak: nevertheless Marais believes it would have been worthwhile for the government to attempt to keep them on the land.[3]

Legal recognition of ten scattered rural areas developed as mission stations and communal reserves for Coloured people was consolidated in a Cape Act of 1909. A series of further enactments made provision for the inclusion of other areas and for changes in the control, administration and development of these areas (Fig. 7.1). They are mostly either small mission stations which are little more than villages, or vast expanses of sparsely populated and semi-desert areas in the north-west Cape. Less than 3 per cent of the Coloured population lives in these rural areas, which had a total area of just over 1·7 million hectares at the beginning of 1975.[4]

Despite the lack of land, the rural Coloured population has remained large in the twentieth century. There are a number of reasons for this. The extension of European fruit and vegetable growing, wine production and mixed farming has provided employment. This is clearly illustrated by the contrast between the wine-producing Paarl district, with a high rate of rural population growth since 1945, and the predominantly wheat-growing Malmesbury District, where mechanisation and modernisation have increased productivity and reduced the need for a large rural Coloured population.[5] Agricultural production in the winter rainfall area of the Cape also demands much seasonal labour. Wage-earners in rural families often seek employment in urban areas of the Western Cape in the off-season, especially if they live within commuting distance, yet statistically they remain rural. African migration to urban areas in the Cape is another factor which helps to explain why so many Coloureds remained on the land. The relatively slow provision of low rent housing for Coloureds in urban areas, with resultant squatting and overcrowding, has also deterred more rapid urbanisation.

Population growth and urbanisation

High fertility rates and decreasing mortality have led to a doubling of the Coloured population between 1951 and the early 1970s: in 1970 it exceeded two million for the first time. A maximum growth rate of 3·31 per cent per annum was attained during the years 1955–56; this was reduced to 3·02 per cent in the late 1960s, owing to reduced levels of

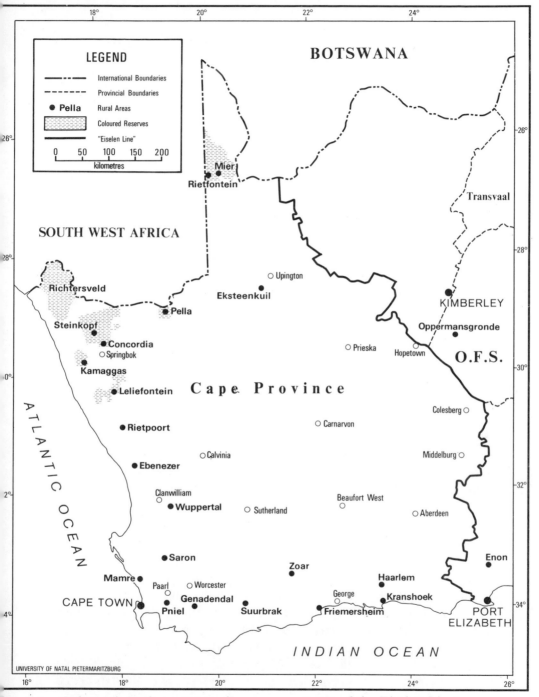

Fig. 7.1   Coloured employment preference area (west of the Eiselen Line) and Coloured rural areas

125

Table 7.1
Coloured urbanisation, 1946–70

Year	Total population	Urbanised (%)
1946	928,060	58
1951	1,103,020	63
1960	1,509,050	67·5
1970	2,021,430	74

Source: Union of South Africa, population censuses, 1946, 1951, 1960; Republic of South Africa, population census, 1970.

fertility.[6] Only a marginally lower rate of increase, 2·99 per cent per annum, is projected for the 1970s.[7] This is because a further anticipated decline in fertility will be partly countered by a further decrease in mortality, whilst the youthful age structure of the Coloured population (44·0 per cent below the age of fifteen in 1970) is such that an increase in the numbers of women in the fecund ages will occur. After 1980 a gradual decline in the Coloured growth rate is envisaged, but this will not prevent a further doubling of population by the year 2000, when it is expected to reach 4,890,000.[8] Professor Sadie's projections suggest that the Coloured population will overtake the White population between 2010 and 2015 AD, in the absence of increased White immigration.[9] The political significance of such projections, viewed against suggestions that Coloured people should be brought 'inside the laager', are evident: already by 1960 Coloureds constituted the majority of the inhabitants of the Western Cape.

The rapid population growth of the 1950s and 1960s has been accompanied by increased urbanisation (Table 7.1), although Coloureds are still some way behind the Indian rate of urbanisation (which reached 86 per cent in 1970). The Coloured rural population is, furthermore, still increasing in absolute terms. It is the 150,000 Coloureds of the Transvaal who are the most highly urbanised: in 1970 95 per cent lived in towns, 55 per cent in Johannesburg alone. Most of these, together with smaller numbers in Natal (67,000) and the Orange Free State (36,000) came originally from the Cape either in the days of the Voortrekkers or subsequently.

In the Cape itself, 29·6 per cent of all South Africa's Coloureds lived in the Cape Metropolitan Area in 1970, and a further 5·3 per cent in Port Elizabeth–Uitenhage: as with Indians, such concentrations coupled with high rates of increase could have political significance disproportionate to overall numbers.

The Coloured housing problem in Greater Cape Town

Poor housing conditions have existed at the Cape virtually since the founding of the settlement in 1652. A government committee of enquiry reporting in 1943 stated *inter alia:*

> Here then, is one of the largest and culturally most outstanding cities of South Africa which for forty years and more has undergone slow metamorphic growth and yet has apparently never at any time made a serious effort to cleanse its fringes once and for all of the fungus of haphazard planning, insanitary housing, disease and crime.[10]

Rapid urbanisation in the ensuing decades has accentuated housing shortages. Professor Cilliers estimates that in 1972 at least 173,388 Coloured people, some 22·6 per cent of the population of Greater Cape Town, were living under squatter conditions.[11] In order to cater for both squatters and others known to be in need of housing in the region, at least 54,908 dwelling units were needed to accommodate an estimated 314,623 people.[12] Inadequate housing is probably the greatest source of insecurity to the Coloured people, and the single most important factor impeding their social and economic advance. It contributes to the instability of Coloured labour, lowers the physical and psychological abilities of workers, and largely negates all the potential benefits to be derived from social, cultural, economic and educational measures aimed at uplifting and advancing the population.

Squatter sites in the Cape Town area include Vrygrond, Crossroads, Werkgenot, Michell's Plain and Lourdes Farm. Some, like Crossroads, house mainly Africans.[13] The majority have no piped water supply and no garbage collection service. There are few access roads for the fire brigade and the police, and almost no services. The squatter population is far from homogeneous: recent migrants probably account for only a quarter of the total. Other groups include families of mixed African and Coloured descent who can be catered for neither in an African nor a Coloured township; people who have left housing estates owing to the anonymous type of housing provided; and those whose level of income is insufficient even to qualify for sub-economic housing.[14] Any strategy for upgrading squatter areas depends above all on increased security of tenure; hitherto, incessant destruction of squatter houses and families, without the offer of alternative accommodation, has left little incentive for squatters to use their own resources, potential and creativity to rehabilitate the communities in which they live. Encouraging developments during 1975 included the establishment of site and service schemes at Vrygrond and Philippi; and the founding by various organisations of a Cape Flats Committee to assist squatters.[15]

The Group Areas Act has contributed substantially to the present crisis proportions of the backlog in housing provision. By the end of 1974, no less than 75,472 Coloured families throughout the country had been disqualified from remaining in their homes, of whom 53,203 had been resettled.[16] In Greater Cape Town, over 10,000 disqualified families will need rehousing if the Act continues to be implemented. If these families were allowed to remain where they were, housing demand would be reduced by one-fifth, which would make the overcoming of the housing crisis by the early 1980s much more feasible. Such an achievement would depend on a number of changes in the current situation. At present the Group Areas Act limits provision of Coloured housing schemes to the public sector. Until a few years ago, institutions such as the Citizens' Housing League were allowed to participate and made a valuable contribution. Furthermore, now that housing for Coloureds is provided increasingly on an economic rather than sub-economic basis, private developers could be encouraged to enter the market. Private enterprise could also build more single accommodation, especially for the rapidly growing category of white-collar workers, were this permitted. More provision of plots for personal home ownership schemes could be made available, and measures taken to ensure that land speculation in such plots is limited as far as possible. Employers of Coloured labour should also be making a greater contribution to the housing of their employees: they are currently enabled to provide such accommodation in Coloured group areas in terms of a scheme whereby they retain the use of the properties for sixty years, and the whole sum spent on them is tax deductible. Their response to these generous provisions has so far been disappointing; this reflects the attitude of South African employers that housing is the responsibility of the government or municipality.

Implementation of the Group Areas Act may also be criticised by urban geographers or planners on two other grounds. First, the established economic and ecological structure of Cape Town militates against the development of separate, full-scale and diversified urban settlements for Whites and Coloureds. Secondly, the allocation of Coloured group areas has been made on the assumption that the Coloured population will continue to be primarily involved in industrial activities. In early years this was a reasonable assumption, but in recent years the economic structure of the Western Cape has changed considerably. The White population of Greater Cape Town increased by only 24 per cent between 1960 and 1970, compared with 34·9 per cent in Durban–Pinetown and 34·4 per cent in the PWV metropolitan area: this was partly due to a low rate of natural increase, but also to relatively low White immigration from rural areas. At the same time economic development has, as elsewhere in South Africa, called for a rapid expansion of employment in the technical, commercial, administrative, professional and semi-professional sectors, which can only be achieved by using Coloured labour. Such jobs are mainly located in central areas, yet no Coloured group areas have been proclaimed near such areas. The proclamation of District Six as White is particularly regrettable in this respect, as this was a predominantly Coloured area already and could have supported at least 50,000 people in the central Cape Town area.[17] As it is, the Cape Town CBD is suffering increasingly from congestion arising from the enforced commuting of Coloured workers. The absence of Coloured group areas in or near central Cape Town also deprives Coloured white-collar workers of access to amenities from their place of work.

The Mamre–Darling and Saldanha Bay developments

The government's response to planning problems in the Cape Peninsula, particularly as they relate to Coloured people, has been to encourage the shifting of industrial development to the Mamre–Darling area (Fig. 7.1). Dassenberg and Darling now qualify for decentralisation assistance in respect of Coloured labour, and a large new Coloured township, which may eventually house 500,000 people, is to be developed at Dassenberg. Ten factories were under construction in 1975.[18] It also appears likely that the Mamre–Silverboom area will gradually be developed as an independent village and seaside resort; the scarcity of good beach facilities and holiday resorts as well as residential property for Coloured people may encourage this process, and also lead to significant retirement of Coloureds to the area. The major question hanging over the Mamre–Darling scheme is the degree of employment self-sufficiency which is attainable if a substantial amount of population growth is siphoned away from the Cape Peninsula. If the growth area can attract only a limited amount of light industry, it will have to depend for employment primarily on the Cape Peninsula (65 kilometres away by present roads, although a shorter route is planned), which will add to the already heavy burden of passenger transport in that area.

The Saldanha development further north will not offer significant numbers of jobs to Coloureds in the 1970s: the ore export scheme alone needs only about 1,000 people for its operation. It appears probable, however, that a steel plant will be built at Saldanha. Longer term opportunities include the export of other minerals, the beneficiation of some of them (especially manganese), the construction of a ship repair yard and its possible expansion for shipbuilding.[19] By 1985 it is expected that linkage effects will begin to materialise, with a consequent broadening and deepening of the industrial and services structure, and a greater multiplier effect. A population of 230,000 in 1990 has been forecast for the Saldanha area, while total employment is estimated to be 100,000.[20] Although some use of African labour is probable, development on this scale would undoubtedly require substantial involvement of Coloured people. It would also significantly strengthen the Cape Town–Mamre–Saldanha axis envisaged in the National Physical Development Plan, which may eventually form part of a new Cape–Johannesburg rail link via Saldanha and Sishen.

Coloured townships in the northern provinces[21]

Coloured Group Areas have been proclaimed in most Cape towns, and in the major cities elsewhere. In the Southern Transvaal, such areas have been proclaimed only in Boksburg, Randfontein and Vereeniging, with similar development envisaged in Alberton, Nigel and Brakpan. Elsewhere in the three northern provinces, government policy since about 1968 has been to create regional townships in towns that are considered to be actual or potential employment growth points. People are being encouraged to move to one or other of these townships from areas where the Coloured community is small and where no housing scheme exists. The populations of these townships should eventually be large enough to support adequate educational, social and other facilities, and to develop local government bodies. Such townships are being developed, or are planned, at Middelburg, Witbank and Standerton in the eastern Transvaal, Klerksdorp and Potchefstroom in the western Transvaal, Estcourt, Ladysmith and Marburg in Natal, and Bloemfontein in the Free State. In order to stimulate employment growth, the government offers incentives to entrepreneurs using Coloured labour who set up or extend establishments in three of these towns – Bloemfontein, Klerksdorp and Ladysmith – and also in Heilbronn and Welkom in the Free State, and Newcastle in Natal. The latter are amongst a dozen or so towns where the development of already proclaimed group areas is permitted for the time being, although subject to controls in most cases. Final decisions appear to have been postponed in several cases pending the report of the Commission of Inquiry into Matters relating to the Coloured Population Group (the Theron Commission), publication of which is expected during 1976. Meanwhile considerable numbers of Coloureds continue to live in the African townships of the Transvaal and the Free State pending eventual resettlement.

A recent survey by the South African Institute of Race Relations found that while there are some Coloured people who do not wish to leave certain of the smaller towns, considerable numbers have already migrated from other towns and rural areas in search of better housing, employment and educational opportunities. This has exacerbated existing shortages in the towns where they now live. Towns reporting abnormal Coloured population increases because of this migration include Johannesburg, Durban, Pietermaritzburg, Ladysmith, Estcourt, Newcastle, Bloemfontein and Heilbronn. Widespread housing shortages affect Coloureds in most towns in the northern provinces. In some cases they are largely due to extended delays in the proclamation of group areas, as in Ladysmith and Dundee, where the proclamations were not gazetted until 1974. Until 1971–72, the only Coloured group area in the East Rand was at Boksburg. In other towns such as Nigel, Springs and Witbank there have been lengthy intervals between the proclamations and the acquisition of land and commencement of building, during which serious overcrowding has occurred in existing housing areas.

Coloured employment in rural areas

Traditionally Coloureds have been manual labourers, craftsmen, market gardeners, agricultural labourers and domestic servants. Their economic position was weakened by the 'civilised labour' legislation of the 1920s (chapter 3), which caused them to lose ground even in some of the traditional fields of employment such as bricklaying, woodworking and building: in 1950, nine-tenths were classified as unskilled labourers.[22]

Agriculture continued to employ just over a quarter of economically active Coloured men in 1970, mainly in the Cape (Table 7.2). In South Africa as a whole, Coloureds in the primary sector have actually

131

outnumbered Whites since 1960. Most are unskilled labourers, especially in the Western Cape. Since 1945, increased African migration to the Western Cape has been the cause of some insecurity for Coloureds, as Africans have been willing to work for even lower wages.[23] Most farmers

Table 7.2
Coloured occupations in 1970

	Percentage of economically active persons			
	Cape		Northern provinces	
	Male	Female	Male	Female
Professional, technical and related	2·0	6·0	2·8	5·7
Administrative	0·2	0·01	0·4	0·003
Clerical and related	5·2	3·9	7·9	7·0
Sales	3·9	3·0	4·1	6·3
Domestic service	5·5	47·2	5·1	25·7
Farm and forestry	27·5	5·2	7·3	0·7
Production and transport	50·7	27·5	59·2	35·4
Others	5·0	7·3	13·3	19·2

Source: Republic of South Africa, *1970 Census, Sample Tabulation: Occupations of Whites, Coloureds and Asians.*

prefer Coloured workers, however, except in dairying and cattle rearing, where the services of Africans are more valued. Coloured farm workers live in tied cottages for which they pay no rent, and may even be given rations of varying value. In the Western Cape the computation of real income is further complicated by the tot system, by which wine is given to Coloured workers not only on wine farms but also on fruit and grain farms. Some farmers claim that they could not keep their labour without it, others that turnover and productivity are unchanged whether they have it or not, and yet others that an all round improvement occurs if milk or cash are substituted for the tot. Cash wages on the farm seldom exceed R30 per month, and are often much less, tending to decrease with distance from Cape Town. Wages for both urban and rural Coloureds reach minimal levels in the north-west Cape, where the expected standard of living is very low.[24]

In the Coloured reserves of the north-west Cape the population consists overwhelmingly of children under eighteen and older people over fifty.[25] There is a strong conservative element amongst the latter, and a fatalism which has accepted the drought and a decline in fishing at Port Nolloth on the Namaqualand coast. For some who have lived their whole lives in rural poverty, the aspirations of the mass of urban Coloureds have little meaning. One of the few commercial activities in the Namaqualand reserves is the mining of both base minerals and precious stones in the areas of Concordia, Steinkopf, Kamaggas and Richtersveld (Fig. 7.1): the rentals of the mining leases provide some income for the local management boards.[26]

Government spending on improvement and development schemes in all the twenty-two Coloured reserves amounted to only R330,841 in 1972–73 and R370,768 in 1973–74.[27] Two further Coloured rural areas were proclaimed in 1975, at Hottentot Kraal in the Swellendam district and Goodhouse in Namaqualand.

The utilisation of Coloured labour

New employment opportunities for Coloureds are largely confined to urban areas. Between 1951 and 1970, over one-third of all new employment was in manufacturing, 20 per cent in commerce and finance, 17 per cent in services and 13 per cent in construction.[28] In the Western Cape the Coloured labour position in these and other employment sectors is protected by the Coloured employment preference area west of the Eiselen Line (Fig. 7.1), in which the employment of Coloureds is officially encouraged with the ultimate aim of removing all Africans from this area, which has traditionally been the preserve of Whites and Coloureds. The short term benefits for Coloured workers are obvious: they are no longer threatened by competition from Africans willing to work for lower wages, whilst fears of unemployment accompanying the rapid rise in the Coloured population are reduced. The number of Coloured employees in state departments and municipalities increased by 82 per cent (28,000) between 1962 and 1973, whilst in the private sector Coloureds increased their share of non-White employment in the Cape Town area from 77 per cent in 1966 to 82 per cent in 1973.[29] In manufacturing industry, Coloured workers have long been important, and now constitute 95 per cent of the manufacturing labour force in the Western Cape. Government policies have confirmed their position in this sector by protecting job opportunities for Coloureds in a number of industries including clothing, footwear, food, catering and motor assembly.[30] Nevertheless the Coloured labour preference policy may be questioned, not only as an obstacle to free movement of labour in a capitalist economy and yet one more barrier to African mobility and advancement, but also in terms of its effectiveness and the long term benefits conferred on the Coloured population. On the one hand, it appears to be achieving little reduction in the African population (in the Cape Town metropolitan area an intercensal increase of 43·5 per cent, marginally greater than that of the Coloureds themselves, was actually recorded in the 1960s). Were the policy to effect a substantial reduction of the African labour force, on the other hand, it is arguable that the absence of a cheap, unskilled and semi-skilled African labour force might decrease the attractiveness of the region for entrepreneurs, and so ultimately limit the economic opportunities of the Coloureds.

The activity rate of Coloured women slightly exceeds that of White women, and is extremely high in relation to the age structure of the Coloured population. Domestic service continues to be a major source of female Coloured employment, especially in the Cape (Table 7.2), where there is a shortage of African servants and where many Whites employ Africans who are not legally resident in the Western Cape. Manufacturing industry is the second major category of employment for Coloured women, whose numbers in the production and transport category increased by 49 per cent in the 1960s.[31] The increase in commercial opportunities for Coloured women has also been rapid since 1950, partly because of the change to self-service and supermarket retailing, and partly because the general labour shortage has tended to siphon White labour away from commerce, leaving opportunities for Coloured replacement. Nevertheless, Coloured female participation in commerce remains low in comparison with that of White women.

In recent years average earnings of Coloured workers have risen more rapidly than those of all other racial groups, but in 1970 four-fifths of all male earners had an annual income of less than R1,000 (i.e. less than the Poverty Datum Line for sole earners of multiple households), whilst only 5 per cent had an income above R2,000.[32] Half of all male workers earned less than R500 per annum, and half of all female workers, many of whom are the sole breadwinners of households, earn less than R240 annually. The low income of these households has far-reaching consequences for standards of nutrition, health, housing and personal care, as well as for the individual's motivation and labour productivity. Low incomes are the root of the 'culture of poverty' which remains characteristic of a wide section of the Coloured community. Although the

134

principle of the 'rate for the job' is gradually being extended to many categories of Coloured and White employment, discrimination in wages and conditions of work is still widespread. This may, however, benefit Coloured workers in the short term, in the sense that lower labour costs encourage White employers to overcome prejudices against employing non-Whites.

It is clear that fundamental structural changes are occurring in the labour force, as manpower shortages necessitate the upgrading of Coloured workers to employment at supervisory, administrative and managerial levels. Statutory job reservation is currently minimal since few determinations (the term used for a government proclamation reserving specific occupations for a given race group) have actually been made and exemptions are easily granted. Conventional discrimination is, for Coloureds as for Indians, far more widespread. It results in practical problems in finding specific types of employment, training or entrance to apprenticeships, as well as restrictions on promotion and attainment of responsibility. A crucial principle in this regard, which is still widely. adhered to, disallows Coloured workers in positions of authority over Whites.

Changes in such conventional attitudes are urgently needed if economic growth is to be sustained in the Western Cape. What is seldom realised by Whites is that many of the factors mitigating against full and effective utilisation of the potential Coloured labour force are similar to those pertaining for any Western industrial working class.[33] Instead, the causes of and remedies for problems such as high rates of absenteeism, lack of a sense of responsibility, high labour turnover and unemployment tend to be sought in racial terms. A more positive approach would be to view these phenomena in terms of the social and economic position of the Coloured population, and to concentrate on measures such as compulsory school attendance, registration and training of young school-leavers, attention to young recruits by employers, and similar measures aimed at producing a more disciplined, responsible and better trained labour force. There is also evidence that ethnic stereotyping by employers leads to job dissatisfaction. Coloureds are a heterogeneous labour force in terms of class, religion and other factors, and should, like any body of workers, be treated as individuals on the basis of achievement, characteristics and personality.

Reformed attitudes to Coloured labour in the Western Cape are all the more necessary in the face of the relatively high earnings level of Coloured workers in the Transvaal, which is already having some effect on Coloured northward labour migration, notwithstanding social and other obstacles which hamper resettlement. With the application of restrictions on the employment of African labour in the Southern Transvaal and other 'controlled' areas (chapter 3), competiton for available Coloured labour between industrial centres may be expected to increase.[34] There has also been a trickle of Coloured emigration, mainly to Canada and Australia, since the late 1960s. Official figures appear unrealistically low, and in any case conceal the potential loss to the Coloured community represented by the large share of professional and other highly skilled people amongst the migrants.

The upgrading of the Coloured labour force also demands the acceleration of education and training programmes.Notwithstanding the rapid population growth of the 1960s, the proportion of school pupils in the total Coloured population increased from 20·8 per cent in 1961 to 25·5 per cent in 1971, reflecting considerable progress in the spreading of basic education.[35] Substantial increases were also effected in the number of pupils at higher standards, although the absolute numbers remain very low. The number and educational standard of teachers is a major obstacle to improvements, whilst the expansion of schools and classroom facilities has not kept up with the rapid increase in pupil number, partly because enforced removals to group areas caused many schools to close down. University education has been seriously hampered by the fact that the Coloured University of the Western Cape has been politically unacceptable to many students, and is of much lower academic standing than the Indian University of Durban–Westville. Technical training also faces some major obstacles, especially the relatively small number of school-leavers with some background in mathematics and the natural sciences. There has, however, been a rapid expansion of student numbers at the Peninsula College for Advanced Technical Education, and at the five other Coloured technical colleges in Cape Town, Port Elizabeth, Kimberley, Johannesburg and Durban. In addition, specialised training opportunities are gradually increasing, including those for workers in the hotel industry and retailing, and for motor mechanics and farmworkers.

Coloured entrepreneurship

Amongst the Cape Malay people independent small traders and artisans have a tradition which stretches back 200 years to the period of slavery and the early days of Cape Town, when White entrepreneurship was relatively lacking. The rest of the Coloured population has, like the Afrikaners, almost no business tradition: both communities were tied to the land, poorly educated, and remote from a business environment. In so far as the Coloured community is intended to develop on separate social and political lines, the absence of a sizeable business element leaves other gaps too, in terms of the fulfilment of leadership functions, the stabilisation of community life, and the contacts with other races which result from mutual business interests.[36]

Thomas estimates the number of Coloured male entrepreneurs in 1970 at 12–15,000: this figure includes owners and managers of small shops and cafés, hawkers, small service establishments, and small clothing, furniture and other factories, as well as independent artisans owning small enterprises such as engineering or maintenance workshops, and construction firms.[37] Most of these businesses are relatively small and risk prone (many of them are one-man ventures), with only limited liquid capital and an intimate dependence on a small group of customers. Such enterprises found it virtually impossible to move when group areas were proclaimed, whilst long periods of uncertainty about relocation and the freezing of expansion years before eviction discouraged growth. Thus most Coloured enterprises affected in this way failed to consolidate and rationalise, whilst many businesses in predominantly Coloured business areas near the town centre (such as District Six and the Malay Quarters in Cape Town and Korsten in Port Elizabeth) were forced out of existence.

Coloured enterprises have nonetheless expanded considerably since the mid-1960s, with individual enterprises increasing in size, and with enterprises as a whole diversifying both horizontally and vertically. Expansion has occurred especially in those enterprises where success is dependent on local demand in Coloured group areas and in the categories where Coloured artisans already had a strong interest. Expansion into manufacturing is very slow, primarily as a result of the greater demands made by such enterprises upon capital as well as managerial and technical expertise, and the severe competition of well-established, large scale White enterprises.

The lack of organisation amongst Coloured entrepreneurs and the reluctance of individual entrepreneurs to merge in order to concentrate capital constitute major problems. The greatest obstacle to Coloured entrepreneurial expansion, however, is the restriction of Coloured businesses to Coloured group areas (although up to 49 per cent Coloured shareholding in mixed enterprises is permitted elsewhere). These areas are residential and have provision only for small shops and other enterprises, which offer no economies of scale and put Coloured businessmen at a disadvantage *vis-à-vis* the CBDs. Competition for the few business premises available also pushes prices to unrealistic levels, whilst a surplus of office space develops in the Cape Town CBD. High crime rates and insecurity in Coloured townships increase insurance rates for Coloured businessmen. The one advantage which Coloureds should theoretically enjoy in the group areas – lack of competition from other races – has proved impossible to implement. Indian entrepreneurs in particular have found various ways of 'infiltrating' Coloured group areas, following their removal from other locations, whilst existing White firms are reluctant to sell out and are not forced to do so.

The overwhelming part of the purchasing power of Coloured people is spent outside their group areas. The considerable expansion of White-controlled downtown and suburban shopping complexes which has occurred in Cape Town, Port Elizabeth and other towns is partially dependent on the Coloured market.[38] Where such development has occurred on the edge of Coloured group areas, it is nevertheless quite impracticable to duplicate it inside; the same applies to free trade zones for Indians, Chinese and sometimes White businesses in areas close to Coloured group areas. The net result is that, whereas Coloured entrepreneurs are not effectively protected inside their own group areas, their expansion into CBDs is restricted far more effectively. Yet the structure of the White–Coloured economy leaves scope for only one major CBD in each town: this is particularly true of smaller towns where Coloured enterprises moved out of integrated business centres have little chance of survival.

In 1962 the government established the Coloured Development Corporation in order to assist Coloured entrepreneurs. By the end of 1974 it had given financial assistance totalling R10·3 million to 297 entrepreneurs.[39] It has also established or bought from Whites the Spes Bona Savings Bank, Superama supermarkets, a hotel and a property development corporation, all of which are used for Coloured management training. Other properties acquired or established by the CDC and its subsidiaries have since been sold or leased to Coloured businessmen. Whilst these activities clearly help Coloured entrepreneurs, they are restricted in scope, and it is unfortunate that Coloureds do not have the same easy access to the general capital market as White firms.

Cultural and social attitudes

Hellmann says of the Coloured reaction to apartheid that:

> . . . the Coloured people . . . whose lives and destinies have always
> been inextricably linked with the White group, and whose loyalties

to South Africa have been unshakeable, are being spiritually lacerated by the rejection they are now experiencing.[40]

On any criteria other than those of descent and the physical characteristics of race, Coloured people belong to the White population from whom they are in part descended, and whose language and culture they share. Even race is so difficult to define clearly that members of the same family have been classified in different racial categories in terms of the Population Registration Act of 1950. 86 per cent of Coloureds speak Afrikaans, although only 37 per cent belong to Afrikaans churches. Economically there was no question of discrimination between Coloureds and Whites until the influx of Whites from the Platteland to the towns in the 1920s produced competition for jobs (chapter 3).

Beyond this general association with European culture and values it is extremely difficult to generalise about Coloured attitudes, as the Coloured population embraces immense variations in background, experience, class and current social situation. Indeed, it is economic diversity which underlies the deep resentment felt by many people at being called 'Coloured' and hence assumed to have more in common with all other Coloureds than with others of comparable social and economic background. As the Coloured People's Convention declared in 1961, 'a Coloured person is one who is discriminated against in a particular sort of way.'[41]

Several components contribute to class differentiation, although poverty alone is an insuperable handicap to upward social mobility. There is a definite advantage in being light-skinned, or straight- or light-haired, particularly if one can occasionally pass as White. Fluency in English is a second index of social class. Few Coloureds speak Afrikaans well; many use the patois known as 'Gam taal' and find it easier to read English-language newspapers. Afrikaans is the language of the 'dominee' (Dutch Reformed minister) and of the oppressor, or when spoken badly the language of the street. Most urban Coloureds believe that English-speaking White South Africans (including and often particularly the Jews) are more reasonable in their treatment of non-Whites. For the better educated people, English is also seen as the universal language which enables one to learn about the world as it really is, rather than through the limited perspective of the Afrikaner.

In the rural areas, where relatively little English is spoken, the social distinction between English and Afrikaans speakers is much smaller. Rather the distinction between urban and rural is itself a status indicator, rural Coloureds generally being poorer, less well educated, more conservative and fatalistic in their outlook: for many of them the past, when land and stock were more plentiful and children more respectful, was better than the present.[42] Urban dwellers, on the other hand, are more concerned with present pleasures or with future economic and social justice.

None of these social indicators are absolute: the main determinants of Coloured status and social class are education, wealth and occupation. Many higher status Coloureds make great efforts to prove to others, including Whites, that they are 'respectable'. The churchgoers amongst them support the larger established churches or, in the case of the Cape Malays, Islam (4 per cent of Coloureds are Moslems). Their attitudes towards Whites are ambivalent: a desire to identify conflicts with revulsion against discrimination and paternalism. Some Coloureds refuse the chance to be classified as White because of the rifts that would arise between them and their families and friends, whilst others refuse to seek reclassification for fear they might fail and be damned for trying. Those who have succeeded in obtaining White identity cards often live in fear that they will be reclassified and possibly lose their jobs, their homes and their friends.

The mass of less well-educated and articulate urban Coloureds face frustration in their attempts to attain the goals of economic and social self-respect which their society idealises. This leads many to feel a sense of impotence and racial inferiority. Such frustrations contribute to alcoholism and the smoking of dagga (cannabis), with short term goals and immediate gratification becoming the norm. Retreat is also found in religion, with a perceptible drift towards emphasis on individual salvation and emotional worship in small churches: the evangelical churches, by tending to regard segregation as almost irrelevant to personal salvation, appeal to the frustrated Coloured man in much the same way as they once attracted poverty stricken White American farmers in the Appalachians.

Coloured political development and 'parallelism'

At the National Convention preceding the Act of Union the political rights of Coloureds were hotly debated. The Orange Free State and the Transvaal were opposed to the extension of the Cape position and the granting of full citizenship. The outcome was a compromise agreement to maintain the *status quo* in each province, although Coloureds were excluded from election to the Union Parliament. Recommendations were made by the Wilcocks Report in 1937 that the franchise enjoyed by

Coloureds in the Cape be extended to Coloureds living in other provinces who possessed the necessary qualifications,[43] but consideration of this recommendation was delayed by the Second World War and it was never implemented. Meanwhile the extension of the franchise to women in 1931 and the lowering of the franchise qualifications in the same year applied to Whites only, thus strengthening the position of the northern provinces. The Nationalist government abolished the common roll and provided for separate Coloured representation in Parliament in 1956, after a prolonged constitutional crisis concerning this measure. Subsequently, Coloured representation in Parliament was abolished altogether in 1968.

This was in accordance with the philosophy of separate development, and the government therefore began to create separate political institutions and to speak of the Coloureds as a separate 'nation' or 'people'. At local level there were 4 Coloured local affairs committees in Natal in 1975, of which 2 were fully elective, and 97 Coloured management committees elsewhere in South Africa, 81 having elected as well as nominated members.[44] At national level the Coloured Representative Council (CRC), established in 1964, was given legislative as well as consultative functions in 1968, although legislation is subject to official scrutiny and approval both before it is introduced and after it is passed by the CRC. Its consultative functions include advising at the request of the government on matters of interest to Coloureds, and making recommendations about any plans intended to benefit Coloureds.

The CRC currently has forty elected and twenty nominated members, but all members will be elected after 1980. In the 1969 election the Federal Coloured People's Party, which supports separate development, gained only eleven seats. It did best in the Free State and the Transvaal, where Coloured people were voting in an election for the first time and felt they were making some political progress, and where there is a strong feeling that the *status quo* is preferable to closer association with Africans. The Labour Party, which opposed separate development, enjoyed strong support in the urban areas and the Coloured 'heartland' in the Western Cape. It won twenty-six seats, but the government gave the Federal Party a majority in the Council by nominating twenty of its supporters. In the 1975 election the Labour Party, fighting on the platform of full Parliamentary representation for Coloureds and rejection of separate development, won a clear majority (thirty-one seats). However, despite its rejection of the CRC, the Labour Party decided after the election to use the Council as a platform from which to make its demands.

These election results suggest that the spirit of accommodation and compromise is weaker amongst Coloureds than Indians, and that active hostility to separate development is more freely expressed. The far smaller Coloured business and trading interest helps to explain this, whilst Coloureds in the Cape Province are sufficiently numerous not to fear 'swamping' by Africans. It may well be, however, that the protection of Coloured labour in the Cape and gradually improving facilities and employment opportunities for Coloureds will encourage more of them to accept their current second-class citizenship, rather than risk losing their advantages over Africans. The discouragement of any form of contact between Coloureds and Africans tends to encourage the development of such an attitude.

What the future holds for Coloured political development is very uncertain. The extent of Coloured urbanisation and integration into the common economy is such as to rule out separate territorial development or a 'Colouredstan'. The government's policy is, by its own admission, not yet fully worked out, and is likely to be influenced by the report of the Theron Commission. The present policy is described as 'parallelism', and envisages separate nationhood, with a Coloured cabinet and parliament paralleling those of the White 'nation', but the sharing of a common motherland. In accordance with this view it was announced in 1975 that the Executive Committee of the CRC would be given cabinet status, and a statutory inter-cabinet council would be established, consisting of the CRC cabinet and an equal number of ministers from the White cabinet under the chairmanship of the Prime Minister. Yet Mr Vorster had pinpointed the realities of the situation in 1974:

> Although the factual situation amounts to the White Parliament and Government being sovereign in South Africa, *and since the same area of land cannot have a second sovereign parliament,* the White Parliament should, in implementing its policy of political development, be prepared, in exercising its sovereign power in the sphere of common interests, to give the Coloured people's political leaders a say in matters mutually affecting the Whites and the Coloureds. (Author's italics.)[45]

Rhoodie believes that the policy is destined (if not designed) to function as an interim one, in the long run evolving unavoidably into a system calculated to regularise progressive integration rather than increasing separation.[46] By means of parallelism the government may be seeking to avoid either the frustration or the promotion of Coloured nationalism: to promote it could lead to demands for a territorial solution to which the government could not possibly agree, whilst to frustrate it could bring

142

nearer the inevitability of White–Coloured integration. Increasing pressures in favour of such integration will be examined in chapter 12.

References

[1]   J.S. Marais (1939), *The Cape Coloured People 1652–1937,* Longman, London, pp. 5–9.
[2]   W.M. Macmillan (1963), *Bantu, Boer and Briton,* Clarendon Press, Oxford, p. 61.
[3]   J.S. Marais, op. cit., pp. 107–8.
[4]   Republic of South Africa (1975), *Progress of a People: the Coloureds of South Africa,* Department of Information, Pretoria, p. 29.
[5]   S.P. Cilliers (1963), *The Coloureds of South Africa: a factual survey,* Banier Publications, Cape Town, pp. 18–19.
[6]   J.L. Sadie (1972), *Projections of the South African Population 1970–2020,* Industrial Development Corporation, Johannesburg, p. 25.
[7]   Ibid.
[8]   Ibid., p. 24.
[9]   Ibid., pp. 13 and 24.
[10] Quoted by S.P. Cilliers (1972) in 'Facing the crisis in housing for the Coloured people', paper read at a meeting of the Cape Chamber of Commerce, 21 November, p. 1.
[11] Ibid., p. 4.
[12] Ibid.
[13] D. Russell (1975), *Crossroads Squatter Camp: a report on the disruption of African family life,* Board of Social Responsibility, Diocese of Cape Town.
[14] F.J. Lund and J.G. Potgieter (1975), 'Squatting: the bigger problem', *South African Outlook,* August, p. 120.
[15] M. Horrell and T. Hodgson (1976), *A Survey of Race Relations in South Africa 1975,* SAIRR, Johannesburg, pp. 76-7.
[16] Ibid., p. 69.
[17] S.P. Cilliers (1973), 'Urban renewal and the needs of the Coloured community', paper read at a symposium organised by the Cape Chamber of Commerce, 6 November, p. 15.
[18] M. Horrell and T. Hodgson, op. cit., p. 76.
[19] W.H. Thomas (1973a), *Greater Saldanha and the Development of the Western Cape,* Bureau for Economic Research, Stellenbosch, for the Syfrets–VAL Group, pp. 79–82.
[20] Ibid., pp. 102–3.

[21] This section is based on the following report: *Some Notes on Regional Townships, Other Group Areas and Housing Schemes for Coloured People in the Northern Provinces,* SAIRR, Johannesburg, 1974.

[22] K. Buchanan and N. Hurwitz (1950), 'The "Coloured" community in the Union of South Africa', *Geog. Rev.* 40, p. 408.

[23] A.L. Müller (1968), *Minority Interests: the political economy of the Coloured and Indian communities in South Africa,* SAIRR, Johannesburg, p. 23.

[24] M.G. Whisson (1971), 'The Coloured people', in *South Africa's Minorities,* SPRO-CAS Publication No. 2, Johannesburg, pp. 63–4.

[25] Ibid., p. 64.

[26] Republic of South Africa, op. cit., p. 32.

[27] M. Horrell, op. cit., p. 180; M. Horrell and T. Hodgson, op. cit., pp. 113–14.

[28] W.H. Thomas (1974), 'Socio-economic development of the Coloured community', privately circulated paper, p. 9.

[29] Republic of South Africa, op. cit., p. 83.

[30] Ibid.

[31] W.H. Thomas (1974), op. cit., p. 11.

[32] Ibid., p. 15.

[33] S.P. Cilliers (1971a), 'The effective utilisation of Coloured labour in Western Cape industry', paper read at a meeting of the Institute of Industrialists (Cape), Cape Town, 17 February, p. 16.

[34] S.P. Cilliers (1971b), *Appeal to Reason,* University Publishers and Booksellers, Stellenbosch, p. 64.

[35] W.H. Thomas (1974), op. cit., p. 17.

[36] For a more detailed analysis of Coloured entrepreneurship see W.H. Thomas (1973b), 'Coloured entrepreneurship and economic development in South Africa', (private circulation).

[37] Ibid., p. 8.

[38] See, for example, E.J. Ter Meulen (1969), 'Shoplocation Claremont: the effects of socio-economic changes as expressed in the development of a surburban shopping centre in Cape Town, Republic of South Africa', *Tijdschrift voor Economische en Sociale Geografie* 59, pp. 208–20.

[39] M. Horrell and T. Hodgson, op. cit., p. 113.

[40] E. Hellmann (1972), 'The crux of the race problem in South Africa', in N.J. Rhoodie (ed.), *South African Dialogue,* McGraw-Hill, Johannesburg, p. 19.

[41] M.G. Whisson, op. cit., p. 64.

[42] Ibid., p. 68.

[43] Union of South Africa (1937), *Report of the Commission of Enquiry*

on the Cape Coloured Population of the Union, UG 54/1937, para. 1158.

[44] M. Horrell and T. Hodgson, op. cit., p. 79.

[45] B.J. Vorster (1974), in an address to the CRC at the official opening of the 7th session, 8 November.

[46] N.J. Rhoodie (1973), 'The Coloured policy of South Africa: parallelism as a socio-political device to regulate White–Coloured integration', *Afn. Aff.* 72, pp. 46–56.

PART IV

BLACK SOUTH AFRICA: THE AFRICAN HOMELANDS

8 Population pressures and migrant labour

Population size and distribution in 1970

Details of the size and distribution of the African population appear in Table 8.1, in which homeland totals relate to land incorporated into the homelands at the time of the 1970 census. Censuses of population in African rural areas face numerous practical difficulties which may lead to considerable under-enumeration. Thus a detailed survey of kraals in the Tugela Location (KwaZulu) in 1968 found the African population to be 27·3 per cent higher than that assumed and planned for by the Department of Bantu Administration and Development, and 89·5 per cent higher than the 1960 census figure.[1] It is generally accepted, however, that homeland enumeration in the 1970 census was much fuller than in 1960.[2] The figures for homeland populations in Table 8.1 may therefore be treated with some confidence, whereas comparison of the 1960 and 1970 homeland populations may be misleading.

Only 48 per cent of the total African population was to be found in the homelands in 1970, even if no allowance is made for the continuing under-enumeration of urban Africans in 'White' South Africa. Of the 7 million Africans living in the homelands, 653,000 (9·3 per cent) were living in homelands allocated to other groups. If the government should decide to make the homelands homogeneous in this respect, large numbers of Tswanas, North Sotho (Pedi and North Ndebele) and Transkeian Xhosa in particular would have to be moved. The 'others' listed in Table 8.1 include primarily the South Ndebele, for whom no homeland had been created in 1970, although one is now planned in the vicinity of Groblersdal in the eastern Transvaal (see Fig. 11.3).

The position of Bophuthatswana is of special interest on account of the absence of the majority of its own citizens and the presence of some 268,000 other Africans, notably North and South Sotho, Shangaan, Zulu and South Ndebele. It appears that the proximity of much of Bophuthatswana to the PWV complex has resulted both in a large efflux of Tswanas from the homeland and an influx of non-Tswana citizens into Bophuthatswana. This latter process could be further stimulated by the

149

Table 8.1
African population of South Africa, 1970 ('000)

Areas	Peoples											Foreign Africans*	Overall Total
	Xhosa/ Transkei	Xhosa/ Ciskei	Tswana	North Sotho	Shangaan	Venda	Swazi	Zulu	South Sotho	Other	Total		
White areas	1,312·2	396·4	1,072·8	602·8	261·1	106·1	361·4	1,878·8	1,218·7	359·5	7,569·8	489·5	8,059·3
African homelands	1,685·2	518·8	607·1	1,003·2	389·2	253·4	110·3	2,139·0	138·2	131·4	6,975·8	22·5	6,998·3
Transkei	1,644·6	–	0·1	–	–	–	–	21·3	59·9	0·1	1,726·0	–	–
Ciskei	–	511·7**	0·1	–	–	–	–	–	13·2	0·1	525·1	–	–
Bophuthatswana	21·0	6·3	596·7	66·1	55·5	5·4	8·9	26·6	24·1	54·4	865·0	16·0	–
Lebowa	2·8	0·8	9·1	899·9	73·6	2·9	10·7	7·4	2·6	73·9	1,083·7	–	–
Gazankulu	–	–	0·2	25·5	231·1	3·5	2·9	1·0	–	0·5	264·7	–	–
Venda	–	–	0·3	7·7	17·7	241·6	–	–	–	0·1	267·4	–	–
Swazi	–	–	–	3·4	10·3	–	81·2	21·1	–	0·3	116·3	–	–
KwaZulu	16·8	–	0·5	0·6	1·0	–	6·6	2,061·6	14·5	2·0	2,103·6	–	–
Qwaqwa	–	–	0·1	–	–	–	–	–	23·9	–	24·0	–	–
Total	2,997·4	915·2	1,679·9	1,606·0	650·3	395·5	471·7	4,017·8	1,356·9	490·9	14,545·6	512·0	15,057·6

*Estimate.
**Includes an unknown number of Transkei Xhosa.
Source: Department of Statistics.

development of border industries at Rosslyn, Rustenburg and Brits and of the homeland growth point at Babelegi (see Fig. 11.3).

Migration

The percentage of each population group actually living in its own homeland varies from 1·8 in the case of the South Sotho to 67·2 for the Venda (see Table 8.2). The situation in Qwaqwa, the South Sotho homeland, is officially regarded as exceptional, 'as the true homeland of the South Sotho is the Kingdom of Lesotho a few kilometres away',[3] which implies that no addition to the present absurdly inadequate provision of land for the South Sotho is intended.

It is not known precisely how many of the additional people who are considered as constituting the *de jure* population of the homelands were temporarily absent migrants in 1970, and how many were living on a more permanent basis in White areas. Figures calculated indirectly from other data appear in Table 8.2. Altogether there were some 1·7 million male workers normally domiciled in the homelands, of whom 630,000 were

Table 8.2
Absence of Africans from their respective homelands, 1970

Peoples	Percentage of citizens in homeland			Number of males aged 15–64 absent	
	Total	Persons aged 15–64		Temporarily	Continuously
		Males	Females		
Xhosa/Transkei	54·9	35·3	62·9	224,500	274,300
Xhosa/Ciskei	55·9	38·1	56·1	37,200	111,800
Tswana	35·5	24·4	32·8	37,600	273,600
North Sotho	56·0	35·0	59·5	91,200	150,500
Shangaan	35·5	18·4	40·7	38,700	91,300
Venda	67·2	40·1	76·1	30,200	17,100
Swazi	17·2	12·5	16·4	5,000	96,100
Zulu	51·3	36·7	53·2	164,300	435,400
South Sotho	1·8	1·2	1·9	2,500	320,300

Source: J.A. Lombard and P.J. van der Merwe (1972), 'Central problems of the economic development of Bantu homelands', *Finance and Trade Review* 10, no. 1, p. 31.

working elsewhere in 1970, whilst 1,770,000 African men were working continuously in White areas. Striking evidence of the homelands' dependence on 'White' South Africa for employment is revealed by the fact that in no homeland were more than 40 per cent of the *de jure* male citizens aged between fifteen and sixty-four actually living in the homeland.

Population growth

Any prospect of the homelands becoming less dependent on White areas for employment appears remote so long as the African population continues to grow at anything approaching the present rate. In South Africa as a whole it increased from 10,928,000 in 1960 to 15,057,000 in 1970, including 489,000 foreign Africans who were working in the Republic. This 37·8 per cent increase represents the fastest growth rate of the country's four major population groups, and one of the highest growth rates in the world. The 0–14 age group is increasing particularly fast, thus the 'demographic drag' (the ratio between percentage increases in the 0–14 and 15–64 age groups) is 1·10 for Africans, compared with 1·04 for Coloureds, 0·76 for Whites, and 0·35 for Indians.[4] Africans appear to be nearing the second recognised stage of demographic development, which is characterised by declining death rates and unchanged birth rates at high levels. This means that, in the normal course of events, they have still to pass through the third stage, in which further declines in death rates and a slowly falling birth rate combine to produce a net rise in rates of natural increase. Coloureds, on the other hand, have already reached this stage, whilst Indians have entered a fourth stage characterised by reduced rates of natural increase. The White population appears to be in the fifth phase, with a low rate of natural increase and an ageing population.[5]

The implications of this situation are summarised in Table 8.3 below. Not only will the White proportion of the total population be halved within fifty years if present trends continue, but the number of Africans will increase to over 37 million within one generation. When Professor Tomlinson drew up his blueprint for separate development in 1955, the projected African population for the year 2000 was only 21 million; of this it was envisaged that, given optimum conditions and development, the proposed Bantustans would be able to support a population of 8–10 million.[6] Not only has Tomlinson's 'optimum development' not yet been attempted (chapters 9 and 10), but such development would in any

Table 8.3
Population projections, 1970–2020

Group	1970 (%)	2000		2020	
		'000	%	'000	%
Whites	17·5	5,726	11·7	7,039	8·9
Coloureds	9·4	4,890	10·0	7,720	9·8
Indians	2·9	1,215	2·5	1,617	2·0
Africans	70·2	37,293	75·9	62,798	79·3
Total		49,124		79,174	

Source: J.L. Sadie (1972), *Projections of the South African Population 1970–2020.*

case support only a quarter of the population now projected.

The actual population of the homelands had reached nearly 7 million even in 1970. Assuming the same growth rate as for the African population as a whole, the homeland population will reach 17,886,000 by 2000 and 37,972,000 by 2020. To these figures must be added further population increases as a result of resettling 'surplus' Africans currently residing in White areas, both rural and urban. Such a policy has been pursued with vigour in the 1960s, as the following figures indicate:[7]

– 340,000 people were removed by the abolition of labour tenancies on White farms;
– 656,000 people were removed by laws preventing squatters on White farms;
– 97,000 people were removed by the elimination of 'Black spots', small scheduled areas and outlying parts of other scheduled areas (Black spots are areas of African settlement surrounded by White farmland; 'scheduled areas' constitute land set aside for Africans in terms of the Native Land Act of 1913);
– 400,000 people were removed through being 'endorsed out' of the urban areas.

The further resettlement of up to half the existing number of Africans in White areas is being seriously contemplated. This would add over 4 million people (1970 figures) to the homeland population, together with the natural increase which this extra population would inevitably generate. In such circumstances the homeland population could exceed 25 million by the year 2000.

Population growth of this order would pose staggering problems for the homelands themselves. Before examining these, however, some reference must be made to the wider implications of the 'population explosion' in South Africa, and to the difficulties which hinder the successful adoption of a vigorous population policy in the context of current racial attitudes.

Some consequences of population explosion

At present South Africa is the only country in Africa able to export food on a significant scale. The neighbouring countries of Botswana, Lesotho and Swaziland are not even self-sufficient in maize, their staple food. The agricultural difficulties of Mozambique may prove relatively short lived: a combination of the ravages of the war against the Portuguese and serious crop failures made the country dependent on Rhodesian grain until Mozambique closed the border for political reasons in March 1976, since when she has been forced to look elsewhere. In Zambia the abandonment of European farms and a growing urban élite are together responsible for rapidly rising imports of dairy produce, meat, sugar and sometimes even maize, most of them obtained from or through South Africa.[8] In such circumstances, South Africa is likely to be progressively called upon to act as the granary of Southern Africa. However, if her own population continues to grow at the present rate, it seems unlikely that she could fulfill this role.

South African agriculture has made tremendous progress since 1945 (chapter 3). In the 1960s, output of plant products increased more rapidly than population, but animal products failed to keep pace.[9] Production from the mainly traditional sector of African stockfarming is thought unlikely to have an important bearing on the pattern of domestic meat production for several decades. The prospects of further large scale expansion after the completion of current schemes, notably the Orange River Project, are poor. Thus it will become increasingly difficult to maintain the current volume of agricultural exports in the face of increasing domestic consumption: yet a substantial reduction in those exports would have severe repercussions on the national economy.

Rapid population growth also poses environmental problems. Van Rensburg fears that the environmental depletion consequent upon meeting food needs for the next thirty years will be paid for in the next century.[10] Water supply will be another area of concern. The Report of the Commission of Inquiry into Water Affairs estimated the 1965 consumption of water for household, municipal, agricultural and industrial purposes at 25 billion litres per day; by the year 2000 this is expected to have increased to 80 billion litres per day.[11] South Africa as a whole is far from well-watered, and such quantities of water, if available, could only be supplied at considerable cost.

The limitation of population

Attempts at birth control are not new in South Africa. The semi-private Family Planning Association of South Africa has been active for forty years, with increasing support from central, provincial and local government. It appears to undertake most educational and motivational activity with regard to contraception, but has handed all but one of its clinics over to local authorities, provincial hospitals, or the Department of Health.[12] Altogether there were 2,338 family planning clinics throughout the country in August 1974, most of them open to all race groups.[13] Success amongst Africans nevertheless remains very localised, although there are indications that urban Africans in particular are becoming more aware of family planning.

A major reason for this lack of success is to be found in the dualistic nature of White attitudes on birth control. A widespread desire to increase the White proportion of the population leads to support only for a selective birth control policy, i.e. one aimed primarily at Africans. It is also felt that a non-discriminatory policy will reduce the strength of those sections of the population responsible for economic growth, which are mainly White. Judged by the historical precedents set by other White populations, however, a further decline in the fertility of Whites is almost inevitable: in the 1960s South African Whites experienced a higher growth rate than most other White populations. Thus they stand only to lose over the coming decades by failing to adopt a vigorous, non-discriminatory birth control policy. Unfortunately, official attitudes have tended to reflect White prejudices hitherto. Africans naturally see the contradiction if government spokesmen ask Whites to 'give a White child to the Republic of South Africa next year',[14] yet urge Africans to have fewer children.

In recent years there have been welcome signs of official realisation that a successful birth control policy must be non-discriminatory. It must also be a policy which, although government-inspired, relies on the persuasion of Africans by Africans. Thirdly, it must be directed at African men as well as women; African husbands who know little of family planning are seldom receptive to their wives' persuasion, and may regard it as an attack upon their virility.

If these requirements are met, there remains one more obstacle to successful family planning: the continuing encouragement of White immigration. Net immigration declined from a peak of over 32,000 in 1969 and 1970 to 17,726 in 1973, but increased to 28,592 in 1974. Such immigrants may help to relieve shortages of skilled workers, but those shortages are themselves largely the result of statutory and non-statutory discrimination against non-Whites. With the removal of such barriers and the improvement of education and training facilities, South Africa could dispense with the need for White immigrants. Such a step appears to be in the long term interests of all population groups.

Alternatives for the homelands

The current size of the 0–14 age group will ensure that, whatever the successes or failures of population policy, the African population will continue to increase rapidly over the next two decades as this generation reaches the reproductive age group. What, then, are the alternatives facing the already overcrowded homelands in the face of further population growth? Six alternative possibilities are recognised below, although they are by no means mutually exclusive.

The most frightening possibility is simply one of increasing poverty, unemployment and even starvation in the homelands. The threat this would pose to White security is aptly summed up in the comment 'If they don't eat, we don't sleep.' White South Africa cannot afford to let such a situation develop, and is seeking an alternative by means of agricultural and industrial development in the homelands. The possibility of this supporting present or future homeland populations is examined in chapters 9 and 10.

Of the remaining alternatives, two demand a fundamental modification of current policies. The first is to give the homelands more land. Increased population will almost certainly lead to louder and increasingly urgent demands for more land, which will be hard to resist with the present argument that 'Never in history have nations and peoples determined their respective political homelands on the basis of population density or natural resources.'[15] A major objection to giving the homelands more land, quite apart from the political difficulties, is that unless a transformation of African agriculture can be achieved in a remarkably short time, such a transfer of land from White farmers would substantially reduce production of the food which is needed to feed South Africa's growing urban population.

The fourth alternative implies the greatest long term changes in current policies, namely the permanent settlement of far greater numbers of Africans in White urban areas. Not only would this exacerbate White insecurity, but it would also become increasingly difficult to deny normal rights to urban Africans on the grounds that they were homeland citizens.

If permanent residence in the towns is to be avoided, there remain two other means of allowing the surplus homeland population to make a living in White areas. One, which has been seriously suggested from time to time, envisages the provision of high speed transport links to major employment centres enabling Africans to travel hundreds of miles a day in a short space of time, and so to continue living in homelands which are remote from large cities.[16] Wilson dismisses such a vision suitably, if with an element of exaggeration, with the remark that 'a society that cannot even afford to pay the majority of its workers a living wage is hardly in a position to turn its entire proletariat into a jet set.'[17]

The final alternative, which in present circumstances seems the most probable, is continuation on a still larger scale of the migrant labour system, always assuming sufficient economic growth to absorb the additional migrants. Some of the many issues raised by this prospect are discussed below.

Migrant labour and the homelands

The extent and current significance of migrant labour in South Africa has been extensively documented, most notably by Wilson.[18] The high level of employment dependency characteristic of the homelands (see Table 8.2) has not surprisingly led to their being described as 'reservoirs of cheap labour for the White economy.'[19] Africans seeking work in White areas are required to register at labour bureaux in the homelands, although a minority circumvent this system and migrate illegally. In most of the homelands the rate of labour migration is increasing: between 1936 and 1970 the number of migrants grew at an average compound rate of 3·1 per cent per annum.[20] As a result, the ratio of migrants to economically active males in the homelands is on average 6:5.[21]

Of the various arguments advanced in favour of the migrant labour system, the following are of particular relevance to the homelands and their inhabitants:

(1) Oscillating migration eases the cultural transition from traditional subsistence society to modern urban life. This was undoubtedly true in the decades after the diamond and gold discoveries, but is of far less relevance today, when an increasing proportion of the African population has considerable urban experience. It is clearly invalid in relation to those 'endorsed out' of urban areas.

(2) Through remittances the migrant system spreads money far afield, thus widening the cash economy to areas that would otherwise have remained isolated for longer. This argument is weakened by the fact that migrant labourers are usually estimated to spend 80 per cent of their wages in 'White South Africa': this money, and the multiplier effects it represents in terms of job opportunities, is lost to the homelands.

(3) When there is unemployment, workers with links to the land have something on which to fall back. In practice, whereas only a very small proportion of the total African labour force would need to be migrant in order to cushion the permanently urbanised workers from unemployment, male migrants constituted 59 per cent of economically active African men in White areas in 1970.[22]

The opposing economic arguments which relate to the homelands include the following:

(1) Poor rural areas are subsidising urban development. This is the result of the rural areas from which men come and the towns in which they work being seen, for political reasons, as separate entities, not as belonging together or having mutual responsibility for each other.[23] Thus migrant labourers are paid lower wages than would be needed for full family support, whilst urban areas and employers are saved the cost of providing family housing, social security and the greater urban infrastructure which the presence of families would demand. In short, the growth points of the economy are able to expand without having to bear the cost 'of the human being behind the labour unit.'[24] The rural areas, on the other hand, become so densely populated with women, children and old people that there is insufficient land for the rationalisation and improvement of agriculture.

(2) The system drains the homelands of their best manpower. This means that homeland educational expenditure benefits the 'White' economy far more than that of the homelands themselves. At the educational level of primary school plus four years, the rate of migration from the homelands reaches 90 per cent.[25] As these migrants are limited to a contract for one year at a time, they receive little training and acquire few skills which they might subsequently apply in the homelands.

(3)   Those left in the homelands may become considerably poorer than they were. The food produced by able-bodied men in the homelands would normally be used to feed the old and crippled as well as wives and children. Not only do migrant workers spend a relatively higher proportion of their earnings on themselves, but their remittances may be used to feed and clothe a tighter family circle than previously.[26]

(4)   Restrictions on the volume of migration create unemployment. This argument is difficult to assess; the basic point is that by prohibiting people from doing jobs in one area, one does not necessarily ensure that there will be opportunities for them to work elsewhere. The shortage of domestic servants in Cape Town (chapter 7) is a case in point.

To these economic arguments might be added a battery of social ones. The break-up of family life and impediments to normal sexual relationships affect some of the most basic human needs: Wilson lists illegitimacy, bigamy, prostitution, homosexuality, drunkenness, violence and the breakdown of parental authority as direct effects of the system, whilst venereal disease, tuberculosis, malnutrition and beriberi are some of the indirect results of the life-style of male migrant labourers.[27] Men are degraded by a system which deprives them of a family rôle, whilst women are left behind feeling lonely and helpless, anxiously waiting for letters, and hopefully for money, from their husbands in town. These and other aspects of migrant labour have led even the Dutch Reformed Church, which in most respects supports separate development, to describe the system in the following terms:

> . . . an evil which ranges thus in the life of the Bantu population must necessarily affect the whole social and religious life of all the races in our fatherland.[28]

Further extension of the migrant labour system is therefore highly undesirable as a means of coping with future population growth in the homelands. The social evils of the system would be multiplied in both town and country. The homeland population would become even more unbalanced than it is now, with an ever-increasing dependency burden and a growing population of women, children and old people sharing the same amount of increasingly impoverished land. A more unpromising human resource base for economic development would be difficult to imagine.

References

[1]   R.E. Schulze (1970), 'A geographical survey as a basis for land

planning in the Tugela Location', *J. for Geog.* 3, p. 630.

[2] M. Lipton (1972), 'The South African census and the Bantustan policy', *The World Today* 28, p. 259.

[3] Republic of South Africa (1974). *South Africa 1974* (official yearbook), p. 300.

[4] N.J. van Rensburg (1972), *Population Explosion in Southern Africa?,* Pretoria, pp. 78-9.

[5] J.A. Lombard and P.J. van der Merwe (1972), 'Central problems of the economic development of Bantu homelands', *Finance and Trade Review* (Volkskas Ltd) 10, no. 1, pp. 7-8.

[6] Union of South Africa (1955), *Report of the Tomlinson Commission on the Socio-Economic Development of the Bantu Areas,* UG 61/1955, pp. 29 and 179.

[7] A. Baldwin (1975), 'Mass removals and separate development', *Journal of Southern African Studies* 2, p. 216.

[8] D.J. Siddle (1971), 'Do-it-yourself policy for rural Zambia', *Geographical Magazine* 43, pp. 569-73.

[9] N.J. van Rensburg, op. cit., p. 66.

[10] Ibid., p. 73.

[11] Republic of South Africa (1970), *Report of the Commission of Inquiry into Water Affairs,* RP 34/1970.

[12] A. Mabin (1976), 'Population policy', in D.M. Smith (ed.), *Separation in South Africa: Peoples and Policies,* Queen Mary College, London, Department of Geography Occasional Paper No. 6, p. 31.

[13] M. Horrell (1975), *A Survey of Race Relations in South Africa 1974,* SAIRR, Johannesburg, pp. 53-4.

[14] M.C. Botha when a deputy Minister in 1965, quoted by A. Mabin, op. cit., p. 31.

[15] Republic of South Africa (1974), *Multi-National Development in South Africa: the Reality,* Department of Information, Pretoria, p. 92.

[16] J.J. Burger (1970), 'Transport systems as a basis for the application of a policy of separate development', paper delivered to the SABRA Congress on 'Homeland Development - a programme for the Seventies', Port Elizabeth, 6 August.

[17] F. Wilson (1975). 'The political implications for Blacks of economic changes now taking place in Southern Africa', in L. Thompson and J. Butler (eds), *Change in Contemporary South Africa,* University of California Press, Berkeley, p. 183.

[18] F. Wilson (1972a), *Migrant Labour in South Africa,* South African Council of Churches and SPRO-CAS, Johannesburg.

[19] See, for instance, M. Lipton (1972), 'Independent Bantustans?',

International Affairs 48, p. 6; and J. Maree (1973), 'Bantustan economics', *Third World* 2, no. 6, p. 29.

[20] J. Nattrass (1976), 'Migrant labour and South African economic development', *SAJE* 44, p. 69.

[21] Ibid., p. 68.

[22] Ibid.

[23] F. Wilson (1972a), op. cit., p. 175.

[24] Ibid., p. 188.

[25] J. Nattrass, op. cit., p. 70.

[26] F. Wilson (1972b), *Labour in the South African Gold Mines 1911–1969,* Cambridge University Press, p. 131.

[27] F. Wilson (1972a), op. cit., pp. 178–86.

[28] *Report of the Committee on Current Affairs,* adopted by the General Synod of the Nederduitse Gereformeerde Kerk, October 1966, p. 50.

9   Homeland agriculture

The physical environment

According to the viewpoint of the writer concerned, the homelands have been variously described as some of the finest well-watered lands of South Africa,[1] and as economically marginal land which is too mountainous, too dry or too remote to be productive.[2] The truth is too complex for such generalisations to be meaningful. If 500 millimetres is taken as the minimum rainfall for successful dry-land crop production, then 76 per cent of the homelands (compared with 35 per cent of South Africa as a whole) are suited to this form of agriculture.[3] Largely on the strength of this factor, the Tomlinson Commission equated the agricultural potential of 100 hectares of land in the homelands with that of 147 hectares in the White areas. The amount of rainfall is, however, only one of several significant factors. Others include the nature and reliability of the rainfall, evaporation rates, steepness of slopes and soil cover. The following comments on each of the homelands provide some indication of the wide variation in agricultural potential which is found.

KwaZulu is probably the best watered of all the homelands. Its various fragments (see Fig. 11.5 for the future pattern) are transversed by several perennial rivers, including the Pongola, Tugela, Umkomaas and Umzimkulu, with resultant irrigation possibilities. In many areas rainfall is episodic and unreliable, however, and high temperatures in lowland areas such as the Tugela Valley result in high evaporation rates and a low effective rainfall. The highly dissected topography of much of KwaZulu also presents problems; in his study of the Tugela Location, Schulze mapped only 8·4 per cent of the land as being soil covered, the remaining 91·6 per cent consisting of rocky outcrops, land generally steeper than a gradient of 15 per cent, or stony areas with skeletal soil in small patches.[4] Mixed farming and stockfarming are KwaZulu's main agricultural activities, with 14·8 per cent of the land classified as arable in 1973 (Table 9.1).

The Transkei is also well-watered, and has several perennial rivers such as the Umtamvuma, Umzimvubu, Umtata, Bashee and Great Kei. Their irrigation potential, coupled with their proximity to some of the best farming land in South Africa, confers on the Transkei an agricultural potential which probably exceeds that of any other homeland. It has the

Table 9.1
Arable and irrigated land in the homelands, 1973

Homeland	Total area (ha.)	Total arable land (ha.)	% Arable land	Irrigated land (ha.)
Transkei	3,854,153	719,000	18·7	2,340
Ciskei	927,208	124,301	13·4	1,000
KwaZulu	3,139,294	465,210	14·8	2,926
Qwaqwa	48,244	9,805	20·3	9
Lebowa	2,144,713	340,457	15·9	7,142
Venda	639,000	55,814	8·7	2,678
Gazankulu	675,710	72,403	10·7	1,141
Swazi	208,735	32,735	15·7	784
Bophuthatswana	3,820,142	255,869	6·7	3,750
Total	15,457,199	2,075,594	13·4	21,770

Source: Republic of South Africa (1974), *South Africa 1974,* p. 294; the proposed South Ndebele homeland has been excluded.

highest percentage of arable land apart from Qwaqwa, the South Sotho's tiny homeland. The Ciskei, further west, suffers from variable climatic conditions. The flow of perennial rivers such as the Keiskama and the Great Kei fluctuates to such an extent that water supply for irrigation is dependent on storage dams. Severe droughts are not uncommon, and cattle farming predominates. Both the Ciskei and the Transkei have much dissected land, and have suffered extensively from soil erosion.

Bophuthatswana is the largest homeland in terms of area, but has an annual rainfall of only 254–500 millimetres.[5] The river beds of the Malopo and Limpopo are no more than dry ditches for a considerable part of the year. The Hartz river, a tributary of the Vaal, flows through the area, allowing it a part in the Hartz–Vaal irrigation scheme. Elsewhere Bophuthatswana is predominantly a cattle grazing area with some mixed farming and dry-land crop production in the vicinity of Mafeking and Lichtenburg.

The three homelands in the northern and eastern Transvaal show considerable variations in physical conditions over relatively short distances. In Lebowa, rainfall varies from 350 millimetres in the west to 710 millimetres in the north.[6] Numerous rivers such as the Olifants and Letaba provide important irrigation potential. Gazankulu is relatively well-watered, and again has important rivers, including the Letaba and Sabie. The Venda homeland has a high rainfall (900 millimetres) on top of the Soutpansberg range which feeds several perennial rivers including the Limpopo, Njelele and Pafuri. These rivers have a large irrigation potential, and some hydro-electric power is generated. By far the largest parts of Lebowa and Gazankulu, and part of Vendaland, are used for stockfarming, but mixed farming is important in the lower lying areas of Vendaland.

The two smallest homelands are those for the Swazi and South Sotho peoples. Mixed farming predominates in the Swazi territories, which have a subtropical climate; the southern block is traversed by the Komati river, which has some potential for irrigation. Qwaqwa, the South Sotho homeland, is a mountainous territory of approximately 1,500 metres above sea level and is characterised by severe winters with snow and frost. Mixed farming is practised; there is a relatively high proportion of arable land, but soil erosion has been severe.

Superimposed upon this variety of environmental conditions is one disadvantage common to almost all parts of the homelands, namely inaccessibility (see Fig. 9.1). The nineteenth-century reserves were ignored by the railway system, which was intended to meet the economic needs of the White population (chapter 2). Relatively few major roads pass through the homelands; an important exception is the route from Durban to the Cape, via the Transkei and Ciskei.

Traditional agriculture in the homelands

Increasing government concern about the deterioration of the reserves led to the establishment of a special technical agricultural service within the Native Affairs Department in 1929. As the task of reclamation was beyond its resources, the technical service concentrated primarily on widespread stabilisation, i.e. the prevention of further deterioration of the soil and its vegetation. The designation of improvement areas was hindered, however, by the reluctance of the inhabitants to agree to this once they realised that it usually entailed the reduction of stock numbers. Within the improvement areas, arable plots and grazing land were demarcated and where possible fenced. Silt traps were built across dongas (gullies) and contour banks constructed. But progress was slow, and by the end of 1952, only 9·4 per cent of the total area of the reserves had been stabilised: at the existing rate, it would have taken 245 years to complete the task.[7]

Attempts to improve methods of cultivation and stockfarming also yielded disappointing results. Despite the use of trained Africans to

164

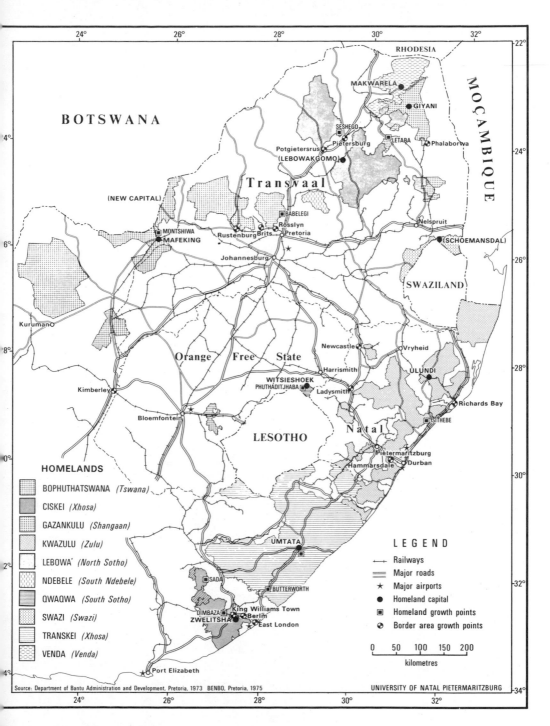

Fig. 9.1   Black homelands – communications

The map legend and labels (as visible on the map):

BOTSWANA

MOÇAMBIQUE

RHODESIA

SWAZILAND

LESOTHO

Transvaal

Orange   Free   State

Natal

MAKWARELA
GIYANI
SESHEGO
Pietersburg
LETABA
Phalaborwa
Potgietersrus
(LEBOWAKGOMO)
(NEW CAPITAL)
BABELEGI
Rosslyn
Nelspruit
MONTSHIWA
Rustenburg Brits
Pretoria
(SCHOEMANSDAL)
MAFEKING
Johannesburg
Kurumano
Newcastle
Vryheid
ULUNDI
Orange
Harrismith
Kimberley
WITSIESHOEK
PHUTHADITJHABA
Ladysmith
Richards Bay
Bloemfontein
ISITHEBE
Pietermaritzburg
Hammarsdale
Durban
UMTATA
SADA
BUTTERWORTH
DIMBAZA
King Williams Town
ZWELITSHA
Berlin
East London
Port Elizabeth

HOMELANDS

- BOPHUTHATSWANA *(Tswana)*
- CISKEI *(Xhosa)*
- GAZANKULU *(Shangaan)*
- KWAZULU *(Zulu)*
- LEBOWA *(North Sotho)*
- NDEBELE *(South Ndebele)*
- QWAQWA *(South Sotho)*
- SWAZI *(Swazi)*
- TRANSKEI *(Xhosa)*
- VENDA *(Venda)*

L E G E N D

- Railways
- Major roads
- ★ Major airports
- ● Homeland capital
- ▣ Homeland growth points
- ⊘ Border area growth points

0   50   100   150   200
kilometres

Source: Department of Bantu Administration and Development, Pretoria, 1973 BENBO, Pretoria, 1975

UNIVERSITY OF NATAL PIETERMARITZBURG

operate demonstration plots and to supervise dipping and inoculation of stock, little interest was aroused, and agricultural production continued to decline. During the period 1946–52, Africans in the reserves produced less than half their normal grain requirements.[8]

Yields have changed little since the Tomlinson Commission reported in 1955. The striking contrast between maize yields on White farms in the Transvaal and in the homelands is shown in Table 9.2 below. Dramatic fluctuations in yields are also noticeable; when bad years result in virtual crop failure, as in 1968 in the Ciskei and 1970 in Gazankulu, the people

Table 9.2
Maize yields* in the homelands, 1967–70

Year	Trans-vaal High-veld	Western Trans-vaal	Cis-kei	Bop-huth-at-swana	Leb-owa	Gazan-kulu	Venda	Swazi	Kwa-Zulu	Qwa-qwa
1967	33·5	27·2	2·8	4·2		2·3 (average)			3·6	n.a.
1968	23·8	17·3	0·3	2·7	0·8	1·9	1·3	1·4	2·2	1·9
1969	14·1	19·0	0·8	2·0	3·5	1·8	3·2	0·5	2·7	1·5
1970	25·2	18·0	1·4	3·4	1·8	†	0·7	1·2	2·9	1·5

* 90·7 kg. or 200 lb. bags per hectare.
† Negligible.
n.a. = Not available.
Source: J.A. Lombard and P.J. Van der Merwe (1972), 'Central problems of the economic development of Bantu homelands', *Finance and Trade Review* 10, no. 1, p. 37.

become dependent on outside supplies. Yet the Transkeian Annual for 1968, reporting that the average maize yield in the territory was 3·5 bags per hectare, comments:

> . . . the incentive to produce more than basic requirements is not there . . . If the season is a good one and a successful crop is reaped it may mean that a man will not plough his land the following year, since he has stored sufficient grain for his requirements . . . That the land is able to produce far more than it is doing at present is beyond all doubt. On experimental bases yields of 67·7 bags per hectare have been obtained, while 19·9 bags per hectare have been reaped from demonstration plots where the rainfall for the growing period of the crops was only 127 millimetres.[9]

Likewise the problem of overstocking has yet to be solved, as overall numbers are still showing a slight upward trend. In view of the increasing population and the continued importance attached to lobola (bride price) this is hardly surprising. The homelands collectively had 3·47 million head of cattle in 1973, together with 3·88 million sheep and 3·14 million goats (1971 figures).[10] In order to promote stock improvement bulls and rams are sold to African farmers at subsidised prices, whilst a few Africans are now able to supply their fellow farmers with well-bred animals. Slaughter cattle are fetching higher prices at sales organised by the Department of Bantu Administration and Development, and such sales have increased steadily in recent years. Since 1974 the Bantu Investment Corporation, in co-operation with the homeland governments concerned, has launched a scheme whereby it buys inferior cattle offered by Africans at auction sales where they fail to fetch a minimum guaranteed price, and keeps them on holding farms until they are marketable. Co-operative shearing schemes have been promoted in wool-producing areas, where farmers receive assistance in classing and marketing their wool. Co-operative dairying schemes have had varying success; in 1971 there were only 1,675 participants in seventy-seven such schemes.[11]

The shortage of personnel in relation to the scale of the problem is an important reason for the slowness of agricultural progress in the homelands. The training of more Africans is particularly urgent. Five agricultural colleges at present serve Africans, but in 1970 there were only 750 qualified African extension workers (one per 9,300 population), of whom 283 were in the Transkei.[12] Relevant degree and training courses have also been available at the University of Fort Hare and at a technical college at Mmadikoti, near Pietersburg since the late 1960s; the numbers of Africans qualifying are as yet very small, however.

Cash crops and irrigation

Commercial crops occupy less than 2 per cent of arable land in the homelands. In 1975 the areas planted included the following (hectares):[13]

Resilient fibres	18,392	Tea	900
Sugar cane	14,349	Coconuts	940
Coffee	205		

The major resilient fibres are sisal and phormium tenax, which are grown on Government plantations as semi-industrial undertakings. One of the largest plantations is at Chloe, near Pietersburg (Lebowa).

Sugar cane is the only cash crop which is grown on a signficant scale by African farmers. It is important largely in KwaZulu, where it is grown for the most part without irrigation. Yields compare unfavourably with those of White farmers, but are improving. African contractors are employed by the planters to cut the cane and deliver it to White-owned mills. The South African Sugar Association has established a R5 million fund to provide low interest loans and helps procure fertilisers and equipment for African and Indian small scale growers, who lack access to normal credit facilities.

Other crops are grown only on a very small, and in some cases experimental, scale. Cotton is grown in the Transvaal homelands, KwaZulu and Bophuthatswana. Tea nurseries have been established by the Transkei government and by the Bantu Investment Corporation in Venda, whilst experimental coffee growing is in progress in several homelands. Coconuts are being grown in northern KwaZulu, where they are planted together with cashew nuts in order to achieve efficient soil utilisation. The Xhosa Development Corporation has established two small tobacco plantations in the Ciskei, and small amounts of citrus fruit are grown on government estates in several homelands.

Timber is at present the most important commercial 'crop' in the homelands. Forests cover just over 2 per cent of their total area: in 1975 this included 225,000 hectares of indigenous forest, 94,500 hectares on which commercial plantations had been established, and 26,000 hectares planted with non-commercial woodlots.[14] Relatively large plantations are found in KwaZulu, Venda and the Ciskei, but only in the Transkei is forestry an important source of revenue. It can generate valuable secondary employment in sawmills, creosoting plants, furniture factories and the pulp and paper industry, but further development is necessarily of a long term nature.

In 1973 less than 22,000 hectares were irrigated throughout the homelands, of which various schemes along the Olifants river in Lebowa accounted for one-third (see Table 9.2). Other notable schemes included those near Taungs in Bophuthatswana and along the Luvuvhu, Phiphidi and Motale rivers in Venda, the Qamata scheme in the western Transkei, the Gxulu scheme near Keiskammahoek (Ciskei), and the Bululwana scheme in the Nongoma district of KwaZulu. Irrigated plots vary according to climatic conditions from about 1·3 to 1·7 hectares. They are leased to settlers on various conditions relating to such matters as payment of rent, beneficial usage, and the number of cattle units which may be kept. Plotholders are urged to rotate their pieces of land, and in

168

addition to maize to grow other crops suited to the locality such as vegetables, fodder crops, wheat, lucerne, tobacco, fruit, sugar cane and groundnuts. Although yields are considerably higher than on dry-lands, the available evidence suggests that few African farmers are showing the industry and enterprise required to make a good living on irrigated land. It is widely reported that new settlers tend to neglect planting after a good harvest, and that advice about crop rotation is disregarded.[15] Certain conditions of tenure, including beneficial occupation and the presence of the plotholder on the irrigation settlement, have proved difficult to enforce; in the case of the latter, it does appear unreasonable to insist that the allotment holder should be present in off-seasons.[16]

The large, recently completed J.G. Strijdom dam at Jozini is planned to irrigate some 35,000 hectares of land in the Makatini Flats along the Pongola river in a wide strip of state-owned land between two African areas in northern Zululand. According to initial government plans for consolidation, this land was to be divided between Africans and Whites, but in the revised official plan, all this land should become part of KwaZulu (see Fig. 11.5). There have been several delays in implementing this scheme, which when operative will probably be the largest irrigation project in any of the homelands.

An interesting attempt began in 1975 to establish South Africa's first silk industry in Gazankulu near Tzaneen.[17] Mulberry trees imported from Japan are being grafted on to an indigenous South African strain. The Lowveld is well suited to the industry, for the trees will bear leaves for up to eight months of the year. Silk is also an ideal peasant farming industry with a high return of R110 per kilogram of raw silk (1975); it is believed that one African family can easily accommodate enough worms to produce this amount every six weeks. If the Gazankulu scheme is successful, the industry may become more widespread in the homelands.

The Tomlinson agricultural strategy

Government agricultural policies in the homelands since 1955 have strongly reflected the views of the Tomlinson Commission. The Commission's brief was 'to conduct an exhaustive enquiry into and report on a comprehensive scheme for the rehabilitation of the Native areas with a view to developing within them a social structure in keeping with the culture of the Native and based on effective socio-economic planning.'[18] In its report the Commission stressed that the essential preconditions for agricultural reform were general economic development, provision of employment to relieve pressure of population on the land, and social development, to produce a climate of opinion in which reform would be possible.

The Commission believed that a sound agriculture implied relatively large holdings (an average of forty-four hectares was recommended) and heavy capital investment. Such holdings would be adequate to enable farming families to earn enough to satisfy their basic requirements, the cash constituent of which was estimated at R120 per annum for mixed farming areas (the majority), R220 on irrigation schemes, R180 in sugar-producing areas, and varying amounts elsewhere. Economic landholdings. were to be determined on the basis of existing farm practices: should an African improve his methods, then he would also be able to increase his income. On this basis, Tomlinson calculated that the homelands could support 307,000 full-time farming families, or 1·8 million people.[19] It has since been widely recognised that the incomes allowed by Tomlinson were unrealistically low if an African peasantry was to be held on the land: even in 1956 the average earnings of Africans in manufacturing amounted to R300 per annum.[20] Tomlinson's population estimates have also proved too low: with a *de facto* homeland population of seven million in 1970, implementation of the Tomlinson proposals would have meant that over five million people would be landless. Even had non-agricultural development proceeded at the pace Tomlinson envisaged, it could not have employed anything like this number by 1970. In the event, the pace of such development has been slow (chapter 10), partly because of the government's rejection of the scale of financial expenditure recommended by the Commission. Likewise, the government's refusal to allow private White entrepreneurship and capital in the homelands has restricted non-agricultural development.

The consequent lack of alternative employment, together with increasing population pressures, has meant that the land reforms carried out to date have not given most families 'economic units', even in Tomlinson's terms. According to official calculations, the size of such plots is considered to include 4·1 hectares of arable land in the Umtata district of the Transkei and between 4·9 and 7·3 hectares in the King William's Town district of the Ciskei: but the median size of arable plot in the Transkeian areas investigated by Maree and de Vos was only 1·9 hectares, and in the Ciskeian areas 1·5 hectares.[21] Many families are currently receiving only one hectare and grazing for two cattle. Admittedly, an attempt is being made to plan these lesser units so that they can ultimately be combined to form full economic units, but it is difficult to foresee a time when enough Africans will leave the land for such units to become the general rule. It is perhaps just as well that the government is not implementing the Tomlinson Commission's recommendation to grant freehold title to the arable holdings, since the present situation is uncertain and may prove to be transitional.

This unpromising outlook should not be allowed to obscure the more positive achievements of the conservation and settlement planning undertaken since 1955. The replanning of settlement and land use has been effected in a considerable proportion of the total area of each homeland (Table 9.3). The procedure is an improved version of that used

Table 9.3
Settlement and planning in the homelands, 1973

Homeland	Percentage of area planned	Diversion banks (km.)	Grass strips (km.)
Transkei	57·4	5,219	215,908
Ciskei	78·8	3,460	12,689
KwaZulu	49·1	949	635
Bophuthatswana	56·1	225	5,992
Lebowa	65·0	1,479	17,801
Venda	77·6	699	4,015
Gazankulu	99·0	134	7,615
Swazi	100·0	42	2,575

Source: Republic of South Africa (1974), *South Africa 1974,* pp. 299, 309.

in improvement areas in the 1930s. The land is divided into arable allotments and grazing areas, the latter camped and fenced so that rotational grazing may be practised. In the Ciskei in particular this practice has allowed the pasture to improve and recover despite severe droughts. In other areas, however, including parts of KwaZulu, soil erosion has reached the point where rehabilitation will be a lengthy process if it is not already too late. Huts are concentrated in villages to permit more effective use of the agricultural land. Stock limitation is enforced, water supplies and dams are provided in each camp, and anti-erosion measures adopted: many miles of contour ridges have been constructed and planted with grass, and where necessary diversion banks have been built. The available arable and grazing land is reallocated to all the inhabitants who previously held land rights, hence the smallness of the plots. Those who previously had neither land nor cattle, and who are known as 'squatters', receive nothing in the redistribution except a hut and a garden, or are encouraged to move to one of the new non-agricultural settlements.

All this is undertaken with the voluntary co-operation of the tribal authorities. The African population is reportedly more willing than in the 1930s to participate in the planning, although in some districts such as eastern Pondoland there has been resistance.[20] Daniel has noted several positive attributes of these land settlement schemes,[23] of which one is the element of self-help involved; many settlement schemes elsewhere in Africa have failed partly because the settlers have had no stake in the scheme in terms of the expenditure of their own effort. South Africa has also avoided the pitfalls of a grandiose approach which can only benefit a small proportion of the people on the land, whilst the relatively low cost means that the average African farmer is not burdened with debt as a result of resettlement. The thoroughness of the preliminary surveys which are undertaken prior to resettlement constitutes another favourable aspect of settlement planning in the homelands.

These not inconsiderable achievements leave the most fundamental problems unsolved. The physical replanning of the land is not sufficient to transform agriculture. Board has shown that there is no significant difference between replanned or 'stabilised' areas and unrehabilitated areas in regard to agricultural practices, productivity and the retention of man on the land.[24] As a result, agricultural incomes remain far below those obtainable in urban areas, even if plots approach the sizes recommended by Tomlinson. When they are much smaller, as is usually the case, existing agricultural practices do not provide for a family's basic needs, thus the head of the family has little choice but to seek work as a migrant labourer in the towns.

An alternative strategy?

From the foregoing it is evident that there is an inherent contradiction which pervades the present agricultural strategy. It is based on large plots and traditional, relatively extensive practices, which implies large scale removals from the land. It is politically unacceptable for the families removed to go to White towns, yet it has so far proved economically impracticable to absorb many of them into non-agricultural sectors within the homelands. Why then has the government not followed the logic of its own intentions, and sought to develop a more labour intensive agriculture? Given the shortage of land, abundance of labour and scarcity of capital, this seems to be the obvious strategy.[25]

Several theoretical calculations suggest that such an approach is capable of solving the problems of the homelands. Lipton criticises Tomlinson for making hardly any allowance for agricultural labourers on large holdings.[26] She suggests that a holding of twenty hectares of good land – the smallest envisaged by Tomlinson – would support ten families of landless labourers even with moderately labour intensive methods. This figure may be questioned, but undoubtedly such a modified intensification of agricultural practices could support more people than at present. If, on the other hand, the size of holdings is drastically reduced and highly intensive methods are adopted, then Lipton suggests that the arable land of the Transkei alone could in theory accommodate 500,000 farming families (60 per cent more than Tomlinson allowed for all the reserves together) on plots of two morgen (1·63 hectares), without allowing for more than 2·6 million hectares of pastoral land.

Afrikaner writers have likewise suggested that with intensive agricultural development the homelands could accommodate many more people. Riekert states that Bophuthatswana could support a population of 6·2 million compared with its 1970 population of 865,000.[27] Grobler calculates the following capacities for the homelands, based on dry-land agriculture:[28]

	Density per hectare	Potential population (millions)
KwaZulu	2·5	7·5
Northern homelands	3·6	10·9
Western homelands	2·4	7·2

Although he does not estimate the number of families which can be absorbed in the agricultural sector *per se,* Grobler believes that this sector can provide adequate scope for the diversification required as a basis for secondary industry.

Even if such estimates are over-optimistic, it would appear that the physical environment is not the fundamental obstacle to the development of a labour intensive agriculture which would substantially reduce the dependence of the homelands on South Africa for employment. The major obstacle is the sheer magnitude of the task in human terms, especially when measured against the time scale in which development is needed.[29] Even the task of carrying out the Tomlinson strategy has been described by Hobart Houghton as calling for 'the energy of Alexander the Great, the wisdom of Solomon and the patience of Job.'[30] How much more overwhelming a task, then, to replan not only the landholdings and settlement pattern but also basic farming methods. Quite apart from the technical and administrative difficulties, this involves changing the behaviour of millions of farmers and farmworkers. The development of peasant agriculture throughout the world is a slow process. South-East Asia has a long tradition of labour intensive cultivation, whereas in South Africa the African agricultural sector, after its initially favourable market response in the 1870s and 1880s (chapter 2) has been forced back to a subsistence or below subsistence level. Social attitudes such as the continuing value attached to cattle would make a 'green revolution' in the homelands very difficult to achieve. Any attempt to do so would, whether carried out by South Africa or by the homeland governments, involve a major transfer of agricultural extension officers from White to African farms. In the short term this would inevitably mean a decrease in overall production and export of agricultural commodities.

It must not be forgotten, either, that despite the success of conservation measures already undertaken many areas of the homelands are still in need of rehabilitation. In some areas this will be a lengthy process, and the implementation of a labour intensive agricultural strategy would be impracticable in the foreseeable future. Meanwhile the resettlement of Africans from White areas inevitably leads to a further deterioration in the ecological balance.

In one respect at least a labour intensive strategy based on very small plots would be little improvement on the Tomlinson strategy: the incomes generated would still be insufficient to hold Africans on the land. To do this in any part of Africa, an agricultural development strategy must work towards a significant reduction of the perceived disparity inherent in a spatial structure polarised between rural and urban areas.[31] Whether the homelands are independent or not will make little difference in this respect, since they, like Botswana, Lesotho and Swaziland, will remain part of the same spatial economic system, which exhibits a high degree of polarisation between core and periphery.

In the absence of a labour intensive agricultural strategy, only the rapid development of other economic activities could enable the homelands to support their *de facto* populations. The prospects for such development will be examined in the following chapter.

References

[1] D.L. Niddrie (1968), *South Africa: nation or nations?*, Van Nostrand, Princeton, p. 145.

174

[2] C. Desmond (1971), *The Discarded People,* Penguin, Harmondsworth, p. 21.

[3] Republic of South Africa (1974), *South Africa 1974* (official yearbook), p. 294.

[4] R.E. Schulze (1970), 'A geographical survey as a basis for land planning in the Tugela Location', *J. for Geog.* 3, p. 626.

[5] J.A. Lombard and P.J. van der Merwe (1972), 'Central problems of the economic development of Bantu homelands', *Finance and Trade Review* (Volkskas Ltd) 10, no. 1, p. 2.

[6] Ibid., p. 3.

[7] Union of South Africa (1955), *Report of the Tomlinson Commission on the Socio-Economic Development of the Bantu Areas,* UG 61/1955, p. 75.

[8] Ibid., p. 84.

[9] Quoted by M. Horrell (1973) in *The African Homelands of South Africa,* SAIRR, Johannesburg, p. 86.

[10] M. Horrell and T. Hodgson (1976), *A Survey of Race Relations in South Africa 1975,* SAIRR, Johannesburg, p. 143.

[11] M. Horrell, op. cit., p. 87.

[12] 'Agricultural development in the Bantu homelands', *Bantu* 17, no. 7 (1970), p. 24.

[13] M. Horrell and T. Hodgson, op. cit., p. 143.

[14] Ibid.

[15] M. Horrell, op. cit., p. 89.

[16] S. van der Horst (1972), 'The economic problems of the homelands', in N.J. Rhoodie (ed.), *South African Dialogue,* McGraw-Hill, Johannesburg, p. 193.

[17] Reported in *Bantu* 22, no. 3 (1975), p. 32.

[18] Union of South Africa, op. cit., p. xviii.

[19] Ibid., p. 114.

[20] S. van der Horst, op. cit., p. 188.

[21] J. Maree and P.J. de Vos (1975), *Underemployment, Poverty and Migrant Labour in the Transkei and Ciskei,* SAIRR, Johannesburg, p. 13.

[22] S. van der Horst, op. cit., p. 189.

[23] J.B. McI. Daniel (1970), 'Rural resettlement schemes in African areas', *J. for Geog.* 3, pp. 645–6.

[24] C. Board (1964), 'The rehabilitation programme in the Bantu areas and its effect on the agricultural life of the Bantu in the eastern Cape', *SAJE* 32, pp. 36–52.

[25] M. Lipton (1972), 'The South African census and the Bantustan policy', *The World Today* 28, p. 264.

[26] Ibid., p. 265.

[27] P.J. Riekert (1970), 'Die Tswana en sy tuisland', *J. of Racial Affairs* 21, p. 137.

[28] J.H. Grobler (1972), 'The agricultural potential of the Bantu homelands', *J. of Racial Affairs* 23, pp. 39–40.

[29] G. Maasdorp (1974), *Economic Development Strategy in the African Homelands: the role of agriculture and industry,* SAIRR, Johannesburg, p. 13.

[30] D.H. Houghton (1973), *The South African Economy,* Oxford University Press, Cape Town, p. 79.

[31] W.J. Davies (1975), 'Politics, perception and development strategy in Tropical Africa', *J. of Modern African Studies* 13, p. 45.

10 Industrial development in the homelands

The resource base: primary products

It will be apparent from the previous chapter that the existing agricultural resource base for industrial development in the homelands is minimal, and shows little sign of rapid expansion. The processing of fibres is the most significant agriculturally based industry at present, supporting nineteen decorticating plants in 1975[1] as well as a sisal factory in Lebowa and a grain bag factory at Butterworth in the Transkei. A maize milling firm has also established a R2 million complex at Butterworth, and several maize mills elsewhere in the Transkei. A tea factory is associated with the tea nursery at Lambasi in southern Pondoland. Timber-based industries included fourteen creosoting plants and nineteen sawmills in 1975,[2] but much of the timber is sent to sawmills outside the homelands. A gradual expansion of commercial cropping may allow further development of agricultural processing industries, particularly where considerable weight loss occurs in the course of production. This is true, for instance, of the sugar industry; thus increasing cane cultivation in KwaZulu may well justify the construction of one or more sugar mills to replace dependence on those in adjacent White areas. Fish farming projects such as the hatchery on the Pienaars river a hundred kilometres north of Pretoria (Bophuthatswana) may lead to the development of canning and freezing industries.

Some homelands may prove to be rich in minerals – Bophuthatswana, Lebowa, Gazankulu, Venda and Swazi all lie within South Africa's mineral rich belt which extends from the northern Transvaal to the northern Cape. Large deposits of titanium ores are thought to exist in KwaZulu, between Richards' Bay and the Mozambique border. Little mining potential appears to exist, however, in the Transkei and the Ciskei. In the past it appears that such areas as Phalaborwa (eastern Transvaal) have been excluded from the homelands because of their mineral resources, but the policy of homeland consolidation has probably proceeded too far for this to be repeated as further resources are discovered. Current production and employment (Table 10.1) are

177

Table 10.1
Mining production (1973) and employment (1975) in the homelands

| | Employment | | Value (R '000) |
	Whites	Africans	
Bophuthatswana	4,085	61,023	8,379·2
Lebowa	687	16,200	6,807·6
KwaZulu	14	307	529·0
Gazankulu	8	151	246·5
Venda	39	425	402·1

Source: M. Horrell and T. Hodgson (1976), *A Survey of Race Relations in South Africa 1975*, SAIRR, Johannesburg, p. 144.

concentrated mainly in Bophuthatswana (platinum, asbestos, chromium, limestone, manganese, vanadium) and Lebowa (asbestos, chromium, platinum, andalusite). The great majority of those employed in the platinum mines near Rustenburg are recruited from other parts of South Africa and neighbouring countries, as the native Tswana have been reluctant to work on the mines.

The Bantu Mining Corporation is currently prospecting in several homelands, together with nearly 200 White and African leaseholders, both companies and individuals. Several significant discoveries were announced during 1975, beginning in January with the discovery of new platinum deposits in Lebowa. The finding of a major anthracite deposit of at least 100 million tonnes in the Nongoma area of KwaZulu was announced in August, and shortly afterwards a contract for its exploitation was signed; this should generate useful employment opportunities in an otherwise remote district. Later in the same month followed the announcement of South Africa's fist significant gold discovery since the Free State goldfields were found in the mid-1950s. The deposit, which is at least twenty kilometres long, is located fifteen kilometres south of Mafeking, and extends into Bophuthatswana. The ore body is so near the surface that it may be possible to mine part of the gold by open cast methods, and thus keep development costs very low.

Although mining is a significant source of employment in Bophuthatswana and Lebowa, and is likely to become so at least in KwaZulu, it seems unlikely at present that it will generate much industrial employment beyond the possible development of basic processing industries. Royalties and prospecting fees currently accrue largely to government bodies, including the Bantu Mining Corporation and the South African Bantu Trust, rather than to homeland governments, but this would naturally cease to be the case on the attainment of independence.

Labour resources

A potential cheap and plentiful supply of labour is the chief economic advantage many border areas and homelands have to offer industrialists as compensation for higher costs in many other directions. There is thus a strong case for permitting 'promotional' or 'development rates' below those laid down in Industrial Council agreements. The two Acts governing wages, the Industrial Conciliation Act (1956) and the Wage Act (1937, amended 1942), permit different minimum rates to be laid down for different areas; thus lower minimum rates may be permissible in border areas and homelands. In addition, since 1971 neither Act has applied to Africans in the homelands, excluding the Transkei; the government of the latter is responsible for its own industrial legislation, but so far has not found it politic to adopt an independent line.[3]

Actual wage rates in the homelands are inevitably influenced by those in core areas of South Africa. The easier the access of workers from the periphery to jobs in the core areas, the more wage rates in the periphery will rise towards those in the core, although there will still be a margin reflecting the cost of movement and the workers' natural preference for staying at home with their families.[4] Where significant earnings differentials do exist, they are not necessarily confined to the homelands, and would in any case tend to be reduced by significant industrialisation in the low wage areas. The real advantage of the homelands must, however, be measured in terms not of wage rates but of wage *costs*. Productivity tends to be lower in border areas and homelands than in established industrial centres. Selwyn, in his study of Botswana, Lesotho and Swaziland, found that, owing to substantially lower productivity and higher training costs, unskilled and skilled wage costs there were actually higher in some cases than in core areas of Southern Africa; only 30 per cent of firms were of the clear opinion that their labour costs were lower than in the core areas.[5]

Most skilled labour in the homelands is currently expatriate; thus wage rates usually include inducement allowances on top of the high wages already paid to skilled Whites in South Africa. The replacement of this highly paid expatriate labour with lower paid local labour is essential if faster industrial growth is to be achieved. Although job reservation does not apply in the homelands, such an aim must be a long term one: in 1974 there were less than 4,000 Africans enrolled on technical and vocational courses throughout the country.[6] The situation is made worse by a government ruling that no African apprentices will be trained outside the homelands, since there are few artisans able to give such training within the homelands. Moreover, only Africans of the ethnic group of a particular homeland are eligible for training and advancement within the homeland: this effectively excludes, for instance, the majority of African miners in Bophuthatswana and Lebowa from such training.

Markets and transport costs

As noted previously, the homelands depend heavily on their transport links with South Africa (see Fig. 9.1). Although the railways and most main roads tend to follow 'White corridors', a reasonable infrastructure of connecting roads has been established. Unfortunately, the monopolistic position of South African Railways poses other problems for homeland industrialists.[7] Road transport permits are required for any industrial products to be transported by truck from decentralised regions to the major South African markets. As a rule these permits are not easily granted, which means that, since industrial goods must start their journey by road in most homelands, trans-shipment is necessary at the nearest railhead. Not only does this result in additional transfer costs, but the SAR tariff structure favours agricultural and, to a certain extent, mining products at the expense of finished industrial products. This favours market orientated location of industries, and thus the core areas of South Africa. Decentralisation incentives do, however, include a 15 per cent rebate on SAR road and rail tariffs in respect of products manufactured in the homelands, which partially compensates for the disadvantages mentioned.

Improved access to the core areas of South Africa would still leave prospective industrialists in the homelands with serious disadvantages. It is a normal feature of core–periphery relationships that the benefits of free movement of goods accrue mainly to manufacturers in the core area, for whom markets in the periphery become more accessible. Homeland firms will usually lack the experience as well as the economies of scale which benefit established firms in the core area; only in special cases (such as that of bulky products with high transport costs) will these advantages be counteracted sufficiently to induce location in the homelands. The fragmentation of homeland territory poses further problems, since communications, including information media, are usually poorer between the various fragments of territory than between each fragment and the core.[8] Thus homeland consumers may be better informed about South African products than about any product produced elsewhere in their own homelands, whilst manufacturers will face transport problems in attempting to serve even the poor domestic market afforded by the homelands. Independent homelands could theoretically protect their domestic markets against South African competition, but this would involve an effective transfer of resources from very poor consumers to producers of manufactured goods.[9] To achieve their objective, levels of protection would need to be greater than those imposed by South Africa herself, which would further increase the burden on consumers.

Agglomeration economies and urbanisation

The homelands lack most of the external economies which characterise major urban areas. The embryonic nature of existing urban and industrial development gives virtually no scope for inter-industry linkages, nor does it offer a base for the development of legal, financial, advertising and other commercial services, and maintenance facilities. Absence of the social advantages of living in or close to developing urban areas may also deter prospective entrepreneurs from establishing factories in the homelands. Admittedly, the homelands are free from the diseconomies of large urban areas, but so too are many decentralised locations in 'White' South Africa. The cheapness of building land in the homelands may be countered by higher construction costs.

Only those parts of the homelands which abut existing metropolitan regions and growth points are well placed to take advantage of agglomeration economies.[10] The following areas fall into this category (see also Fig. 11.3):

(1) Part of the Ciskei, which abuts the East London metropolitan region, including Berlin and King William's Town.
(2) The Bophuthatswana townships of Garankuwa and Mabopane, and the Babelegi growth point, which are close to Pretoria. Other parts of Bophuthatswana abut the smaller White growth points of Rustenburg and Mafeking.
(3) Parts of KwaZulu which abut the Durban–Pietermaritzburg

corridor, the developing port and industrial complex of Richard's Bay and its communication links with Durban and Johannesburg, and the lesser growth centres of Newcastle and Ladysmith.

It has been pointed out that KwaZulu will soon be 'surrounded by a triangle of economic development unequalled in Africa' with its apices at Johannesburg, Durban and Richard's Bay, and that rapid urbanisation of the Zulu within their own borders is likely.[11]

Unfortunately, the greatest need for employment in the homelands is found not in or near those promising growth areas within the sphere of influence of existing industrial centres, but in remoter parts of the Ciskei, KwaZulu and other homelands. If industrial growth is concentrated in the former areas, the urbanisation process will involve a considerable redistribution of population within the homelands. Other homelands such as Lebowa and Gazankulu have only less important White towns such as Pietersburg and Phalaborwa near their borders, whilst all urbanisation within the Transkei will have to be supported by secondary and tertiary industry within the homeland itself. The Venda and Swazi homelands together with Qwaqwa have the poorest prospects of all for urban development.

The underdeveloped, rural character of the homelands is attested by the fact that in 1960 they possessed only thirty-one townships with a total population of 49,855.[12] Since then township construction has proceeded rapidly. Much of it has occurred in areas bordering White towns and cities, particularly in Bophuthatswana, KwaZulu and Lebowa, where despite the speed of township construction it has often failed to keep up with population growth. Some townships, however, are resettlement camps with almost no urban functions (e.g. Sada and Ilingi near Queenstown, Ciskei – see Fig. 11.4). By 1970 there were eighty-six townships in the homelands, with a total population of 582,356 (Table 10.2), equivalent to 8·3 per cent of the *de facto* population of the homelands. This figure includes Umlazi near Durban (121,160) which was re-zoned as part of KwaZulu. The only other town with over 50,000 people is Mdantsane near East London, which with an official population of 66,380 had 12·6 per cent of the population of the Ciskei: its actual population was probably nearer 100,000. The Transkei, although it has more townships than any other homeland, is one of the least urbanised homelands (2·6 per cent in 1970), owing to its remoteness from White towns. Even Butterworth, which has experienced considerable industrial growth since 1970, is very small in comparison with townships abutting major urban areas. On the basis of present evidence it seems highly

Table 10.2
Number and size of towns in the homelands, 1970

	Number of towns according to size of population									Total number
	Below 500	500 +	1,000 +	2,000 +	5,000 +	10,000 +	20,000 +	50,000 +	100,000 +	
Transkei	6	6	7	5	–	–	1	–	–	25
Ciskei	2	–	1	1	–	1	1	1	–	7
Bophuthatswana	–	2	3	2	3	2	2	–	–	14
Lebowa	–	1	5	4	1	3	–	–	–	14
Gazankulu	–	1	1	1	–	–	–	–	–	3
Venda	–	1	–	–	–	–	–	–	–	1
Swazi	–	1	1	1	–	–	–	–	–	3
KwaZulu	–	3	4	4	3	–	3	–	1	18
Qwaqwa	–	–	1	–	–	–	–	–	–	1
Total	8	15	23	18	7	6	7	1	1	86

Source: J.A. Lombard and P.J. van der Merwe (1972), 'Central problems of the economic development of Bantu homelands', *Finance and Trade Review* 10, no. 1, p. 34.

improbable that a significant degree of urban development and urbanisation can be generated in the remoter parts of the homelands.

Industrial decentralisation policies: border industries

As early as 1936 the Board of Trade and Industries considered the encouragement of industry as a means of ameliorating the poverty of the reserves, but its recommendations were restricted to industries which would not be competitive with those in other areas. The Tomlinson Commission recommended that, in order to create the necessary number of employment opportunities in secondary industry (estimated at 20,000 annually), industries should be established both within the reserves and on their borders. A majority of the Commission's members considered that such development was not practicable within the homelands without White capital and entrepreneurial expertise. The government rejected this recommendation on the grounds that African enterprise should be allowed to develop in the homelands unimpeded by White competition.

It concentrated instead on the development of industrial areas on the borders of the reserves. Border industrial areas were defined as selected underdeveloped regions to be developed through White initiative, and situated near African areas so that African workers could maintain their homes and families in their own areas, commuting daily or, if this was impossible, weekly. Various concessions would be offered to industrialists willing to establish or expand concerns in border areas. The existing Industrial Development Corporation would assist in the development of the border industrial areas, but a new body, the Permanent Committee for the Location of Industry, was established to implement the plan, assist industrialists and investigate applications for assistance. This committee began functioning in 1960; in 1971 it was renamed the Decentralisation Board.

Initially the committee concentrated its attention on the most accessible border areas 'in order to break down prejudices and make a breakthrough with the programme'.[13] Such areas included Hammarsdale (between Durban and Pietermaritzburg), Rosslyn near Pretoria, and Pietermaritzburg itself. Durban–Pinetown was excluded, as industrialists needed little inducement to establish concerns there. In its report for 1968, the committee stated that all available land at Hammarsdale had been sold, that Rosslyn was approaching that stage, and that satisfactory progress was being made in Pietermaritzburg.[14] Rosslyn and Hammarsdale, which were little more than bare veld in 1960, employed 9,300 and 6,600 persons respectively in manufacturing industry by 1970.[15]

After 1968, therefore, attention was focused on areas situated further away from metropolitan complexes, notably the following (adjacent homelands are shown in parenthesis):

East London, Berlin, King William's Town, Queenstown (Ciskei, see Fig. 11.4)
Newcastle, Ladysmith, Colenso, Richard's Bay, Empangeni (KwaZulu, see Fig. 11.5)
Pietersburg, Potgietersrust (Lebowa, see Fig. 11.3)
Tzaneen (Gazankulu and Lebowa)
Phalaborwa (Gazankulu)
Brits, Rustenberg, Zeerust, Mafeking (Bophuthatswana)

The remaining homelands, including the Transkei, received no 'commuter income' in 1967;[16] East London is the nearest border industrial area to the Transkei, but as it is sixty kilometres from the nearest part of the homeland, daily commuting is virtually impossible. While the Transkei is an especially difficult case, in general the border area growth points are not within commuting distance of large parts of the labour supply areas which they are meant to serve. There is still a need for migration of African workers from the interior of the homelands to African townships

184

like Mdantsane and Garankuwa which supply labour to border area growth points. Thus the urban population of the homelands is becoming increasingly concentrated at residential townships just within their borders: in 1970, some 60·9 per cent of the urban population was found in only eight such townships, namely Umlazi (Durban), Mdantsane (East London), Garankuwa (Rosslyn), Madadeni (Newcastle), Clermont (Pinetown), Mabopane (thirty-two kilometres north of Pretoria), Zwelitsha (King William's Town) and Hammarsdale (forty kilometres from Durban).[17]

Between June 1960, when the border industry began, and the end of 1966, 57,100 jobs were created in border industries, 44,600 of them for Africans.[18] This represents only 8,785 jobs per year. The border industry concessions were relatively greater after March 1966, and in September 1968 a number of additional positive inducements were announced. Despite these measures, however, only 30,400 further jobs were created between 1967 and 1970, 23,900 of them for Africans.[19] This represents a slightly lower rate of job creation (7,800 jobs per annum) than in the earlier period. The total increase in border area employment in the 1960s was 87,500 jobs, but of this Bell estimates that only 23,000 (2,200 per annum) are directly attributable to government intervention. By the end of 1974 African employment in border industries was 78,100,[20] only 9,600 more than in 1970, which suggests that the employment growth rate in border industries has slowed down. Whether or not this proves to be temporary, the performance of the border industry policy clearly falls pitifully short of the 20,000 jobs per year which Tomlinson considered necessary. The discrepancy is even greater if allowance is made for population increases in the homelands considerably above those anticipated in the Tomlinson Report (chapter 8).

In seeking an explanation of these disappointing results, Bell has drawn unfavourable comparisons between the nature and value of the concessions available in border industrial areas and those available to Italian firms which move to the Mezzogiorno.[21] Too small a proportion of the benefits accrued in the first one or two years after moving, when they are most valuable. There has been a heavy emphasis on tax rebates and tax allowances, whereas the Southern Italian experience suggests that direct subsidies on machinery and plant, customs exemption, low interest loans and tax exemptions on reinvested profits are more effective incentives. Bell also points out that most of the inducements, such as tax allowances, low interest loans and subsidised rentals, are capital related which tends to maximise the cost of achieving the primary object of the policy, namely increasing employment.[22] The government has also reduced the effectiveness of its policy by showing concern to avoid 'unfair competition'

185

between assisted firms and others; in the early 1960s, for instance, the government was reluctant to assist clothing firms, despite the fact that the clothing industry is the most significant of the more easily divertible industries.[23] Finally, the selective basis of assistance introduces the bargaining skill of firms, and gives rise to charges of inconsistency and arbitrariness; the psychological impact of concessions which are automatically available, as are most of those in the assisted areas of the United Kingdom, is much greater.

If the border industry policy is viewed not merely as an instrument of employment creation but in terms of homeland development, much more fundamental criticisms must be made. Since the border areas are surrounded by more productive White farming areas, they are unlikely to provide a significant market for homeland agriculture.[24] Nor do they provide the homelands with either a corporate or an individual tax base.[25] Much of the money earned is spent in White areas, and because of these leakages the multiplier effect on the homelands is weak: thus Best notes that the border industries of Rosslyn have had little multiplier effect on the commercial growth of Garankuwa because wages are spent in Pretoria.[26] In short, border industries reinforce the economic dependence of the homelands on South Africa.

The rôle of corporations in the homelands

Having rejected private White capital investment in the homelands, the government sought to encourage African entrepreneurs by creating the Bantu Investment Corporation (BIC) in 1959. Its objects were defined as the encouragement of existing industrial, commercial, financial and other undertakings, and the promotion of new ones, the provision of financial, technical and other assistance and expert advice, and the encouragement of thrift and capital accumulation. The Bantu Homelands Development Corporations Act of 1965 subsequently empowered the Minister of Bantu Administration and Development to establish a development corporation for each homeland. These corporations might themselves undertake projects, as well as stimulating and helping Africans to do so. The Xhosa Development Corporation (XDC) was accordingly established in 1966 to operate in the Transkei and the Ciskei, where it took over most of the activities of the BIC. In December 1974 it was announced that development corporations were shortly to be established for each homeland.[27]

The corporations grant loans to Africans to enable them to purchase, establish or expand trading businesses, service concerns or light

186

industries, and to buy stock in trade. Applications are carefully investigated, and in fact the majority are refused. Since most of the loans are granted without normal security, regular training and 'aftercare' is undertaken by officials of the corporations. Although most of the African entrepreneurs have resided and worked in White urban areas for a considerable length of time,[28] virtually none have started significant industrial concerns: between 1960 and 1966, only thirty-five new industries employing 945 Africans were established in the homelands.[29] This clearly confirms the majority view of the Tomlinson Commission concerning the necessity of White capital and entrepreneurial experience in establishing secondary industry in the homelands.

The corporations themselves are responsible for a considerable proportion of these industrial concerns, including furniture factories, breweries, bakeries, grain mills and vehicle repair works. Several hundred retail trading stores have been acquired from Whites, especially in the Transkei, and many of them subsequently sold to Africans. The XDC has also acquired garages and hotels. Amongst the varied concerns acquired or established by the BIC is a holiday resort for Whites which has been established in the mountains of Witsieshoek in order to provide a source of revenue for Qwaqwa. The BIC also controls commercial facilities at the Manyeleti Game Reserve for Africans (which borders the Kruger National Park) and at two African holiday resorts. Both corporations operate savings banks, generally with African managers, at a number of centres.

Whilst the work of the corporations is clearly valuable, they cannot be expected to make a large impact on the employment needs of the homelands with the limited resources at their disposal. The BIC in particular has been criticised by homeland leaders for its monopolistic position and failure to involve people sufficiently in development, together with the absence of African directors on its board. The homeland corporations have likewise been criticised for the minority position of Africans on their controlling boards, and because direct control by homeland governments has been denied.

White capital and homeland growth points

As it became clear that the employment opportunities being created in border areas and within the homelands were far below the numbers needed, the government modified its position in regard to the use of private White capital and entrepreneurship, initially (1968) to encourage mining in the homelands, and in the following year to promote industrial development as

187

well. In terms of the Promotion of Economic Development of Homelands Act (1968) Whites may enter the homelands as agents or contractors to the South African Bantu Trust or one of the corporations. Contracts are usually for periods of twenty-five years (fifty in the case of mining concerns), at the end of which the corporation concerned has the option of purchasing the enterprise, or it may be sold to an African entrepreneur if one is available, or the contract may be renewed.

Homeland industries established as a result of the agency policy have been concentrated in a number of growth points. The main ones are shown in Fig. 11.3; a few factories have also been started at other places including Dimbaza, a resettlement township in the Ciskei now designated a growth point. The concessions available in approved cases are slightly more advantageous than those offered in border industrial areas. Umtata and Butterworth (Transkei) and Isithebe (KwaZulu) have been singled out for particularly favourable treatment, but it is doubtful whether the availability of relatively small additional inducements will be enough to overcome the problem of an unsatisfactory distribution of diverted employment. Thus Babelegi, although less favourably treated, was responsible for 46·1 per cent of all employment at homeland growth points in 1974 (see the projected figures in Table 10.3 below); its proximity to Pretoria, making it by far the best located of the growth points, is clearly the reason. The success of Babelegi as a growth point for the Tswana economy is, however, compromised by the fact that the labour force is comprised of only about 20 per cent Tswana.[30] Paradoxically, there appears to be a shortage of labour in Babelegi and the border areas contiguous to Bophuthatswana; the available evidence suggests that the government has over-concentrated its industrial decentralisation efforts upon these areas.[31]

Thus it is only in Bophuthatswana that the total employment created in *five years* of White investment approaches the *annual* requirement for job opportunities. The absolute shortfall is greatest in KwaZulu and the Transkei; it is particularly serious in the latter owing to the lack of employment in border industrial areas. The magnitude of the task of meeting employment needs in the 1970s and 1980s is suggested by Professor Reynders' estimates of new job opportunities needed annually, which are as follows:[32]

	(1)	(2)
1970–80	40,700	88,000
1980–90	53,000	114,000

Column 1 is concerned only with new entrants to the labour market within the homelands, whereas column 2 also includes Africans becoming available for the labour market in White areas in addition to the current labour force in those areas. It should be remembered that even the column 2 estimates fall short of the stated aim of government policy, i.e. the *reduction* of the African labour force in White areas. Reynders' estimates are in any case conservative: it is generally accepted that the current demand for jobs *within* the homelands is increasing by 60,000 annually. Since the creation of each new job opportunity in the homelands was costing R8,000 by 1974,[33] this implied that an expenditure of R240 million per year would be needed to satisfy job needs within the homelands, even allowing for a 100 per cent multiplier effect. The actual figure would be greater still, since higher incentives would be needed to persuade sufficient industries to move to the homelands.

Table 10.3
Projected employment in homeland industries, 1974

Homeland	Projected no. of jobs, 1974
Transkei:	
Butterworth	2,651
Umtata	609
Elsewhere	986
Ciskei:	
Dimbaza	108
Elsewhere	225
KwaZulu:	
Isithebe	1,654
Qwaqwa:	
Witsieshoek	161
Bophuthatswana:	
Babelegi	5,009
Lebowa:	
Seshego	248
Gazankulu:	
Letaba	181
Total	11,832

Source: Republic of South Africa (1974), *South Africa 1974,* p. 296.

Two recent developments would appear to anticipate the independence of the homelands (chapter 11). In July 1974 the BIC embarked on a campaign to attract British and German money to the homelands. The following October the government announced that henceforth the homeland governments themselves should decide under what conditions business should operate in their areas.[34] Neither measure appears significantly to improve prospects for homeland industrial development. Foreign investment is unlikely to be substantial, given the limited potential of the homelands. The restrictions imposed by agency schemes may have held back investment to some extent, but a substantial increase in White South African investment could only be expected if incentives were raised to impossibly high levels.

The theoretical alternative to such high levels of positive inducements is to strengthen those elements of decentralisation policy which are based on negative controls and restrictions. Under the Physical Planning and Utilisation of Resources Act of 1967, industries in the 'controlled areas' must already apply for permission to increase their African labour force. This would normally be refused for industries with an African:White labour ratio exceeding 2·5:1 if established before 1 June 1973, or 2:1 if established later. In practice, as was seen in chapter 3, a relatively low proportion of applications has been refused, and a large number of industries have been exempted from these provisions. As far as homeland development is concerned, such policies are in any case of dubious value: first because they merely induce the use of capital intensive techniques in metropolitan areas, thus reducing overall African employment; and secondly because decentralising industries have many non-homeland locations open to them.

The fundamental disability of the homelands is their position as the least developed and least promising locations within the South African space economy, which is dominated by a small number of metropolitan areas.[35] In comparison with the USA, the intra-metropolitan periphery of South Africa is proportionately larger, and the national income 800 times smaller.[36] The success of a growth centre strategy in South Africa may well apply only to those areas where the potential for immediate and foreseeable growth is considerable. To apply such a strategy in the homelands is, in effect, to put the 'worst first'.[37] It has little chance of success over wide areas of the homelands, where small service centres are the highest form of urban development that can be expected. The actual location of growth points is a reflection of this: several are near White growth points, and all except Umtata, which has the advantage of rail access, are on the periphery of their respective homelands. The surest way to provide new and viable growth centres around which the homelands could develop would be the incorporation of existing White towns which lie near the borders of the homelands, such as Queenstown (Ciskei), Empangeni (KwaZulu), Rustenburg, (Bophuthatswana) and Phalaborwa (Gazankulu). Such a possibility is, however, politically unacceptable at present.

References

[1]   M. Horrell and T. Hodgson (1976), *A Survey of Race Relations in South Africa 1975*, SAIRR, Johannesburg, p. 144.
[2]   Ibid.
[3]   S.T. van der Horst (1972), *Separate Development: is consensus possible?*, SAIRR, Johannesburg, p. 15.
[4]   P. Selwyn (1975), *Industries in the Southern African Periphery*, Croom Helm, London, p. 55.
[5]   Ibid, pp. 61–2.
[6]   M. Horrell (1975), *A Survey of Race Relations in South Africa 1974*, SAIRR, Johannesburg, p. 261.
[7]   J.H. Lange (1973), comment in a discussion following a paper by R.T. Bell (see ref. 17, below), *SAJE* 41, p. 436.
[8]   G. Maasdorp (1974), *Economic Development Strategy in the African Homelands: the role of agriculture and industry*, SAIRR, Johannesburg, p. 19.
[9]   Ibid., p. 20.
[10] Ibid., p. 17.
[11] Republic of South Africa (1974), *South Africa 1974* (official yearbook), p. 304.
[12] P.S. Hattingh and M.L. Hugo (1971), 'Tendense van Bantoeverstedeliking in Suid-Afrika', *J. of Racial Affairs* 22, p. 124.
[13] Permanent Committee for the Location of Industry (1966), *Report*, quoted by R.T. Bell (see ref. 17 below), p. 405.
[14] Quoted in M. Horrell (1973), *The African Homelands of South Africa*, SAIRR, Johannesburg, p. 105.
[15] M. Horrell (1972 and 1973), *A Survey of Race Relations in South Africa 1971* and *1972*, SAIRR, Johannesburg, pp. 218 and 283 respectively.
[16] J.A. Lombard and P.J. van der Merwe (1972), 'Central problems of the economic development of Bantu homelands', *Finance and Trade Review* (Volkskas Ltd) 10, no. 1, p. 35.

[17] R.T. Bell (1973a), 'Some aspects of industrial decentralisation in South Africa', *SAJE* 41, p. 406.

[18] R.T. Bell (1973b), *Industrial Decentralisation in South Africa,* Oxford University Press, Cape Town, p. 212.

[19] Ibid., p. 233

[20] M. Horrell and T. Hodgson, op. cit., p. 181.

[21] R.T. Bell (1973b), op. cit., pp. 217–18.

[22] Ibid., p. 220.

[23] Ibid., p. 221.

[24] R.T. Bell (1973c), 'Bantustan economic development', *Third World* 2, no. 6, p. 32.

[25] G. Maasdorp, op. cit., p. 10.

[26] A.C.G. Best (1971), 'South Africa's border industries: the Tswana example', *AAAG* 61, p. 335.

[27] M. Horrell and T. Hodgson, op. cit., p. 148.

[28] G. Hart (1972), *Some Socio-Economic Aspects of African Entrepreneurship,* Institute of Social and Economic Research, Rhodes University, Grahamstown.

[29] R.T. Bell (1973a), op. cit., p. 405.

[30] C.M. Rogerson (1974), 'Growth point problems – the case of Babelegi, Bophuthatswana', *J. of Modern African Studies* 12, p. 127.

[31] Ibid., pp. 127–8.

[32] H.J.J. Reynders (1970), 'The employment potential of the Bantu homelands with special reference to industrial decentralisation', *Bantu* 17, no. 11, p. 27.

[33] M. Horrell (1975), op. cit., p. 275.

[34] *Financial Mail,* 4 October 1974, p. 37.

[35] C. Board et al. (1970), 'The structure of the South African space economy: an integrated approach', *Regional Studies* 4, pp. 367–92.

[36] T.J.D. Fair (1973), discussion paper in *Proceedings of the Urban and Regional Development Seminar,* South African Geographical Society, Johannesburg, p. 158.

[37] Ibid.

11 The political geography of the homelands

Economic dependence

It has been amply demonstrated in the last two chapters that the homelands, as peripheral areas within the South African space economy, are likely to remain dependent on the core areas of 'White South Africa' for the employment of a large and probably increasing proportion of their *de facto* population. Employment dependency is inevitably far greater in terms of the *de jure* homeland population; no less than 1,770,000 African males between the ages of fifteen and sixty-four were officially classified as 'continuously absent' from the homelands in 1970.[1]

At present the homelands also depend heavily on the South African Treasury for budgetary support (Table 11.1). Most showed a slight improvement in this respect between 1970–71 and 1973–74, although the deterioration in the Transkeian position is notable. This would appear to reflect increased expenditure by the South African government to prepare the Transkei for independence in October 1976, since the total budget increased much faster than those of the other homelands, more than doubling in three years. It is indeed frequently pointed out in official publications that the Transkeian budget exceeds those of a dozen independent African countries.[2]

'Homeland income' is at present an elusive concept and may be measured in at least three different ways.[3] The *gross domestic product* (GDP) of an area is the total value added by goods and services in the area during a particular year. The *national income* is the total income from work, property or enterprise received by all members of a given ethnic group, irrespective of where they happen to be in South Africa. The *area national income* of each homeland community consists of the domestic product of the homeland minus the share of Whites in this product, plus the income of commuters and remittances to the homeland by migrants (usually estimated at 20 per cent of earnings) and by continuously absent members of the ethnic group (estimated by Lombard and van der Merwe at 5 per cent: this is questionable, as many of those continuously absent may not have retained links with their homelands). National income is by

193

Table 11.1

Sources of income of homeland governments

Homeland	1970-71			1973-74		
	Own income (%)	RSA Treasury (%)	Total budget (Rm.)	Own income (%)	RSA Treasury (%)	Total budget (Rm.)
Transkei	25·5	74·5	24·8	17·1	82·9	53·8
Ciskei	16·8	83·2	9·3	24·4	75·6	15·8
KwaZulu	n.a.	n.a.	n.a.	25·7	74·3	45·5
Qwaqwa	6·7	93·3	1·5	78·3	21·7	2·4
Bophuthatswana	14·1	85·9	13·8	26·7	73·3	20·2
Lebowa	11·9	88·1	11·4	25·0	75·0	21·8
Venda	8·4	91·6	4·3	23·2	76·8	6·0
Gazankulu	20·0	80·0	4·6	29·1	70·9	7·5
Total	18·1	81·9	69·7	23·7	76·3	173·0

n.a. = Not available.
Source: Republic of South Africa (1974), *South Africa 1974,* p. 310.

far the largest of these three measures, but the overwhelming part of it was earned in White areas in 1967 (Table 11.2). Area national incomes were also considerably greater than the GDP, owing to the large number of Africans working outside their homelands. On the other hand, Whites and 'other Africans' made a smaller but significant contribution to the GDP, particularly in Bophuthatswana, Lebowa and Swazi.

Area national income is clearly a significant and useful measure, which might be expected to differ significantly from the GDP even in European countries such as Ireland, Spain or Yugoslavia where the remittances of migrant workers are also important. National income as defined here may appear to be a meaningless abstraction, but its relevance is perhaps greater than it seems, at least for fiscal purposes. According to Lombard and van der Merwe, the Bantu Homelands Citizenship Act (1970) 'more or less implies' that a homeland government may claim the total national income accruing to its citizens as the basis of its taxation.[4] This has already been recognised in South African legislation governing direct taxation of Africans throughout the country, and it may well be that formulae for the identification and transfer to homeland governments of indirect taxation such as excise and sales taxes may follow. If this does indeed occur, it will make the homelands far less dependent on South African budgetary aid. Instead, they would in effect become dependent on South African willingness to retain such unusual fiscal arrangements.

Table 11.2
GDP and national income of African 'nations', 1967 (R million)

Product and income	Xhosa/ Trans- kei	Xhosa/ Ciskei	Tswana	North Sotho	Shan- gaan	Venda	Swazi	Zulu	South Sotho
Gross domestic product:	68·4	13·7	22·6	24·1	5·9	5·9	2·6	50·3	0·6
Homeland citizens	51·9	11·0	11·9	16·5	4·3	4·4	1·5	40·8	0·5
Other Africans	2·6	0·3	5·6	3·4	0·6	0·5	0·6	0·8	–
Whites	13·9	2·4	5·1	4·2	1·0	1·0	0·5	8·7	0·1
National income:	296·4	73·2	142·5	120·3	48·2	22·6	62·0	361·0	142·6
Income from GDP	54·5	11·3	17·5	19·9	4·9	4·9	2·1	41·6	0·5
Commuter income	–	5·9	5·8	5·3	–	–	–	12·5	–
Migrant income	76·0	18·5	26·1	35·9	12·9	11·3	3·0	70·1	0·6
Income of continuously absent workers	165·9	37·5	93·1	59·2	30·4	6·4	56·9	236·8	141·5
Area national income	78·0	22·7	33·2	35·4	9·0	7·5	5·5	80·0	–

Source: J.A. Lombard and P.J. van der Merwe (1972), 'Central problems of the economic development of Bantu homelands', *Finance and Trade Review* 10. no. 1, p. 35.

A development strategy for the homelands

The disadvantages for the homelands of the migrant labour system are so great that any development strategy for independent homelands must be employment orientated. Homeland governments should clearly reconsider present agricultural policies with a view to developing a more labour intensive approach (chapter 9). They should also seek to generate more employment in the secondary and tertiary sectors. The encouragement of labour intensive techniques is clearly implied, but the circumstances in which the homelands find themselves may not always permit this. The majority of potential entrepreneurs are South African, and their activities in the homelands usually form only a small part of their total operations; it is therefore unlikely that they will make special efforts to develop labour intensive techniques for their homeland operations.[5] Homeland governments might reasonably try to influence them by changing the system of inducements to one which was less capital related, but wages would need to be sufficiently high to encourage Africans to remain in the homelands. The latter are, moreover, in a weak bargaining position, because prospective industrialists usually have a choice of countries in which to locate, including Botswana, Lesotho and Swaziland as well as the nine homelands and South Africa itself.[6]

Considerable scope appears to exist for greater local employment and entrepreneurship in building and construction, including road building, in the homelands. For this potential to be realised some revision of building codes and standards is needed. Hitherto, as in many developing countries, the building industry in the homelands has derived its practices from wealthier countries: standards and designs are often unrealistic, and operate against small local builders.[7] In the service sector, homeland governments might well question the desirability of such developments as large supermarkets, which put local shopkeepers out of business, and computerised accounting systems in banks, which reduce employment opportunities.

Any economic development programme for independent homelands would require both professional people and those with middle ranking skills. For the former, the homelands would inevitably continue to depend heavily on expatriates in the foreseeable future, but with the allocation of sufficient resources to commercial, technical and vocational education, the homelands should be able to provide most of their trained manpower needs in the medium term. This assumes the availability of sufficient Whites who are willing to train Africans to do the jobs in question, particularly where college training is inappropriate or insufficient: the White mining unions have proved particularly unco-operative in this respect.[8] It also assumes that the drain of more skilled and educated homeland Africans to more attractive opportunities in White areas, which has long been a problem, can somehow be halted. If not, the homelands would in effect be training labour for the benefit of the South African economy. Theoretical solutions would be for the governments concerned to insist that trainees work for a stipulated period in the homelands, or even to refuse passports to skilled workers who are badly needed in the local economy.[9]

As has been suggested earlier, those homelands which do not abut White urban areas offer relatively limited scope for urbanisation. In other homelands, the urbanisation policies adopted could have important social and economic implications. Homeland residential townships close to White employment centres need not be subject to influx control regulations. Where boundaries have been redrawn to include such townships in the homelands – as in the cases of Thlabane, adjacent to Rustenburg (Bophuthatswana), and most notably Umlazi (KwaZulu), or where such re-zoning is intended, as at Imbali (Pietermaritzburg) and KwaMashu (Durban) – the homeland governments will be free to lift influx control and grant freehold rights. Men who have lived in the hostels of Umlazi and KwaMashu would instead be able to lead settled family lives in an urban environment. This would mean a rapid increase in the urban population of perhaps 50 per cent, imposing a serious housing and infrastructure burden on the KwaZulu government.[10] The use of site and service schemes would be one essential in such circumstances if scarce funds were not to be diverted to mass housing.

Such population movements would alleviate population pressure in rural areas and facilitate agricultural development, but it would remain important for homeland governments to control the rate at which *new* migrants flow to the urban areas seeking work. To do this by voluntary means implies narrowing rural–urban income differentials. This would depend on the success of both rural development policies and urban wage restraint within the homelands. The homeland governments could, however, do little to restrain wages in adjacent White areas, which might lead to excessive urbanisation in adjacent homeland townships in the absence of controls on rural–urban migration. Large numbers of squatters have already streamed into the Bophuthatswana townships of Garankuwa, Mabopane and Temba, as well as the nearby Winterveld area, and a commission of enquiry appointed by the Bophuthatswana Legislative Assembly has reportedly recommended some form of influx control.[11]

A related question of considerable importance for those homelands which abut White metropolitan areas concerns the degree to which they should encourage the concentration of urban and industrial growth in townships such as Mdantsane (Ciskei) and Umlazi, rather than at growth points further within the homelands. In relation to KwaMashu and Umlazi, Maasdorp and Ellison conclude that the generative impact of Durban has been directed mainly to the modern sector, whilst its growth has contained parasitic elements as far as African areas are concerned.[12] They therefore advocate that an independent KwaZulu should seek to develop KwaMashu and Umlazi as generative cities in their own right at the top of an incipient urban hierarchy.[13] They would be well-placed to take advantage of both the agglomeration economies and transport facilities of the Durban metropolitan area, and their proximity to Durban harbour gives them a particularly favourable export position. An attempt could be made to create a CBD in each township by the encouragement of African-owned businesses and services and branches of South African firms. White entrepreneurs have opposed the granting of trading and manufacturing licenses in the townships hitherto, but this need be no problem for independent homeland governments. The commercial and industrial development of townships such as KwaMashu and Umlazi would not, however, reduce their short term dependence on White metropolitan areas for 'quaternary' services such as commercial banking,

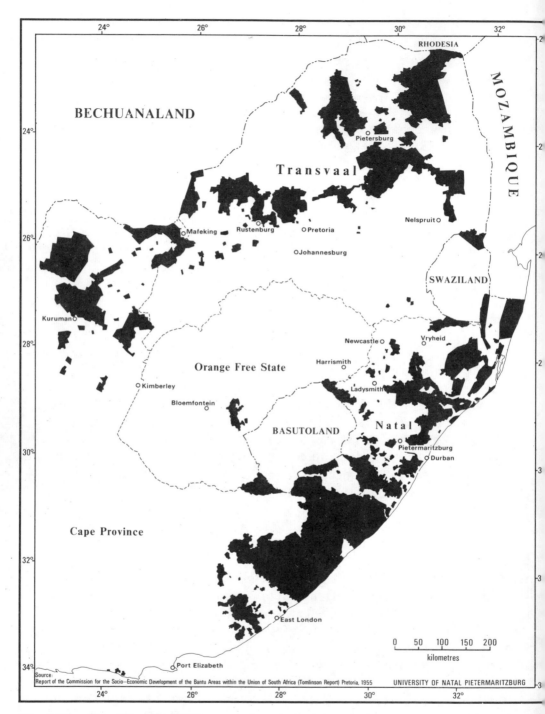

Fig. 11.1   Bantu areas, 1955

198

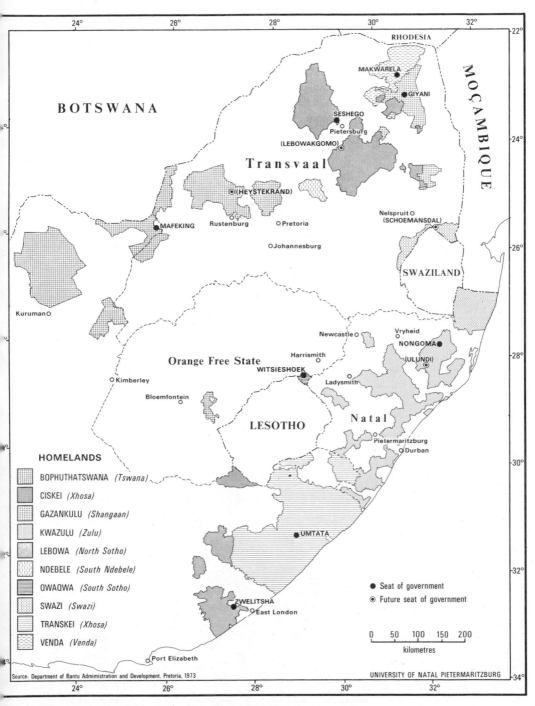

Fig. 11.2   Black homelands – 1973 consolidation proposals

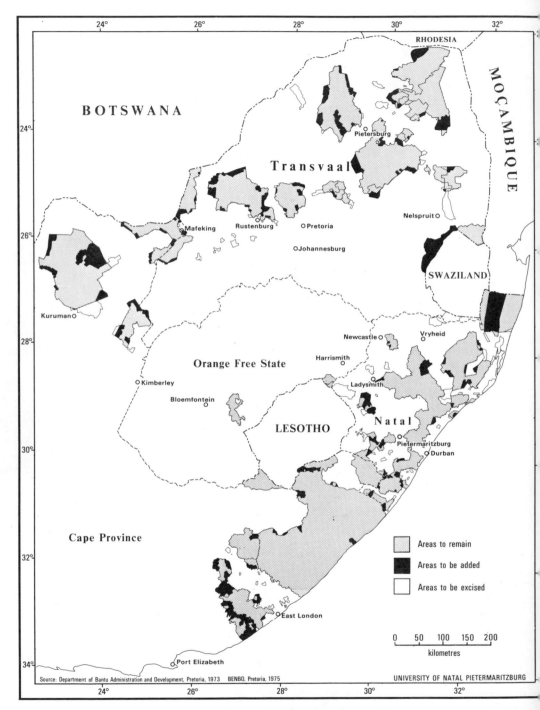

Fig. 11.3   Black homelands – 1975 consolidation proposals

insurance, financial, legal and import–export services.

Such a concentration of industrial and commercial development in townships close to White urban areas would contrast sharply with the mainly interior locations chosen for capital cities (see Fig. 11.3). Such a spatial separation of export base and central place functions has been criticised by C.M. Rogerson on the grounds that it would seem to preclude the immediate prospect of large scale urban development in the new capitals.[14] This is true, but it may be doubted whether the latter could attract significant industrial development whatever the urbanisation strategy pursued by homeland governments. Of the nine new capitals, only Umtata represents the takeover of an established White town.[15] Makwarela is the only urban area in the proposed Venda homeland with the amenities essential for further growth. Giyane (Gazankulu) and Witsieshoek (Qwaqwa) are existing small towns which had a population of less than 1,500 in 1970. The five remaining capitals are virtually, if not actually, new places. The sites chosen are comparatively central and in most cases optimal in relation to the proposed homeland boundaries, but more realistic choices would have included some of the small and medium sized White towns which are instead intended to remain outside the homelands.[16] Such towns range from Melmoth and Eshowe (KwaZulu) and King William's Town (Ciskei) to Pietersburg (Lebowa), Barberton (Swazi) and Mafeking (Bophuthatswana). It is difficult to envisage most of the chosen capitals becoming more than humble administrative centres.

Fragmentation and consolidation

The choice of homeland capitals is just one reflection of the government's unwillingness to add further land to the homelands beyond that promised in the 1936 Native Trust and Land Act (chapter 3). The purchase of the remaining territory owed to Africans under this Act has been speeded up in recent years in order to accelerate the political realisation of separate development, but 1,191,521 hectares were still outstanding at the end of 1974.[17] A considerable degree of consolidation is also intended, as a comparison of the African reserves in 1955 (Fig. 11.1) and the 1973 consolidation proposals (Figs. 11.2 and 11.3) clearly demonstrates; even in 1970 the homelands still consisted of about 100 pieces of land. Yet only three of the smallest homelands – Venda, Qwaqwa and that proposed for the South Ndebele people – will consist of a single block of territory. For the rest, the magnitude of the administrative problems posed by fragmented national territory can be easily imagined, particularly in

KwaZulu and Bophuthatswana, where the fragmentation and dispersal of territory is most extreme. Customs complexities would probably be eased by the homelands joining the Southern African Customs Union, as the Transkei intends to do, but passport control could present considerable difficulties.

The Tomlinson Commission recommended the consolidation of the African reserves into seven ethnic blocks, including one for all Xhosa and a combined Venda–Shangaan block.[18] Instead, the government takes the view that successful implementation of separate development is dependent on national, not geographical, units; thus the 1973 proposals leave thirty-nine pieces of land divided amongst ten homelands. This continuing fragmentation calls into question the intended rôle of the homelands as independent states. All are effectively landlocked, since even those with a coastline contain landlocked blocks (six out of ten in the case of KwaZulu). There are no other states in the world which are both fragmented and landlocked, whilst Lesotho and the micro-states of San Marino and the Vatican are the only other countries wholly surrounded by the territory of another state. Not only are the homelands dependent on South African transport facilities, but the main information media are centred in the South African core areas, and telecommunications links between homeland blocks traverse White areas. The homelands obtain their imports from and through White areas, and their comparatively small volume of exports is sold to South African firms and distributed through South African marketing channels, sometimes on the basis of quotas determined by White interests, as in the case of sugar from KwaZulu.[19]

No homeland possesses a port, although Chief Buthelezi has unsuccessfully urged that Richard's Bay should be developed as a seaport for KwaZulu, whilst Chief Matanzima has declared that 'it is absolutely essential that we should have our own port.'[20] Should any of the three homelands with a coastline attempt to develop a port, it would need to be of an international standard, otherwise transhipment at a South African port would be necessary and no real independence achieved. The largely rural hinterlands of the homelands certainly do not justify such ambitious port construction, and it seems improbable that either South African or foreign interests will provide the necessary capital.

Few changes have so far been made to the 1973 consolidation proposals, which received Parliamentary approval in two stages, some in 1973 and the rest in 1975. The government has, however, conceded one of Chief Matanzima's demands in agreeing that the White enclave of Port St Johns will be incorporated into the Transkei. Although insignificant as a port at present, it will probably be the site of an international port if one is developed. The Transkei will also benefit from a decision of the Ciskeian Legislative Assembly in March 1975 to cede the districts of Herschel and Glen Grey to the Transkei in return for alternative land between East London and Queenstown.[21] Inhabitants of the two areas concerned who wish to remain Ciskeian citizens will be offered alternative land in the new areas to be added to the homeland, but how the government intends to find such land without alienating its own supporters in the area is unclear. Whilst the Glen Grey area already adjoins the Transkei (Fig. 11.3), the acquisition of the Herschel district bordering Lesotho means that the Transkei will comprise three blocks of land instead of two. The Ciskei, on the other hand, will consist of only one, unless the area to be added is not contiguous with its existing territory (Fig. 11.4).

The current consolidation proposals are subject to major criticisms, even if the concept of separate development is accepted. First, the government's claim that the proposed homelands correspond to the 'traditional' homelands of the Bantu peoples is not substantiated by the history of contact between White and Black in South Africa (chapter 2), from which it is clear that Africans are entitled to considerably more than 13·8 per cent of the land. Secondly, the reserves envisaged in the 1936 Native Trust and Land Act were not expected to provide a territorial base for independent states, but merely a home for the rural African population, including those migrant workers residing in the reserves between periods of paid employment. Thirdly, these reserves were, as has been seen, similar in extent to those regarded by the Beaumont Commission in 1916 as necessary for an African population of just over 4 million, whereas the current African population (1976) exceeds 18 million.

A further trenchant criticism can be made if the present distribution of this population is examined. Recalling the principles on which nation states were delimited after the First World War, it might be expected that areas in which more than half the total population belonged to a given tribal group might be allocated to the appropriate homeland. Instead, as Christopher has shown in a series of maps based on the 1970 census, the area in which more than half the total population belongs to each tribal group greatly exceeds the area of its proposed homeland in all cases except Gazankulu and Venda.[22]

It is therefore not surprising that no homeland leader has accepted the consolidation proposals as they stand. Chief Matanzima, although he has accepted independence for the Transkei, intends to continue pressing for more land. He has previously claimed East Griqualand, which would join

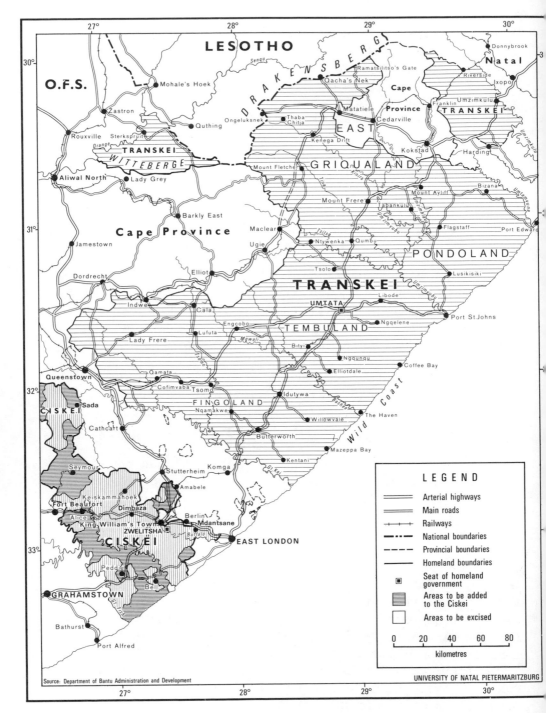

Fig. 11.4   Transkei and Ciskei

204

the Transkei with its detached Umzimkulu region, together with the White farming areas of Elliot and Maclear to the south. The other eight homeland leaders initially took the view that acceptable arrangements about land and jobs should form part of an independence settlement and not be left over for later bargaining and negotiation, believing that their case would be weakened if they accepted independence first. The first homeland to break the ranks was Bophuthatswana, which in November 1975 decided to approach the South African government with a view to independence negotiations.[23] Bophuthatswana's mineral wealth and its relatively successful industrial growth point at Babelegi make it arguably the most economically viable homeland, which may have contributed to the decision to seek independence. It remains to be seen whether other homelands follow suit and so hasten the Balkanisation of South Africa.

It is not difficult to understand the South African government's reluctance either to carry out further consolidation or to add more land to the homelands. Even the purchase of land still due under the 1936 Act is proving very expensive, and is constantly escalating: whereas a figure of R200 million was quoted by Lipton in 1972,[24] three years later the cost of buying the remaining one million hectares of White-owned land was an estimated R500 million.[25] Only R25 million has been authorised for 1975–76,[26] thus the completion of the land purchase programme still appears distant. Consolidation of territory is extremely costly in human terms. It is not known how many people will have to move in order for the present plans to be implemented, although it will probably be between 500,000 and 1,000,000. The implications of greater consolidation have been effectively illustrated for KwaZulu (Fig. 11.5) by Best and Young.[27] Consolidation of KwaZulu into two blocks of territory, leaving a White corridor linking Durban and Pietermaritzburg, but incorporating Richard's Bay, would require 476,000 Africans to move from 'excised' African areas. Consolidation into a contiguous block north of the Durban–Pietermaritzburg corridor would involve the removal of 948,000 Africans (45·3 per cent of the *de facto* population) and 45,000 others. Such ambitious schemes are financially impracticable and almost inconceivable in human terms.

There is, however, an alternative approach. Several homeland leaders have made it clear that the enlargement of the homelands need not mean that Whites already settled in the areas concerned would necessarily be dispossessed. At the annual Council Meeting of the South African Institute of Race Relations in January 1974, Chief Mangope emphasised that 'we would heartily welcome Whites as citizens in our midst. And not only for the sake of their know-how and their capital, but as people.'[28]

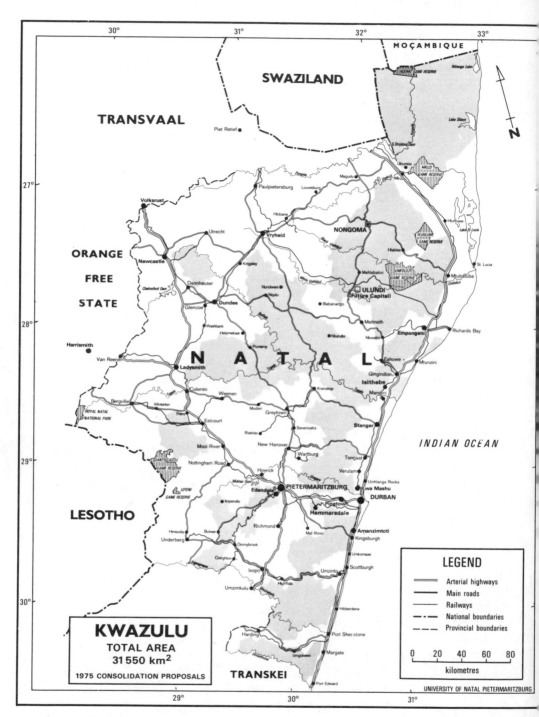

Fig. 11.5   KwaZulu

206

One of the most ambitious claims based on this principle has been made by Lebowa, which has laid claim to about one-third of the Transvaal, including twenty White towns, as well as parts of Gazankulu and Bophuthatswana.[29] Such ideas are currently unacceptable to most Whites; they imply a completely new approach to the problems of pluralism in South Africa (chapter 12).

The meaning of independence

Independence is a relative concept which is not easily definable. It has a range of indicators, and it is difficult to single out even its essential attributes. Most states recognised as independent by the international community suffer considerable restrictions on their control of monetary affairs, defence and foreign policy. Both economic dependence and political subservience are common characteristics of the international scene. In Southern Africa the existence of three former High Commission Territories (Basutoland, Bechuanaland and Swaziland) as independent states which exhibit a strong economic dependence on South Africa suggests comparisons with the homelands. Indeed supporters of separate development argue that the granting of independence to the homelands is merely a continuation of the process of decolonisation begun by Britain in Lesotho, Botswana and Swaziland; when Botswana achieved independence Dr Verwoerd, the then South African Prime Minister, actually sent a telegram of congratulations which justified Botswana's independence in terms of the Bantustan model. Botswana, Lesotho and Swaziland do not suffer from fragmented national territories, but Lesotho is entirely dependent on transit rights through South Africa and Botswana would find reorientation of her trade routes extremely difficult even if the Rhodesian situation were resolved. Whilst it may be difficult to take Qwaqwa or the proposed South Ndebele homeland seriously as prospective independent states, the larger homelands have a greater area, a larger population and a higher budget than many independent states, including Lesotho and Swaziland (Botswana is much larger in area, but consists mostly of desert). Ignoring for the moment all questions of the rightness or fairness of the proposed allocation of territory, it does appear meaningful to ask what degree of independence the larger homelands in particular might be able to achieve.

Despite their many handicaps, independent homelands would not be bereft of political cards to play. Economic stagnation accompanied by mass unemployment could lead to further political instability on South

Africa's borders, which she would be anxious to avoid. This could provide the homelands with bargaining power in relation to continuing South African development aid. The homelands might in addition reduce their dependence on South Africa by obtaining foreign aid and investment. Whether such aid will be forthcoming is questionable; foreign governments will have to decide whether or not to help these weak developing countries, and perhaps gain political and ideological influence in so doing, but at the risk of bolstering the success of South Africa's separate development policies.

The importance of the homelands as providers of labour for the South African economy creates a two-way dependence; the shortage of mine labour which has affected South Africa since 1975 underlines this, and points to the potential negotiating strength of the homelands in relation to the conditions under which their nationals work in South Africa. The homelands cannot press their case too far, however, first because of their dependence on South Africa for skilled labour, capital investment and entrepreneurial ability, and secondly because South African employers could point to the scope for introducing labour saving technology. In this as in other respects, the bargaining strength of individual homelands would be increased if they acted in collusion in order to obtain a better deal for their migrant and commuter workers.

Four homelands have common borders with foreign states (Fig. 11.3): Bophuthatswana (with Botswana), Transkei (with Lesotho), and KwaZulu and Swazi (with Mozambique and Swaziland). Botswana and Lesotho make no practical difference to the degree of independence which the first two homelands might exercise. Lesotho will no longer be surrounded entirely by South Africa, but the formidable Drakensberg escarpment makes the use of a Trankeian port by Lesotho improbable. Some reorientation of northern KwaZulu towards Maputo (Lourenço Marques) is possible, as is the development of a Swazi outlet through Mozambique; it should be remembered, however, that only the exploitation of sizeable iron ore deposits led to the construction of the Swaziland railway to Maputo in 1964.[30] It is interesting that, whilst permitting these common borders, South Africa has retained a five kilometre wide strip of territory between Venda and Rhodesia (Fig. 11.3); so far she has not responded to the change of government in Mozambique by creating similar corridors to seal off KwaZulu or Swazi.

South Africa's own concern that her policies be seen to succeed is a strong card in the hands of the homeland leaders. Legality and the consequences of formal status as a sovereign state have always played a large part in the South African government's own political statements.

South Africa will thus be extremely reluctant to apply political or economic, much less military, pressures on independent homelands. If a homeland went to the length of harbouring guerrilla fighters, however, South Africa would almost certainly intervene: but this applies equally to Botswana, Lesotho and Swaziland too.

The example of the latter states could become an important factor in the success or failure of the homelands in achieving meaningful independence. Within Southern Africa, these countries set themselves no more than the modest aims of multi-racialism and co-existence with South Africa. Internationally, however, their situation is different. In the case of Botswana, Henderson shows that whilst recognising its vulnerability, the country has at the same time manipulated the international system as an independent entity.[31] Since Henderson wrote, the rôle played by Botswana in Southern African détente and the Rhodesian question has amply justified his view that states like Botswana can develop an independent foreign policy. The example of Lesotho, which has strongly opposed détente in Southern Africa, is equally instructive. The significance of these international rôles, particularly that of Botswana, has depended on the formal status accorded the country concerned by the international community; this includes equal voting rights in the United Nations and the Organisation of African Unity, Commonwealth membership, and the right to seek and accept foreign aid from any source. This may prove to be the critical difference between Botswana and the homelands. Authorisation by the South African Parliament alone will not be sufficient to guarantee recognition by the international community and willingness to allow the homelands to manipulate the international system. Even where, as in the Transkei, most if not all the normal requirements for an international state appear to be present, international hostility to apartheid is such that recognition is likely to be withheld.

Transkeian elections*

As the Transkei approaches independence day (26 October 1976), it is appropriate to conclude this chapter by reviewing the voting patterns which characterised its first three elections. It has enjoyed partial self-government since 1963 through the provisions of the Transkei Constitution Act.[32] Legislative power is vested in a single Legislative Assembly which currently consists of forty-five elected members and

---

* This section has been contributed by Owen Williams.

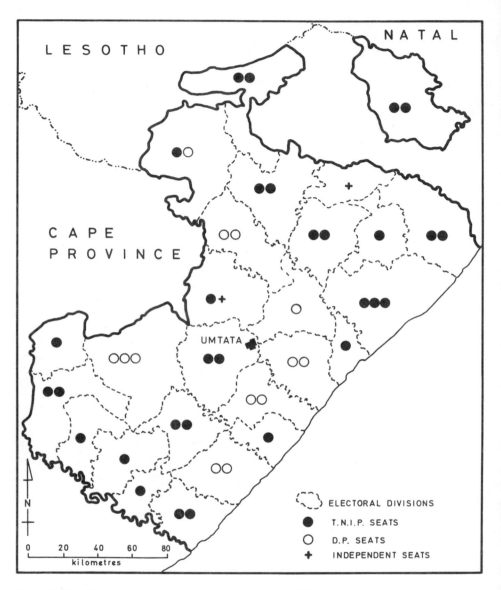

Fig. 11.6   Transkei general election results, 1973
Source: 'Geographic perspectives on Transkeian elections 1963–73'[38];
Transkei Economic Review [36]

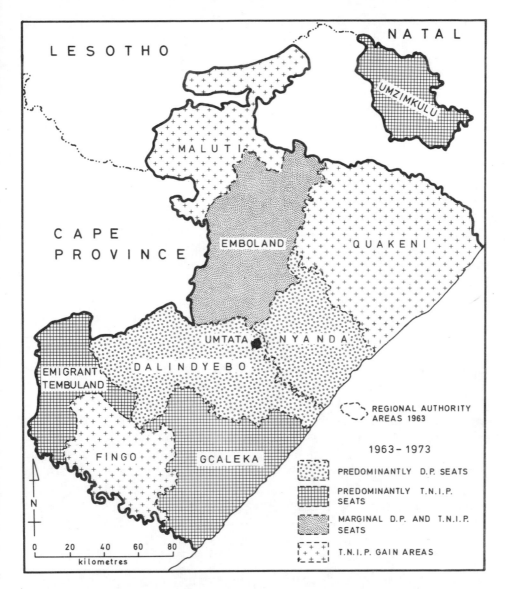

Fig. 11.7   Transkei general election results, 1968 and 1973
Source: 'Geographic perspectives on Transkeian elections 1963–73'[38];
Transkei Economic Review[36]; *South Africa's Transkei*[33]; 'Transkeian
General Election' [35]

211

sixty-four *ex-officio* paramount chiefs and chiefs (an increase to seventy-four chiefs and fifty elected members will allow for representation of Glen Grey and Herschel when these are added). Executive authority lies in the hands of a cabinet chosen by the Chief Minister who is elected by members of the Assembly. The franchise is enjoyed by all African citizens over twenty years of age (over eighteen in the case of taxpayers), who are registered on a voters' roll. Elections took place in 1963, 1968 and 1973. A further election is expected shortly before independence, when further constitutional changes may be expected.

In 1963 the nine regional authority areas served as electoral divisions, and the number of members elected from each was proportionate to the number of registered voters in the region. There were no organised political parties, and the election was a contest for popular support between recognisable groups led by the main contenders for the post of Chief Minister, Chief (Paramount Chief from 1965) Matanzima and Paramount Chief Poto. *Inter alia* the former supported separate development in relation to the Transkei, whilst the latter maintained that the Transkei should remain part of a multi-racial South Africa.[33] The result went in favour of Poto, and between thirty and thirty-eight of his supporters (as near as may be judged) were elected to the forty-five contested seats. Nevertheless, at the ensuing meeting of the Legislative Assembly, clearly through the support of its *ex-officio* members, Matanzima was elected Chief Minister. Within a few months the differences between the two protagonists and their supporters led to the formation of two political parties representing their respective views. The Democratic Party (DP) was led by Poto (who resigned in 1966 on grounds of advanced age and ill-health) and the Transkei National Independence Party (TNIP) by Matanzima. Later elections were contested on this political party basis, since a third party, the Transkei People's Freedom Party, proved to be shortlived.

The 1968 election was concerned with the same issues as that of 1963. The twenty-six magisterial districts served as constituencies, as they did again in 1973. The result was a clear victory for the TNIP which secured twenty-eight of the elected seats; the DP won fourteen seats and three Independent candidates were also successful. In addition, the TNIP enjoyed the support of some fifty-seven of the *ex-officio* members of the Assembly.

The most recent election of 1973 was again conducted on party political lines, and fought on similar issues, but the matter of independence was also at stake, although only after the election was it announced that the Transkei would actually seek independence before 1980.[34] There were 952,000

212

registered voters (447,000 men and 505,000 women) and a 43 per cent poll; all the candidates were resident within the Transkei, whereas in 1963 some were from urban areas in White South Africa.[35] The result was again a TNIP victory. The party still enjoyed the support of most *ex-officio* Assembly members. In terms of the elected seats, after a by-election in one constituency, the TNIP secured 26, the DP 11, and Independents 8.[36] The latter were mostly party rebels with TNIP affiliations who continued to support party policies after the election. Thus a more realistic assessment of the party situation, based on subsequent voting in the Assembly, would be the following: TNIP 30 seats, DP 13, Independents 2.[37, 38] Figs. 11.6 and 11.7 are based on these figures. In any event, the TNIP held a clear mandate to seek early independence.

Fig. 11.6 depicts the 1973 election result in terms of elected members. It suggests a clear dominance of TNIP support in all but some of the central constituencies. Fig. 11.7 reviews the three elections on the basis of the regional authority areas common to them all. The pattern shows an extension of TNIP representation through successive gains from its 1963 northern and southern areas of strength. This increasing strength may be explained, *inter alia,* by the retirement of Poto from the political scene, by the efficiency of the party's campaign organisation, and by the increasing political stature of Matanzima. But most important of all were probably the increasing acceptance of TNIP policies and the promise of early independence, in accord with the wishes of the South African government, together with the tangible improvements in the economic and social infrastructure of the Transkei made by that government.

Tribal allegiances have not been reflected in the election results as might have been expected, although they may still be relevant with regard to the *ex-officio* Assembly members. For elected members such factors as improved communications (which have allowed increasing freedom of movement, settlement and intertribal mixing), the introduction of a common educational system, the presence of only two parties and the general intertribal co-operation which has been progressively built into the Transkeian administrative system appear to have cut across tribal affinities and rendered them less significant in relation to voting patterns and party politics.

References

[1]   J.A. Lombard and P.J. van der Merwe (1972), 'Central problems of the economic development of Bantu homelands', *Finance and Trade Review* (Volkskas Ltd) 10, no. 1, p. 31.

[2]   See, for example, *South Africa 1974,* p. 307; and *Multi-National Development in South Africa: the reality* (1974), Department of Information, Pretoria, p. 79.

[3]   J.A. Lombard and P.J. van der Merwe, op. cit., p. 11.

[4]   Ibid.

[5]   G. Maasdorp (1974), *Economic Development Strategy in the African Homelands: the role of agriculture and industry,* SAIRR, Johannesburg, p. 21.

[6]   G. Maasdorp (1975), 'An economic development strategy for KwaZulu: some questions to be resolved', in *Focus on KwaZulu,* SAIRR, Johannesburg, p. 22.

[7]   Ibid., pp. 22–3.

[8]   M. Horrell (1973), *The African Homelands of South Africa,* SAIRR, Johannesburg, pp. 98–100.

[9]   G. Maasdorp (1975), op. cit., p. 25.

[10] G. Maasdorp and P.A. Ellison (1975), 'Towards KwaZulu', in G. Maasdorp and A.S.B. Humphreys, *From Shantytown to Township,* Juta, Cape Town, p. 141.

[11] *Rand Daily Mail,* 18 March 1975.

[12] G. Maasdorp and P.A. Ellison, op. cit., pp. 139–40.

[13] Ibid., pp. 141–3.

[14] C.M. Rogerson (1974), 'Industrialisation of the Bantu homelands', *Geography* 59, p. 263, and 'New towns in the Bantu homelands', *Geog. Rev.* 64, p. 581.

[15] A.C.G. Best and B.S. Young (1972a), 'Capitals for the homelands', *J. for Geog.* 3, pp. 1043–54.

[16] Ibid.

[17] P.S. Hattingh (1976), 'Homeland consolidation, with special reference to Bophuthatswana', part of a Queen Mary College, London, Department of Geography Occasional Paper.

[18] Union of South Africa (1955), *Report of the Tomlinson Commission on the Socio-Economic Development of the Bantu Areas,* UG 61/1955, pp. 180–3.

[19] G. Maasdorp (1974), op. cit., p. 8.

[20] *Sunday Times* of South Africa, 7 September 1975.

[21] M. Horrell and T. Hodgson (1976), *A Survey of Race Relations*

in South Africa 1975, SAIRR, Johannesburg, pp. 117–8.

[22] A.J. Christopher (1972), 'South Africa and the nation state', *Zambezia* 2, no. 2, pp. 23–37.

[23] 'Bophuthatswana opts for independence', *South African Press Mirror* 2, no. 36 (1975), pp. 1–2.

[24] M. Lipton (1972), 'Independent Bantustans?', *International Affairs* 48, p. 6.

[25] *Financial Mail,* 21 February 1975.

[26] M. Horrell and T. Hodgson, op. cit., p. 124.

[27] A.C.G. Best and B.S. Young (1972b), 'Homeland consolidation: the case of KwaZulu', *South African Geographer* 4, pp. 63–74.

[28] Quoted in M. Horrell (1975), *A Survey of Race Relations in South Africa 1974,* p. 183.

[29] 'Lebowa's claims', *South African Press Mirror* 1, no. 15 (1974), pp. 12–14.

[30] G. Whittington (1966), 'The Swaziland railway', *Tijdschrift voor Economische en Sociale Geografie* 57, pp. 68–73.

[31] W. Henderson (1974), 'Independent Botswana: a reappraisal of foreign policy options', *Afn Aff.* 73, pp. 37–49.

[32] W.D. Hammond-Tooke (1975), *Command or Consensus: the development of Transkeian local government,* David Philip, Cape Town.

[33] G.M. Carter, T. Karis and N.M. Stultz (1967), *South Africa's Transkei,* Heinemann, London.

[34] W.J. Breytenbach (1974), 'Recent elections and the political parties in the homelands', *SAJ of Afn Aff.* 4, no. 1.

[35] H.J. Kotze (1973), 'Transkeian General Election', *Africa Institute Bulletin,* no. 9.

[36] Republic of South Africa (1975), *Transkei Economic Review,* Bureau for Economic Research *re* Bantu Development, Pretoria.

[37] Republic of South Africa (1974), *Transkei Government, Debates of the Transkei Legislative Assembly, First and Second Session, Third Assembly (TLA Hansard) 1973–4,* Elata Commercial Printers, Umtata (and previous issues).

[38] A. van Schalkwyk (1975), 'Geographic Perspectives on Transkeian Elections 1963–73', unpublished honours seminar paper, University of Natal, Pietermaritzburg, Geography Deparment.

PART V

THE FORCES OF CHANGE

12   Change from within

Democratic and divided pluralism

The sources and possible directions of change in South Africa cannot be considered meaningfully without at least a basic understanding of theoretical models of pluralism. The American school of political pluralists, arguing from studies of the American democratic system, denies that a heterogeneous society, be it culturally, racially or ethnically diverse, is incompatible with democratic ideals or institutions.[1] The achievement of such ideals in a plural society does, however, depend on the existence of cross-cutting cleavages, affiliations and loyalties which further common values between, and a competitive balance of, diverse groups. Such characteristics will, it is argued, ensure a stable democracy and prevent major conflict or the disintegration of the homogeneous society.[2]

This 'open pluralistic' model has been contrasted with the 'divided plural society' found in South Africa, where racial cleavages generally coincide with the lines of economic exploitation, political domination and social stratification.[3] In such a situation dissensus and divisive conflict is emphasised, and non-democratic regulation or domination is apparently needed for the political stability of the society. Thus Furnivall, who originally developed the theory of the plural society, emphasised the importance of domination by the colonial power for maintaining the involuntary union of the tropical plural society.[4] Smith in his classic study of the West Indies defines the plural society as necessarily dominated by one of its subsections, and held together by regulation in the absence of the social cohesion derived from consensus.[5] Similarly, Van den Berghe concludes that plural societies 'have often been held together by a mixture of political coercion and economic interdependence.[6]

Such polarised models clearly cannot provide full descriptions of actual societies. In practice, just as the American plural society has its divisive elements,[7] so in South Africa even the most apparently divided society in the world is characterised by elements of convergence and common values. Church allegiances cut across racial groups, as does the increased sharing of many elements of a common culture by large numbers of all races. The small but growing African, Indian and Coloured professional middle classes also represent a significant movement towards more open pluralism. The fundamental question facing those who seek change in South Africa is whether and how the country can move much further from a divided plural to an open pluralistic society. Much the most detailed formulation of a model for transition is that made by the Political Commission of SPRO-CAS,[8] to which only brief reference can be made here. The alternative strategies offered by the political parties are, necessarily perhaps, formulated in much more general terms. Many scenarios have been outlined by academics, including no fewer than nine in a single recent work.[9] The present chapter can provide but a brief analysis of the sources and directions of change, and of some suggested alternatives to separate development which emanate from South Africa itself, paying particular attention to their spatial significance.

Revolutionary change

Political scientists, historians and sociologists have written a great deal about the existence of 'revolutionary preconditions' in South Africa. Such studies, written under the impression of widespread unrest in the 1950s and early 1960s, underestimate the effects of what Adam calls 'an increasingly streamlined and expanding system of sophisticated dominance',[10] which hampers revolutionary change precisely where it seems theoretically most likely. The fear of revolution, if it ever existed, has receded as the state's armed might has increased. A highly efficient police and military machine is complemented by the banning of radical opposition groups. The efficient, tentacular activities of the security police make it extremely difficult for any of them to regroup on an underground basis, let alone to build up the mass support which an overthrow of the state would require.[11] Even the threat of localised urban revolution in townships such as Soweto is contained by, *inter alia,* strategic location of controls for services such as electricity and water supply in White cities, whilst road planning in the vicinity of such townships is influenced by strategic factors. Spontaneous outbursts of violence will probably occur in urban townships, and perhaps also in rural areas, but their effect is likely to be limited and local.

As Brinton points out in his classic study of revolution:

> . . . no government has ever fallen before revolutionists until it has lost control over its armed forces or lost its ability to use them effectively; and, conversely . . . no revolutionists have ever succeeded until they have got a predominance of effective armed force on their side.[12]

Such possibilities appear remote in the present South African situation. Banned organisations such as the African National Congress, the Pan-Africanist Congress and the Communist Party are admittedly committed to the use of violence to overthrow or subvert the state, and will probably engineer sporadic outbursts of sabotage and guerrilla activities, but these are unlikely to do more than stiffen White resistance to any meaningful political change in the foreseeable future.

The 'platitudes of violence', as Kuper aptly describes them,[13] must be viewed in relation to South African society as it actually is, and not, as so often happens, in relation to a theoretical model of complete polarisation. Kuper emphasises the forces countervailing open racial warfare, above all economic interdependence in an advanced industrial society and crosscutting loyalties, arguing that:

> There is too much interdependence to sustain the threat of severance or divisive conflict. In fact, apartheid restructures the society by an elaboration of intercalary institutions and structures, which bind together, as with hoops of steel, the units-in-separation.[14]

This increasing binding together might conceivably continue until eventually the groups explode in sudden violence. To be widespread and successful in overthrowing the state, however, such an explosion would need to be organised rather than spontaneous, which seems impossible in present circumstances. Indians and Coloureds are most unlikely to participate in revolutionary action, since they are as vulnerable to the power of Africans as to the power of Whites. Africans themselves are so fragmented by their different life situations and by their different modes of incorporation that they are unlikely to mobilise racial violence effectively.

One further point is often overlooked. People involved in a social system often closely reflect that system in their values and attitudes. Despite obvious reasons for conflict and resistance, and despite evidence of discontent, a considerable degree of consensus or compliance can still exist. Thus to assume that Africans in South Africa are in a constant ferment over the injustices perpetrated upon them is to underestimate the effectiveness of the very oppression and conditioning to which they are subjected.[15]

Strike action

African workers have been strongly discouraged from forming trade unions and those which exist are not legally recognised. Their activities are, moreover, severely circumscribed; strikes by African workers are illegal, and until they became more widespread vigorous steps were always taken to frustrate strike action. More recently, however, the widespread strikes among the Ovambo in South-West Africa and the wave of strike action in Natal at the beginning of 1973, which proved to be the harbinger of similar action in other industrial centres, have demonstrated that the Black population is not without economic bargaining power. Could this power be used to extract political concessions?

There have been other occasions when Africans have gone on strike, as in the gold mines in 1946 and after Sharpeville in 1960 when almost the entire African labour force in Cape Town went on strike for nearly two weeks. Similar action occurred in other centres, but in none of these cases were political concessions granted. Localised strike action, even if a ripple effect does occur and unrest spreads, does not represent a unified flexing of the muscles of African economic power. The strikers may be visited with repression, including penal action, mass dismissals and the planting of informers in the factories, although such measures are viewed by many Whites as anachronistic. Strikes will undoubtedly continue to occur and will secure economic gains as well as engender a greater spirit of militancy, but only a prolonged nationwide general strike could produce significant political concessions. Such a strike would involve massive organisation and the accumulation of substantial strike funds; under present conditions the Whites would undoubtedly be capable of continued existence as an economically viable group for longer than the strikers could survive, although under considerable stress. It is, however, possible that the psychological impact of such a strike would persuade many Whites of the wisdom of change.

Economic forces

Several distinct arguments may be advanced in support of the view that economic forces will gradually erode apartheid; three of the most important ones will be mentioned here. One argument holds that the sustained growth of the South African economy will make it increasingly less true that there is insufficient wealth to go round; rather an expanding economy will be seen to have something in it for everybody. Gradually a climate will develop in which Whites feel less threatened and better able to carry out political reforms. It is, however, by no means clear that industrial and economic maturity automatically propels a society towards democracy: South Africa certainly offers no evidence of this as yet. It may indeed be argued that improved living standards help to preserve the political system intact by dampening the drive to revolutionary change.[16]

A second argument maintains that 'there must be some point at which an equilibrium can no longer be maintained between economic growth and political rigidity.'[17] In particular it is held that there is a contradiction between economic goals, such as sustained growth and profit maximisation, and the maintenance of White supremacy in the labour market. As the colour bar is increasingly punctured and modified to allow non-Whites to perform more skilled work, so the latter will become more indispensable and acquire greater bargaining power, which may be used to obtain political concessions. Unlike the average African labourer who cannot afford to be 'endorsed out', this increasingly large non-White middle class, increasingly impatient with arbitrary restraint, would be well placed to challenge the White monopoly of political power.

This argument too is open to strong objections. Blumer argues that, according to all empirical experience, a race order existing prior to industrialisation may be taken over, continued, and if necessary further cemented.[18] Thus it seems perfectly consistent with the processes already observed in South Africa for the colour bar in industry to be *lifted* but not abolished, without endangering the supremacy of White workers and without permitting other workers to organise into effective unions. It is true that South African industrialists have expressed disapproval of some aspects of apartheid, but an empirical survey by Adam suggests that both entrepreneurs and government agree on the basic principles of White rule.[19] This being so, it seems probable that the means can be found to adapt the structures of separate development to changing labour needs without granting fundamental political concessions.

A third area of argument concerns the growing consumer power of Africans, Indians and Coloureds. It is likely that the incomes of all these groups will rise substantially over the next few years in response to a combination of pressures (including strikes, moral pressures such as the Wages Commission set up by South African university students and pressures on foreign firms emanating from their home countries and those business interests such as clothing manufactures and food chain stores for whom the costs of higher wages are outweighed by an increased consumer market).[20] The possible effects of such increased consumer power are twofold. In mobilising their consumer power Blacks could force changes in, for example, the employment practices of large firms. Even this requires organisation, however, and it is difficult to see how such consumer power could be effectively used for wider political ends. More important is the possibility that increasing Black consumption and incomes will stimulate what Wilson calls 'the closing of the culture gap', a process already begun by urbanisation.[21] This would be an important part of the transition from a divided plural to an open pluralistic society. In itself, however, the closing of the culture gap must be regarded as a necessary but not sufficient condition for political change.

The alternative strategies of White political parties

Five political parties contested more than one seat in the 1974 general election. Three offered what may be termed alternative strategies to separate development. The exception was the Herstigte Nasionale Partie, which stands for national unity around the core of Afrikanerdom (English-speakers being regarded as Afrikaners in the making). The party believes that international forces making for racial integration must be resisted, and economic forces militating against separate development must be countered: industrialisation should be checked if it is overstimulated by foreign capital and labour. Such views, with their extreme emphasis on Afrikaner cultural identity even at the expense of economic growth, have found little favour with the electorate.

The United Party formulated a new policy of race federation in 1972.[22] This envisages that, after consultation and negotiation with all communities, the present Parliament will draw up a new constitution creating a federal structure consisting of community states and a federal assembly. Initially there would be at least four White community states corresponding to the existing provinces, and a minimum of seven African community states covering both the homelands and Africans elsewhere in South Africa. There would also be two Coloured and one Indian community states. Each community state would have its own local government institutions, and a legislative assembly to handle 'its own intimate affairs'. These assemblies would replace the existing provincial councils, homeland authorities, the Coloured Representative Council and the South African Indian Council. Consultative committees would be set up to give each community 'a direct line of communication with Parliament' through its legislative assembly. In addition, each assembly would elect representatives to a federal assembly. The White Parliament would act as regulator in the delegation of powers both to the legislative and federal assemblies. It is clearly stated that power over matters affecting the internal and external safety of the state will not be transferred to the federal assembly without the consent of South Africa's present White electorate.

These proposals have been criticised from various standpoints. To liberals they are unacceptable because they continue to emphasise the group at the expense of the individual, and because they offer political representation and powersharing to non-Whites on conditions laid down by Whites.[23] This is not surprising, since the United Party claims to stand, *inter alia,* for 'White leadership not in the sense of one group exercising *Baasskap* over others, nor in the self-interest of any one community, but in the service of all communities and for the maintenance of orderly political, economic and social progress.'[24] The SPRO-CAS Political Commission concludes that the United Party measures 'amount to so many opportunities for Whites to contain or veto the claims for political change advanced by other and unspecified (but presumably Black) political forces.'[25] Geographers must also criticise the proposals for failing to tackle problems of territorial consolidation of the homelands, and for creating Coloured and Indian Legislative Assemblies which, like the present Councils, would have no territorial base apart, presumably, from group areas.

Schlemmer accurately sums up race federation as 'a rather uncomfortable attempt to offer an alternative to the Nationalist Party's promise of a total solution to the colour issue.'[26] In so far as existing United Party support is based more on its policies relating to economic and living conditions than on its race policies, the Party probably does not need to formulate any grand blueprints; but to have any hope of winning the Afrikaner support necessary to achieve a parliamentary majority it will almost certainly have to do so.

The Democratic Party was formed by Mr Theo Gerdener, a former Nationalist cabinet minister, in 1973. It advocates a 'twin stream' policy, with the gradual political and economic assimilation of Coloureds and Indians into the White group, although social and biological integration is seen as highly improbable.[27] For Africans, sovereign states would be created; large urban African townships such as Soweto and Langa might become autonomous city states or integral parts of homeland states. The party stands for the consolidation of the homelands into large blocks, but without any mass population removals: Whites could remain in the new states if they wished. Considerable emphasis is placed on the economic development of the new states, and the need to include genuine urban growth points within their boundaries is realised. Federation is criticised as possibly leading to race conflict;[28] rather a 'Commonwealth' of independent states is envisaged, in which the political independence of the member states would be combined with co-operation in economic, technical and administrative matters.

The Democratic Party came close to winning Pietermaritzburg North in the 1974 general election, but has otherwise made little impact. Its policies do, however, contain elements of realism which may conceivably influence the direction of 'verligte' thinking in the Nationalist Party. The solution proposed for urban Africans is perhaps the least acceptable element of the party's policy.

The Progressive Reform Party stands for an open society in which there would be no officially sanctioned racial discrimination, although the rights of individuals to choose segregated facilities or of institutions such as universities and trade unions to restrict their membership would be upheld.[29] The colour bar in employment would be abolished, and equal pay for equal work introduced: the racial basis of influx control measures would be removed, and the migrant labour system phased out. The party advocates a federal system consisting of self-governing states, linked through a rigid constitution together with a bill of rights interpreted by a powerful independent judiciary. Some of the states, those homelands which have not chosen independence, would be predominantly African; in the others, the existing provinces, all races would share the franchise. The degree of homeland consolidation envisaged has not been made explicit, but presumably the non-racial basis of the states would enable extensive consolidation to take place. Considerable decentralisation is proposed, with the Federal Parliament exercising only such powers as are essentially national in character; it would consist of two chambers, a House of Assembly and a Senate. Half the members of the former would be elected on a basis of proportional representation, with all citizens who possess basic literacy eligible to vote. The other half would be elected on the present constituency system but with a qualified franchise, the criterion for the vote being ten years of schooling (Standard 8 or its vocational training equivalent). Subject to a certain minimum, the number of seats allocated to each state would be proportionate to the number of voters in that state who were registered to vote on a constituency basis.

Given that the Progressive Reform Party also intends to make Standard 8 the level of free compulsory education which the state should provide, it is clear that, even in the unlikely event that a majority of the homelands has already opted for independence, these constitutional proposals would eventually lead to a non-White majority in the Federal Assembly. They are thus bolder than those of any other White political party, and also place far less emphasis on group identity and correspondingly more on the individual. For precisely these reasons, they are unlikely to meet with widespread White acceptance, for 'so long as the political parties and the polity itself remains predominantly White, proposals for extending the vote to qualified Blacks is [sic] bound to be ineffectual since at odds with

226

the basic competition for power.'[30] But similar objections may well apply to all proposals for the peaceful democratisation of a divided plural society. The Progressive Reform proposals do appear to succeed better than the former Progressive policy, which was more wholly dependent on a qualified franchise, in meeting the detailed criticisms levelled at liberal constitutional solutions.[31] They are also much less open to the accusation of sharing power on essentially White terms.

Change within the Nationalist Party

It will be evident from the above that other White political parties have accepted some aspects of separate development, particularly the existence of the homelands, whether independent or otherwise. Indeed, despite Nationalist rejection of federation, separate development in some respects prepares the way for a transition from a centralised to a federal system. It contains a number of structural elements which tend to decrease the intensity of conflict and improve the conditions for rational negotiation in ways not provided for by the Westminster model.[32] These include the granting of local autonomy to various groups, the creation of subsystems of representative government on a non-competitive basis, the restriction of direct popular involvement and the growing emphasis on consultation and even contestation between established representative leaders. Separate development might therefore be seen, embryonically at least, as the basis for a new potential common political system structuring conflict in South African society not on the Westminster model, but in terms of bargaining and mutual accommodation between groups.[33]

For such a system to be democratic, the relative power of the components is all important, and here the present Nationalist blueprint clearly falls down by any standards. Within the Nationalist Party, however, there is considerable divergence between 'verligte' and 'verkrampte' positions. Some Nationalists belong to an all-party group known as Verligte Action, formed in 1973 with the object of mobilising enlightened opinion of all parties to facilitate change. Some prominent Nationalist thinkers, whilst accepting the basic philosophy of separate development, wish to see it assume a much more equitable character. This suggests three possible developments. First, the Nationalist Party itself might pursue increasingly 'verligte' policies: however, such a change would almost certainly be restricted by fears of another split to the right. Secondly, the 'verligte' Nationalists might break away and form a new party.[34] Thirdly, some form of coalition with the United Party may be a possibility. This would make possible the implementation of more equitable separate development with the backing of more broadly based United Party support to counter the large 'verkrampte' element in the Nationalist Party. It is, however, difficult to see the Nationalist leadership permitting so 'unpolitical' a move.[35]

The SPRO-CAS model

The detailed transition model put forward by the SPRO-CAS Political Commission has two stages.[36] The first aims at the greatest measure of non-discrimination and equality possible in the present society and a progressive pluralistic devolution of power starting from the present political system. The proposed programme of socio-economic and educational development would, *inter alia,* further decentralise economic growth and stimulate the creation of maximum employment opportunities: it is recognised that the problem of increasing unemployment may be one of South Africa's greatest economic problems in the next decade, and one which has immediate social and political implications. Influx control would be progressively revised, restrictions on the regional mobility of African labour reduced, and the migrant labour system phased out. In the towns there would be a progressive extension of property acquisition and ownership rights of Africans, Indians and Coloureds outside the existing group areas, with emphasis on the creation and enlargement of racially 'open' areas. Stage one also includes a series of measures aimed at the liberalisation and democratisation of society. The accompanying constitutional proposals include the progressive devolution of powers from central government to subsystems of representative government. These would include regional authorities not constituted on a strict ethnic basis, as well as communal authorities for Africans, Indians and Coloureds in 'the common area' (i.e. outside the homelands). In addition, regional planning and co-ordinating committees would represent all groups in the common area.

Preparatory to the second stage of the model, preliminary constitutional consultations and negotiations would take place between the regional and communal authorities and the central government. The probable outcome of these deliberations is seen as a federal, multi-racial political system. With the displacement of the White Parliament, White communal authorities would be created alongside those for other groups. These constitutional measures would be accompanied by the creation of a more open pluralistic society, but one which permitted a degree of optional segregation.

228

These proposals go well beyond those of the United Party and embrace many positive directions of change. They nevertheless emanate from the conviction that a liberal constitutional strategy is impracticable in the context of a divided plural society. The resultant emphasis on the group at the expense of the individual is rejected in a minority report by Dr Edgar Brookes, an 'unreconstructed' liberal, as attempting 'to cast out Beelzebub by Beelzebub', and as 'yet one more example of South Africans evading the real issue of human equality, and going along flowery garden paths.'[37] Certainly the Commission's proposals appear a complex and – to use Schlemmer's word again – uncomfortable alternative to separate development, and bear the unmistakeable stamp of White authorship.

Marquard's concept of federation

Many aspects of the federal proposals of SPRO-CAS and the United Party, and more particularly those of the Progressive Reform Party, are found in Marquard's bold if less precise ideas for federation in Southern Africa.[38] He points out that, just as it was the desire for a uniform Native policy that made South Africa opt for union rather than federation in 1910, so today it may well be the impossibility of maintaining that policy (apartheid, as it has since become) which strengthens the need for federation.[39] Marquard's proposals involve two operations which need not be simultaneous: redrawing the internal boundaries of South Africa to create eleven regions within a federal structure, and federating this new federation with Botswana, Lesotho, Swaziland and South-West Africa. The second stage undoubtedly makes sense in terms of economic geography, in so far as South Africa's neighbours are, like the homelands, peripheral areas within the Southern African economic system. But to induce three independent states and a fourth territory within which some form of independence is unlikely to be long delayed to enter a federation which must, to be successful, allay the fears of White South Africans, would be extremely difficult if not impossible.

Unlike the political parties, Marquard emphasises that the implementation of partition and federation within South Africa itself would be dependent on the majority support of all adult South Africans. He implicitly recognises, however, that Whites would have to be satisfied first before handing over to the population at large this fundamental constitutional decision. The requirement of a reasonable degree of economic balance between the eleven regions would require a radical redrawing of existing internal boundaries. Marquard purposely avoids producing a map to guard against drawing 'as many red herrings across the trail as there are new boundaries.'[40] He regards the Xhosa, Zulu, Tswana and South Sotho homelands as the nuclei of four of his regions, but conceives of more than one way of accommodating other groups and the urban Africans, leaving this important question unresolved. The franchise would have to be based on a common role, albeit with some form of qualification. The Progressive Reform proposals appear to conform and in some ways improve upon Marquard's ideas in this respect; they also resemble Marquard in their reliance on a constitution, bill of rights, and independent judiciary. The greatest difficulty facing both sets of proposals is to persuade White South Africans that their position 'as a minority in a federation would be far healthier and more secure than under a unitary system with exisiting policies.'[41] White perception and evaluation of the external threat to South Africa, upon which Marquard lays great emphasis, has clearly so far failed to produce widespread support for radical constitutional change.

Black federation and the common area

Just as the concept of federation is increasingly common to all shades of 'verligte' opinion – including many Nationalists in private conversation, according to Professor H.W. van der Merwe[42] – so too it is becoming general practice to refer to what is officially 'White South Africa' as 'the common area'.[43] Implicit in this term is the permanence of all four ethnic groups within the common area, and the need for a strategy which gives due recognition to this fact. It follows logically that, for the homelands, as areas which are not common to all races, a different strategy may be appropriate.

A solution along these lines has been most clearly enunciated by Cilliers,[44] who advocates not separate development *per se,* nor transition to a common society *per se,* but the simultaneous evolution of both. Basically he suggests the accommodation of the *de facto* and possibly part of the *de jure* African population in genuinely consolidated homelands, which would advance to independence along currently envisaged lines. In the remainder of the country, he believes that Whites have sufficient in common with Coloureds, Asians and permanently urbanised Africans to form the basis of a shared society:

> In fact, it should be quite clear that those among these population groups who share what is commonly called Western civilisation and

culture, would form such a comfortable majority that a political system accommodating all these elements could be developed that would have a reasonable chance of survival.[45]

The concept of White–Coloured solidarity is nothing new: General Hertzog, the former South African Prime Minister, saw the Coloured group as a natural ally of the Whites and favoured its economic, political and cultural assimilation. A recent opinion poll by the Afrikaans newspaper *Rapport* found that two-thirds of Afrikaners regard the Afrikaans-speaking Coloured man who belongs to the Dutch Reformed Church as an Afrikaner.[46] An earlier poll showed that 57 per cent of all Whites believe that Coloureds should be represented in Parliament and that their representatives should be Coloured.[47] The major problem has always been that such solidarity would present a new dilemma, since it would be impossible to uphold a rigid race ideology with regard to Indians and 'educated' Africans. Cilliers, by advocating a common society within the common area, is effectively dismissing this dilemma as no longer relevant.

His ideas do, however, pose disturbing questions. Reliance on the majority within the common area sharing Western civilisation is in effect substituting class division for racial division; many would decry this, although it would certainly go some way to bringing South Africa into line with the rest of the world. A more intractable problem might be the consequences of Cilliers' ideas in terms of social geography. To perpetuate and strengthen the division between the homelands and the common area would probably accentuate the already growing cleavage of material interests between Africans with urban residential rights in the common area ('insiders') and migrant workers and peasants in the homelands ('outsiders') to which reference was made in chapter 4. This has perhaps already become noticeable in the vehement resistance of some urban African leaders to seeking common political cause with the homeland leaders.[48] The danger is that inequality between White and Black will merely be replaced by geographical inequality between common area and homeland.

This fear could be at least partly countered by extensive consolidation (including realistic urban growth points) and greatly increased expenditure on homeland economic development. Given these prerequisites, Cilliers' ideas have one massive advantage over ideas of multi-racial federation: it is conceivable that they might evolve from present Nationalist Party policy and therefore stand a better chance of implementation than any other strategies considered here. It is doubtful whether the separation of the homelands could ever be acceptable to liberals, but it is not beyond the bounds of possibility that the homelands might gain international acceptance if properly consolidated.

Such an outcome would perhaps be more likely in the event of some form of homeland federation. This is already under consideration: in November 1973 six homeland leaders or their deputies convened in Umtata to review the problems and prospects of forming a Black federation in Southern Africa. The South African government has stated that it has no objection to Black federation once the homelands achieve independence, but federation before that is constitutionally impossible.[49] Whilst Qwaqwa is the only homeland to have repudiated federation, considerable differences of opinion still exist between homeland leaders on the purpose, form and function of federation.[50] Tribal and ethnic identities still predominate, and only a limited leadership is currently committed to federation for its own sake. Economic links and interpersonal contact are virtually non-existent, whilst 'a federation of poor states does not produce a strong one.'[51] A viable federal 'raison d'être' is therefore lacking at present, but a federation of properly consolidated and economically more developed independent homelands alongside a multi-racial state (federal or unitary) in the common area must be regarded as a practicable if long term alternative to present policies.

References

[1]   See, for example, W. Kornhauser (1959), *The Politics of Mass Society,* Routledge and Kegan Paul, London, pp. 78–82.
[2]   See, for example S. Lipset (1960), *Political Man,* Heinemann, London, pp. 88–9; and A. Lijphart (1968), *The Politics of Accommodation,* University of California Press, Berkeley, pp. 7ff.
[3]   SPRO-CAS Political Commission (1973), *South Africa's Political Alternatives,* SPRO-CAS Publication No. 10, Johannesburg, pp. 82–5.
[4]   J.S. Furnivall (1948), *Colonial Policy and Practice,* Cambridge University Press, p. 307.
[5]   M.G. Smith (1965), *The Plural Society in the British West Indies,* University of California Press, Berkeley, pp. 62, 86, 90.
[6]   P.L. Van den Berghe (1967), *Race and Racism,* Wiley, New York, pp. 138–9.
[7]   See, for example, H.S. Kariel (1961), *The Decline of American Pluralism,* Stanford University Press; and N. Glazer and D. Moynihan

(1963), *Beyond the Melting Pot,* MIT Press, Cambridge (Mass.).

[8] SPRO-CAS Political Commission, op. cit.

[9] C. Potholm and R. Dale (eds) (1972), *Southern Africa in Perspective: Essays in Regional Politics,* The Free Press, New York, pp. 321–31.

[10] H. Adam (1971), *Modernizing Racial Domination: the dynamics of South African politics,* University of California Press, Berkeley, p. 15.

[11] SPRO-CAS Political Commission, op. cit., p. 47.

[12] C. Brinton (1952), *The Anatomy of Revolution,* Prentice-Hall, New York, pp. 98–9.

[13] L. Kuper (1971), 'Political change in White settler societies: the possibility of peaceful democratization', in L. Kuper and M.G. Smith (eds), *Pluralism in Africa,* University of California Press, Berkeley, p. 169.

[14] Ibid., p. 182.

[15] SPRO-CAS (1971), *Directions of Change in South African Politics,* SPRO-CAS Occasional Publication No. 3, Johannesburg, p. 13.

[16] I.T.M. Snellen (1967), 'Apartheid: checks and changes', *International Affairs* 43, p. 303.

[17] L. Kuper (1968), 'The political situation of non-Whites in South Africa', in W. Hance (ed.), *Southern Africa and the United States,* Columbia University Press, New York, p. 103.

[18] H. Blumer (1965), 'Industrialisation and race relations', in G. Hunter (ed.), *Industrialisation and Race Relations,* Oxford University Press, London, pp. 220–53.

[19] H. Adam (1971), 'The South African power-élite: a survey of ideological commitment', in H. Adam (ed.), *South Africa: sociological perspectives,* Oxford University Press, London, pp. 89–90.

[20] F. Wilson (1975), 'The political implications for Blacks of economic changes now taking place in South Africa', in L. Thompson and J. Butler (eds), *Change in Contemporary South Africa,* University of California Press, Berkeley, p. 193.

[21] Ibid., p. 194.

[22] See *The United Party's Federation of South African Peoples* (1972) and *Federation: your only way to security* (undated).

[23] A. Paton (1971), 'Some thoughts on the common society', in SPRO-CAS (1971), op. cit., p. 46.

[24] *The Aims and Principles of the United Party* (1973), as accepted by the Central Congress of the Party, November 1973.

[25] SPRO-CAS Political Commission, op. cit., p. 183.

[26] L. Schlemmer (1971), 'Future political implications of present

trends', in SPRO-CAS (1971), op. cit., p. 28.

[27] Democratic Party (1974), *Policy and Aims.*

[28] Democratic Party (undated), *Policy Letter no. 2.*

[29] The principles and policy of the newly-formed Progressive Reform party were set out in a joint statement (May 1975), and subsequently elaborated by its leader, Mr Colin Eglin, in his inaugural speech (July 1975). Both were reported extensively in the South African press.

[30] SPRO-CAS Political Commission, op. cit., p. 138.

[31] Ibid., pp. 127–43.

[32] Ibid., p. 170.

[33] Ibid., p. 191.

[34] This was advocated by W. Kleynhans in the *Rand Daily Mail,* 8 December 1970, quoted by L. Schlemmer, op. cit., p. 31.

[35] L. Schlemmer, op. cit., p. 32.

[36] SPRO-CAS Political Commission, op. cit., pp. 222–42.

[37] E. Brookes (1973), Minority report following the Majority Report of the SPRO-CAS Political Commission, op. cit., pp. 243–4.

[38] L. Marquard (1971), *A Federation of Southern Africa,* Oxford University Press, London.

[39] Ibid., p. 34.

[40] Ibid., p. 127.

[41] Ibid., pp. 125–6.

[42] H.W. van der Merwe (1975), 'Some things political leaders dare not say publicly', *Race Relations News* (April), p. 4.

[43] See, for example, *Race Relations News* (1975), February, pp. 2–6, March, pp. 4–6, April, pp. 3–4.

[44] S.P. Cilliers (1971), *Appeal to Reason,* University Publishers and Booksellers, Stellenbosch.

[45] Ibid., p. 8.

[46] Reported in *Race Relations News,* November 1975, p. 7.

[47] *The Times,* 6 February 1975.

[48] L. Schlemmer (1975), 'The devolution theory examined', *Race Relations News,* April, p. 3.

[49] A.C.G. Best (1976), 'Black federation in South Africa', part of a Queen Mary College London, Department of Geography Occasional Paper.

[50] Ibid., pp. 14–17.

[51] Ibid., pp. 26–7.

13 External pressures on South Africa

Economic sanctions

As the decolonisation of Africa accelerated in the late 1950s and early 1960s, opposition to apartheid mounted and became more militant. South Africa was excluded, at the insistence of the Afro-Asian bloc, from a wide range of international agencies and conferences. She was increasingly isolated within the United Nations and became the object of an economic boycott by most African and many Asian countries. They hoped that their efforts would be widened into universal economic sanctions, with UN support, which would eventually bring a new dispensation in South Africa.

This scenario was never realistic and utterly failed to materialise. Even without the protection provided by Western political and economic interests (see below), South Africa's wealth of resources and growing self-sufficiency are such as to enable her to withstand any foreseeable economic pressures almost indefinitely, although not without economic strains. She is better able to feed herself than most if not all her neighbours. Production of steel and most chemicals is catching up with local demand, and the electronics industry is flourishing. The one major commodity so far lacking is oil, but only one-fifth of South Africa's energy requirements come from imported oil. The boycott imposed by the Arabs in 1973 had a minimal effect, since almost all imported oil comes from Iran. When the second oil from coal plant in the eastern Transvaal Highveld comes into operation in 1980, the Republic will be able to supply 40 per cent of her oil requirements; she has also stockpiled enough oil to meet four years' demand. Coal supplies are sufficient for well over a century ahead, and nuclear power, gas turbines, pumped storage and hydro-electricity will be producing substantial quantities of power within a decade from now. South Africa also appears to have developed the capacity to manufacture most of her defensive armaments and, although there are important constraints in this regard, she has the capability (including ample resources of uranium) to develop an independent nuclear deterrent: she has indeed refused to ratify the Nuclear Non-Proliferation Treaty for this reason.

Western financial interests in South Africa are on such a scale that withdrawal is inconceivable. Total foreign liabilities doubled between 1967 and 1972, when they reached R7,800 million; the 1976 figure probably exceeds R13,000 million. With growing American and Japanese investment, the share of the Sterling Area has been gradually decreasing, but it was still 56 per cent in 1972. Withdrawal of these investments, which yield large revenues for important companies and foreign exchange for the balance of payments, would seriously damage Britain's already ailing economy. It is widely believed that South African investments are more profitable than most overseas investments, because of cheap labour as well as stable conditions. Although precise statistics are lacking, the available evidence tends to confirm this.[1] South Africa is important to the multinational corporations as the only major industrial base in Africa from which goods may be exported to various parts of Africa and even to the Mediterranean. Western and Japanese trading interests in South Africa are also growing. By 1972 Britain, the United States, West Germany and France alone exported goods worth R2,300 million to Southern Africa, most of this to South Africa herself; the German share has grown particularly fast. Most Western countries have favourable trade balances with Southern Africa, but the Michaelis Report, presented to the EEC in late 1972, indicated that in the future the EEC will be critically dependent upon South Africa for strategic raw materials.[2]

The 'moral lobby' against British and American investment in South Africa appears to have weakened since the early 1970s in favour of the argument that investment is permissible provided that the foreign company sets a good example in such things as wage rates, union recognition and working conditions. This approach has not been ineffective, although its significance may be rather as a catalyst in association with internal forces such as more widespread strike action than as a primary cause.

A recent development of this 'positive impact' school of thought is the argument in favour of foreign investment in the homelands.[3] It is argued that the homelands provide the only effective political and economic training ground for Africans. The rise of Black governments on South Africa's borders has undoubtedly boosted African morale, and leaves the homeland leaders no choice but to lead the movement for change. Their chances of securing effective political change will arguably be strengthened by the rapid economic development of their own territories. In this way, and by helping to reduce homeland dependence on South Africa, foreign aid may be regarded as representing not collaboration with apartheid but an essential element in the fight against it. On these grounds Blausten even argues that the homelands should, as developing countries, be included as signatories to the EEC's Lomé Convention.[4] Whilst these arguments are not without substance, there is little doubt that foreign aid and investment in the homelands would please the South African government. It also seems doubtful whether existing or likely inducements will be sufficient to encourage substantial investment of private foreign capital in the Southern African periphery.

Western political interests in Southern Africa deter thoroughgoing opposition to apartheid. As Gervasi points out, the foundation of Western political influence in the area is the system of political power that now prevails there:[5] the collapse of that system could well produce a régime hostile to Western interests. This would threaten the security of the Cape sea route, which is vital for most Middle East oil imports and a great deal of other trade. Russia's growing naval power in the Indian Ocean makes this no idle speculation. Furthermore, given South Africa's industrial powerbase, a hostile régime could exert great influence and threaten Western interests throughout Africa.

Gervasi maintains that Western countries were so alarmed by the successes of guerrilla movements in the territories north of the Republic that, far from withdrawing South African investments or imposing economic sanctions, they actually began to pursue a strategy of containment aimed at forestalling revolution at the end of the 1960s.[6] This strategy includes discreet aid to the White régime and preparation for assistance to it in the event of military conflict spreading to the Republic. It also includes an element of reform, but the reforms envisaged are marginal, and intended to assist the open presentation of the strategy as promoting peaceful, evolutionary change through accelerated economic growth. What matters in these terms is not whether economic growth actually induces change, but whether it is believed to do so. Nolutshungu regards such Western pressures as 'anti-revolutionary reformism', and correlates their efforts with a class analysis of South African society.[7] From this he deduces that, since members of the Afrikaner élite are now major capitalists with international affiliations, the Nationalist Party has become more responsive to the interests of big business and is no longer primarily representative of the White workers and lower middle class, most of whom are Afrikaners. It is therefore quite willing to promote reforms of the sort desired by Western governments, which include concessions to an African bourgeoisie whose growing separation from workers and peasants gives it distinctive interests.

This cynical view entails what amounts to an international capitalist conspiracy involving Western governments, the South African government and Afrikaner élite, and the Black South African bourgeoisie.[8] It ignores the fact that moderate reforms may ultimately generate fundamental changes in the distribution of power and wealth in South Africa. Even on its own terms, the Gervasi–Nolutshungu theory underestimates the importance to Western governments of maintaining good political and economic relationships with the rest of Africa; the African tour of Dr Kissinger, the American Secretary of State, in April 1976 made this clear: Dr Kissinger committed the USA to outright support for Rhodesian majority rule, Namibian (South-West African) independence, and the ending of apartheid in South Africa.[9] Recent events have also shown that external deterrents to Western support for the White régime may be strengthened by pressures from Arab oil producers or perhaps from combinations of Third World producers of other raw materials. The débâcles in Suez, Algeria and Vietnam have in any case produced domestic constraints which make it very difficult for any British, French, or American government to intervene militarily in Southern Africa in support (or for that matter against) a White régime or its protégé, as events in Angola during the first half of 1976 clearly demonstrated. The likelihood is, in the words of South Africa's *Financial Mail,* that 'there will be no U.S. embrace of South Africa. Nor will there be any noticeable retreat from the present stance.'[10]

South African policies in Africa

South African policies in relation to the rest of Africa have been far from static. Nationalist governments openly opposed decolonisation until it became clear, in the late 1950s, that the process was irreversible. In so far as their policy was outward looking, it laid stress on the idea of a pan-African organisation which might knit together the various co-operative efforts of colonial governments, such as the Commission for Technical Cooperation in Africa south of the Sahara established in 1950.[11] South Africa continued to support colonial and settler governments where they survived, and the general Afrikaner attitude was inward looking and defensive in relation to a threatening environment.

In the late 1960s a new self-assurance developed, born of the belief that no obstacle, however threatening, was insurmountable.[12] Backed by economic and military strength, South Africa felt able to look beyond the 'laager' and meet the world on its own terms. It was realised that South Africa was not only *in* Africa but *of* Africa, and that her security lay in normalising relations with other British African states. The export of

South African capital increased as investors took advantage of emerging opportunities in the rest of the continent. The homeland policy was gradually developed as South Africa's answer to decolonisation. Malawi became the focal point of a 'dialogue' policy, but successes were also achieved in relation to Lesotho and the Malagasy Republic, with which a series of economic and trade agreements were concluded in 1970. Most important perhaps was the support for dialogue of seven Francophone countries led by the Ivory Coast, whilst debt-ridden Ghana increased its trade with South Africa more surreptitiously. As Dalcanton points out, whereas South Africa's willingness to engage in dialogue arose from growing self-confidence, the dialogue-orientated African leaders were motivated by the conviction that all else had failed.[13] African régimes which were no longer revolutionary or even radical were in any case apprehensive of the radicalisation of the continent that might follow a revolution in South Africa. The Lusaka Manifesto, adopted by the Organisation of African Unity in September 1969, was notable for its relatively conciliatory tone.

After the 1970 general election, the Nationalists once again found themselves threatened. At home they had for the first time lost seats, a trend which continued in subsequent by-elections. A series of successful African strikes began at the end of 1972 (chapter 3). The South African economy turned inflationary and separate development came under increasing attack from homeland leaders. Internationally, countries such as Ghana, Malawi and the Malagasy Republic became more critical of the Republic. Above all, the 1973 coup in Portugal threatened to bring African governments to power in Mozambique and Angola.

The electorate responded to these threats in 1974 by giving the Nationalists an increased majority (chapter 5). This enabled the Prime Minister, Mr Vorster, to launch his détente policy in a memorable speech to the South African Senate on 23 October 1974. Emphasising South Africa's identity as an African state, Mr Vorster expressed South Africa's willingness to contribute as far as possible to the development of other African countries. The Zambian President's reaction was equally notable: Dr Kaunda hailed Mr Vorster's speech as 'the voice of reason for which Africa and the rest of the world has been waiting.' The subsequent revelation of Mr Vorster's secret visit to the Ivory Coast in September 1974 took the world by surprise, as did his Liberian visit in February 1975 (the Ivory Coast Information Minister subsequently visited South Africa in September 1975). But the greatest success of détente to date has undoubtedly been Mr Vorster's historic meeting with Dr Kaunda and their joint participation in the Rhodesian constitutional discussions on the

Victoria Falls Bridge in August 1975.[14] Two years before Mr Vorster had declared that 'we know what to do if our neighbour's house is on fire',[15] but by 1975 'Realpolitik' was clearly evident in South African pressures on the Rhodesian government. The longer the latter survived with the aid of South African co-operation, the more fragile détente would become. With the closure by Mozambique of her Rhodesian border in March 1976, Rhodesian dependence on South African rail links became complete.

The greatest damage to détente has, however, resulted from South Africa's intervention in the civil war which followed Angolan independence in November 1975. The sequence of events remains controversial, but the most accepted version suggests that UNITA, the movement based in southern and central Angola, asked South Africa to intervene militarily to stop the Russian-backed MPLA. South Africa appears to have done so only with the prior approval of Zaïre, Zambia and the Ivory Coast, and very possibly the United States. The rapid success of a South African-led flying column appears to have prompted a massive influx of Russian military equipment and Cuban soldiers which subsequently enabled the MPLA to achieve victory, the South Africans refusing to continue the battle without American help which was not forthcoming, and in the face of widespread condemnation. At the end of March 1976 South Africa withdrew the troops still defending the Calueque and Ruacana dams, part of the Cunene River Project, in return for the vaguest of guarantees. This failed, however, to avert the passing of a UN resolution condemning South African aggression but remaining silent on the intervention of Cuban forces. The consequences of these events appear to be threefold: the weakening of détente, the turning of the spotlight on South-West Africa (Namibia), and the renewed hardening of White South African attitudes following the biased UN verdict.

Economic interdependence in Southern Africa

South Africa's closest economic relationships in the subcontinent are with Botswana, Lesotho and Swaziland: indeed, one strong argument against an economic boycott is the damage which these countries, especially Lesotho, would suffer. They form both a customs and a monetary union with South Africa. The original customs agreement was based on the ratio of total customs duties collected by each territory to the total customs revenue for the entire area between 1906 and 1908, but in 1970 a new agreement came into force, as a result of which the annual revenues received by Swaziland more than doubled and those of Lesotho increased by 500 per cent. Ironically, these new revenues only increase the countries' dependence on the Republic, since British grants in aid are no longer necessary to balance their budgets and Britain has been able to reduce the level of her aid.

Lesotho is the most dependent on South Africa in terms of employment (chapter 3) and trade; in addition, South Africa is to provide the major financing for Lesotho's Maliba-Matso water development project. Swaziland, like Lesotho, obtains 80 per cent of her imports from South Africa, but Japan, Britain and the United States take a major share of her exports. Botswana's economy has been transformed by the exploitation of diamond and copper-nickel deposits, which have reduced her dependence on South Africa as an export market, although dependence on South African exports and on the Anglo-American Corporation as the major source of private investment in Botswana's mineral deposits is notable.

The Swaziland railway to Maputo, completed in 1964, significantly reduces Swaziland's infrastructural dependence on South Africa, particularly in relation to exports; South Africa had rejected earlier proposals to link Swaziland with the South African rail system until Swaziland became part of the Union,[16] and again indicated that a proposed rail link was not feasible in 1973.[17] South Africa continues to dominate Swaziland's links with the outside world, however: all international telephone traffic goes through Johannesburg, whilst mail and telecommunications go through Pretoria. Most of Swaziland's road network, bus routes and cable car system (for asbestos export) terminate in South Africa, and together carry nearly 80 per cent of Swazi imports.

Botswana and Lesotho are now attempting to modify the infrastructural patterns of Southern Africa. Lesotho is seeking to construct a new international airport near Maseru to develop direct service to Zambia and Botswana: this might give the government some options with regard to refugees from South Africa and some degree of psychological independence, but little else. Botswana has constructed a tarred highway to link Gaberones and southern Botswana with Livingstone in Zambia by means of the Kazangula ferry; an earlier proposal for a bridge has, however, not been implemented in the face of South Africa's refusal to accept the existence of a common border between Botswana and Zambia at the eastern end of the Caprivi Strip. With only a ferry link, significant reorientation of Botswana's trade towards Zambia and East Africa seems unlikely. Such a reorientation would be much more feasible, although costly, given Black rule in Rhodesia, using the existing railway which is currently controlled by Rhodesian Railways.

Since Rhodesian UDI in 1965, Zambia has made substantial progress in its policy of reorientating trade and transaction flows away from the Southern African subsystem, which may have substantial impact on Botswana and Malawi in the long term. Paradoxically, however, UDI had the effect of making several countries in Southern and Central Africa *more* dependent for their external trade on South Africa. Zambia and Zaïre are both in considerable economic difficulties at present (1976), largely owing to the collapse in world copper prices. Neither can afford to ignore the fact that the cheapest supplier of equipment and spares is South Africa, with which Zambian trade is known to be expanding rapidly, whilst Zaïre is certainly trading clandestinely with South Africa. That Rhodesia provides transit facilities for this trade is one of the many paradoxes of the current South African situation.

The independence of Mozambique in June 1975 and of Angola the following November inevitably invited speculation concerning future political and economic relationships in Southern Africa, the more so since both the Frelimo government in Mozambique and the eventually triumphant MPLA in Angola have clear leanings towards the Eastern bloc. The two cases are in reality quite distinct, owing to Mozambique's far more extensive economic ties with South Africa. The Republic is Mozambique's second largest trading partner after Portugal, supplying 37·5 per cent of Mozambique's imports in 1972,[18] including iron and steel products, lubricating oils, chemicals, plastics and electronic equipment: replacement of these from other sources would be more costly. Some 116,000 Mozambicans worked in South Africa in 1972, mainly in the goldmines. Of their estimated earnings of R45 million, about R20 million were remitted in gold at the artificially low official price, an arrangement highly favourable to Mozambique. The convention governing conditions for workers recruited for South Africa stipulates that 40 per cent of South African tonnage in the 'competitive area' (between Maputo and Durban) should pass through Maputo. In 1972 Mozambique's harbours and railways earned about R50 million from South Africa alone, which equalled the combined total for the transit trade of Swaziland, Rhodesia, Malawi and Zambia. Mozambique's foreign exchange earnings from tourism amounted to between R20 million and R40 million in 1972, when 59 per cent of the visitors were South Africans. This source of revenue has, however, virtually dried up since the change of government.

Altogether, these sources of income represented over 40 per cent of Mozambique's foreign exchange earnings. The parlous state of her economy will hardly permit her to endanger this income by supporting open hostilities against South Africa in the foreseeable future. Nor could Mozambique afford, in view of serious unemployment problems, to prohibit migrant labour to South Africa. She is much more likely, given South African dependence on this labour, to demand renegotiation of the Mozambique Convention. She may also increase rail tariffs as Zambia has done, and possibly port dues too, but as the capacity of Richard's Bay expands Mozambique will have less room for manoeuvre in this respect.

The most publicised South African interests in Mozambique and Angola are the Cabora Bassa and Cunene schemes respectively. It has been suggested that such projects may increase South Africa's vulnerability, particularly in relation to power supplies,[19] but this is not supported by the facts. Although South Africa is contracted to buy 73 per cent of Cabora Bassa power by 1979, this represents only 8 per cent of her total needs, which could be met from several alternative sources. It is rather Mozambique which is vulnerable, as she could hardly find alternative markets for the amount of power involved. Likewise the South African sponsored pipeline to transport natural gas from Mozambique is not essential to South Africa's needs. The Cunene scheme in Angola benefits only South-West Africa. South Africa's main economic interest in ensuring the unhindered development of these projects is the under-standable wish to get some return on her substantial investment .- approximately R217 million for the South African section of Cabora Bassa (plus credits to Portugal) and R412 million for Cunene.

Angola's diamond production is currently marketed through De Beers. It is reported that Russia has designs on the marketing of diamonds from both Angola and South-West Africa, in which case she would compete with De Beers overall.[20] Otherwise Angola has few important economic ties with South Africa, which leaves her relatively free to support guerrilla or other military action to free South-West Africa from South African control.

The military threat to White rule in South Africa

If and when White rule collapses in Rhodesia, South Africa (with South-West Africa) will face potentially hostile neighbours along a frontier stretching over 3,000 kilometres across the continent from the Cunene River to Delagoa Bay. For reasons already explained, Mozambique, Swaziland, Lesotho and Botswana are unlikely to harbour guerrillas operating against South Africa in the foreseeable future. With these states at least the Republic will probably preserve a normal working relationship. South African 'Realpolitik' with regard to Rhodesia is clearly designed to moderate the policies of an African government in Zimbabwe, which would certainly have much to gain from economic co-operation with South Africa; the Limpopo is in any case more easily defensible than the Zambesi. The crucial border would appear to be that between Angola and South-West Africa. At the time of writing Cuban troops remain in Angola. Their successful operation in that country raised serious fears that a race war might be starting in Southern Africa. A 40 per cent increase in defence expenditure in the South African budget for 1976–77, bringing the share of defence to more than one-sixth of total government expenditure, reflected these fears.

In these circumstances the position of South-West Africa is clearly all-important. Currently, the South African government is committed to allowing the eleven ethnic groups which have been taking part in constitutional talks in Windhoek to decide the territory's future. South Africa insists that the conference shall have the option of breaking up the territory into several independent African states and one White state, a solution which is totally rejected by the major nationalist organisation SWAPO as well as by the United Nations. The idea of yielding the northern half of the territory has often been suggested, but this too would be unacceptable to SWAPO. Whilst Mr Vorster has not ruled out unitary independence for South-West Africa if the Conference so decides, the likelihood of it doing so is small without SWAPO participation. South Africa would, it seems, be well advised to permit this. Whatever the problems in relation to the 90,000 South-West African Whites, the withdrawal of South Africa from an independent Namibia would remove a major source of international criticism and leave South Africa with a far more easily defended border. It would, above all, substantially reduce the possibility of Cuban or Russian intervention.

It is unlikely that White rule in South Africa will ever be overthrown by guerrilla forces alone. For one thing, the terrain in the vicinity of her borders is for the most part treeless or sparsely wooded savanna, which affords guerrillas scant opportunity for concealment. More fundamentally, the South African situation is not one of convincing a metropolitan government that it was in its interests to withdraw, as was the case with France and Portugal, nor of a weak and corrupt system in a pre-industrial state such as Batista's Cuba.[21] In resisting 'terrorists' South Africa has the ardent support of over four million Whites who consider that their survival is at stake; she also has a powerful industrial base and far more formidable military equipment than any government hitherto overthrown by guerrilla forces. This very strength is likely to

244

deter direct Soviet intervention in South Africa proper. It would mean a struggle utterly different in scale from those which Russia has supported elsewhere, and one which, in view of the strength of Western economic and political interests in South Africa, Russia would hardly dare enter. She must, moreover, be aware that many African states are increasingly alarmed by her evident African ambitions. This seems likely to dissuade Russia from doing more than supporting endemic guerrilla warfare against South Africa where practicable. It is to be hoped that such a situation, if it materialises, does not further harden White resistance to internal change.

Conclusions

Except in the improbable event of Soviet-backed intervention on a massive scale, no external pressure seems likely to do more than act as a catalyst and secondary cause of change, reinforcing internal pressures. Thus it is to South Africa itself that one must look for change: to all internal pressure groups and White political parties, strengthened hopefully by outside opinion, but more particularly to "'n Afrika-horende volk' (a people belonging to Africa), as the Afrikaners justifiably regard themselves, and to the dynamics of the system which they have created. Whilst many of their attitudes may stem from the colonial period, White South Africans are not settlers. Only one attempt at evacuation ever took place, when Arkansas, Colorado and Wyoming offered the Boers land in 1900.[22] Such an offer would be no more acceptable today than at the turn of the century: indeed in many ways less so, for the Whites have built a modern industrial nation in Africa. They have built it, however, with the aid of all races, who cannot ultimately be denied citizenship in the country which they and their fathers have helped to create.

References

[1] 'South Africa', *Financial Times* survey, 25 February 1975, p. 21.
[2] S. Gervasi (1975), 'The politics of "accelerated economic growth"', in L. Thompson and J. Butler (eds), *Change in Contemporary South Africa,* University of California Press, Berkeley, p. 353.
[3] R. Blausten (1976), 'Foreign investment in the Black homelands of South Africa', *Afn Aff.* 75, pp. 208–23.
[4] Ibid., p. 216.

[5]   S. Gervasi, op. cit., p. 352.

[6]   Ibid. pp. 355–9.

[7]   S.C. Nolutshungu (1975a), 'The impact of external opposition on South African politics', in L. Thompson and J. Butler, op. cit., pp. 369–99.

[8]   L. Thompson (1975), 'White over Black in South Africa: what of the future?', in L. Thompson and J. Butler, op. cit., p. 403.

[9]   *The Times,* 28 April 1976.

[10] *Financial Mail,* 5 September 1975.

[11] S.C. Nolutshungu (1975b), *South Africa in Africa: a study of ideology in foreign policy,* Manchester University Press, p. 58.

[12] D.C. Dalcanton (1976), 'Vorster and the politics of confidence, 1966–1974', *Afn Aff.* 75, p. 163.

[13] Ibid., pp. 169–70.

[14] O. Geyser (1975), 'Détente in Southern Africa', *Afn Aff.* 75, pp. 205–7.

[15] *Africa Research Bulletin* 11, no. 8 (August 1973), p. 2961, quoted by L. Thompson, op. cit., p. 407.

[16] G. Whittington (1966), 'The Swaziland railway', *Tijdschrift voor Economische en Sociale Geografie* 57, pp. 68–9.

[17] *Times of Swaziland,* 19 January 1973, quoted in C. Potholm (1975), 'Effects of change in contiguous territories' in L. Thompson and J. Butler, op. cit., p. 337.

[18] The 1972 statistics quoted in this paragraph are all published in the *Africa Institute Bulletin,* no. 6 (1974).

[19] See, for example, C. Potholm (1975), op. cit., (ref. 17), pp. 334–5.

[20] *The Economist,* 6 March 1976, p. 77.

[21] L. Thompson, op. cit., p. 408.

[22] E. Waugh (1960), *A Tourist in Africa,* Chapman and Hall, London, p. 41.

Select bibliography

Apartheid and its ramifications are the subject of a vast literature. Only the more basic books are listed below, as comprehensive bibliographies appear in H. Adam (ed.) (1971), *South Africa: sociological perspectives* (items published between 1960 and 1970) and in L. Thompson and J. Butler (eds) (1975), *Change in Contemporary South Africa* (items published between 1970 and 1974). The *Annual Survey of Race Relations in South Africa,* published by the South African Institute of Race Relations, is invaluable, whilst the Institute also publishes the monthly newspaper *Race Relations News,* and many other papers and pamphlets. The South African Bureau of Racial Affairs tends toward the government viewpoint and publishes the *Journal of Racial Affairs.* The South African *Financial Mail* is a valuable source of economic news. The quarterly journal *African Affairs* is useful both for its papers and for the select bibliography of recent books and articles in each issue. Other useful journals include: *Africa Institute Bulletin, Africa Quarterly, Journal for Geography* (more recently *South African Geographer*), *Journal of Modern African Studies, Journal of Southern African Studies , South African Geographical Journal, South African Journal of African Affairs, South African Journal of Economics, South African Outlook, Standard Bank Review.* An invaluable source of reference for the subcontinent is the *Standard Encyclopaedia of Southern Africa,* published by Nasionale Opvoedkundige Uitgewery Ltd, Cape Town. Novels and short stories concerned with South African society, past and present, include those by Olive Schreiner, Pauline Smith, Alan Paton and Nadine Gordimer.

Adam, H. (1971), *Modernizing Racial Domination: the dynamics of South African politics,* University of California Press, Berkeley.

Adam, H. (ed.) (1971), *South Africa: sociological perspectives,* Oxford University Press, London.

Ballinger, M. (1969), *From Union to Apartheid: a trek to isolation,* Juta, Cape Town.

Barber, J. (1973), *South Africa's Foreign Policy 1945–1970,* Oxford University Press, London.

Barratt, J., et al. (1974), *Accelerated Development in Southern Africa,* Macmillan, London.

247

Bell, T. (1973), *Industrial Decentralisation in South Africa,* Oxford University Press, Cape Town.

van den Bergh, P.L. (1965), *South Africa: a study in conflict,* Wesleyan University Press, Middletown (Conn.).

Board, C. (1962), *The Border Region: natural environment and land use in the Eastern Cape* (2 vols), Oxford University Press, Cape Town.

Brandel-Syrier, M. (1971), *Reeftown Elite: a study of social mobility in a modern African community on the Reef,* Routledge and Kegan Paul, London.

Brookes, E.H. (1968), *Apartheid: a documentary study of modern South Africa,* Routledge and Kegan Paul, London.

Brookes, E.H. (1974), *White Rule in South Africa 1830–1910,* University of Natal Press, Pietermaritzburg.

Brookes, E.H. and Webb, C. de B. (1965) *A History of Natal,* University of Natal Press, Pietermaritzburg.

Carter, G. (1962), *The Politics of Inequality: South Africa since 1948,* 3rd ed., Praeger, New York.

Carter, G., Karis, T. and Stultz, N.M. (1967), *South Africa's Transkei: the politics of domestic colonialism,* Heinemann, London.

Cilliers, S.P. (1971), *Appeal to Reason,* University Publishers and Booksellers, Stellenbosch.

Cole, M. (1961), *South Africa,* Methuen, London.

Desmond, C. (1971), *The Discarded People,* Penguin, Harmondsworth.

Drury, A. (1967), *A Very Strange Society: a journey to the heart of South Africa,* Trident Press, New York.

Duggan, W.B. (1973), *A Socio-Economic Profile of South Africa,* Praeger, New York.

First, R., Steele, J. and Gurney, C. (1972), *The South African Connection: western investment in apartheid,* Temple Smith, London (also published by Penguin, 1973).

Fisher, J. (1969), *The Afrikaners,* Cassell, London.

Giniewski, P. (1961), *Bantustans: a trek towards the future,* Human and Rousseau, Cape Town.

Green, L.P. and Fair, T.J.D. (1962), *Development in Africa,* Witwatersrand University Press, Johannesburg.

Hahlo, H.R. and Kahn, E. (1960), *The Union of South Africa: the development of its laws and constitution,* Juta, Cape Town.

Hailey, W.M. (1963), *The Republic of South Africa and the High Commission Territories,* Oxford University Press, London.

Hance, W. (ed.) (1968), *South Africa and the United States,* Columbia University Press, New York.

Heard, K.A. (1974), *General Elections in South Africa 1943-1970,* Oxford University Press, London.

Hepple, A. (1966), *South Africa: a political and economic history,* Pall Mall Press, London.

Hill, C.R. (1964), *Bantustans: the fragmentation of South Africa,* Oxford University Press, London.

Hoagland, J. (1972), *South Africa: civilization in conflict,* Allen and Unwin, London.

Houghton, D.H. (1960), *Economic Development in a Plural Society: studies in the Border region of the Cape Province,* Oxford University Press, Cape Town.

Houghton, D.H. (1973), *The South African Economy* (3rd ed.), Oxford University Press, Cape Town.

Houghton, D.H. and Dagut, J. (1972, 3rd vol. 1973), *Source Material on the South African Economy 1860-1970* (3 vols), Oxford University Press, Cape Town.

Hurwitz, N. and Williams, O. (1962), *The Economic Framework of South Africa,* Shuter and Shooter, Pietermaritzburg.

Hutson, H.W. (1973), *Majority Rule - Why? Co-operation not Confrontation in South Africa,* Johnson, London.

Hyam, R. (1972), *The Failure of South African Expansion 1908-48,* Macmillan, London.

van Jaarsfeld, F.A. (1961), *The Afrikaner's Interpretation of South African History,* Simondium, Cape Town.

Keppel-Jones, A. (1975), *South Africa: a short history* (5th ed.), Hutchinson, London.

de Kiewiet, C.W. (1941), *A History of South Africa: social and economic,* Oxford University Press, London.

The Kissinger Study of Southern Africa (1975), Spokesman Books, Nottingham.

de Klerk, W.A. (1975), *The Puritans in Africa,* Rex Collings, London.

Kuper, H. (1960), *Indian People in Natal,* Natal University Press, Pietermaritzburg.

Kuper, L. (1965), *An African Bourgeoisie,* Yale University Press, New Haven (Conn.).

Kuper, L. and Smith, M.G. (1971), *Pluralism in Africa,* University of California Press, Berkeley.

Kuper, L., Watts, H. and Davies, R. (1958), *Durban: a study in racial ecology,* Jonathan Cape, London.

Leftwich, A. (ed.) (1974), *South Africa: economic growth and political change,* Allison and Busby, London.

Legum, C. (1975), *Southern Africa: the secret diplomacy of détente, South Africa at the crossroads,* Rex Collings, London.

Lever, H. (1972), *The South African Voter,* Juta, Cape Town.

Maasdorp, G. and Humphreys, A.S.B. (eds) (1975), *From Shantytown to Township.* Juta, Cape Town.

McCrystal, L. (1969), *City, Town or Country: the economics of concentration and dispersal, with particular reference to South Africa,* A.A. Balkema, Cape Town.

Mackler, I. (1972), *Pattern for Profit,* Lexington Books, Lexington (Mass.).

Macmillan, W.M. (1930), *Complex South Africa,* Faber, London.

Macmillan, W.M. (1927), *The Cape Colour Question,* Faber, London.

Macmillan, W.M. (1963), *Bantu, Boer and Briton: the making of the South African Native Problem,* Clarendon Press, Oxford.

Marais, J.S. (1939), *The Cape Coloured People 1652–1937,* Longman, London.

Marquard, L. (1969), *Peoples and Policies of South Africa* (4th ed.), Oxford University Press, London.

Marquard, L. (1971), *A Federation of Southern Africa,* Oxford University Press, London.

Mayer, P. (1961), *Townsmen or Tribesmen,* Oxford University Press, Cape Town.

Meer, F. (1969), *Portrait of Indian South Africans,* Avon House, Durban.

Ngubane, J.K. (1963), *An African Explains Apartheid,* Pall Mall, London.

Niddrie, D.L. (1968), *South Africa: nation or nations?* Van Nostrand, Princeton.

Nolutshungu, S.C. (1975), *South Africa in Africa: a study of ideology in foreign policy,* Manchester University Press.

Pachai, B. (1971), *The International Aspects of the South African Indian Question 1860–1971,* Struik, Cape Town.

Paton, A. (1969), *Portrait of South Africa,* Lutterworth, London.

Pollock, N.C. and Agnew, S. (1963), *An Historical Geography of South Africa,* Longman, London.

Potholm, C. and Dale, R. (eds) (1972), *Southern Africa in Perspective: essays in regional politics,* Free Press, New York.

Randall, P. (ed.) (1970), *Anatomy of Apartheid,* SPRO-CAS, Johannesburg.

Randall, P. (ed.) (1971), *Directions of Change in South African Politics,* SPRO-CAS, Johannesburg.

250

Randall, P. (ed.) (1971), *Education beyond Apartheid*, SPRO-CAS, Johannesburg.

Randall, P. (ed.) (1971), *Some Implications of Inequality*, SPRO-CAS, Johannesburg.

Randall, P. (ed.) (1971), *South Africa's Minorities*, SPRO-CAS, Johannesburg.

Randall, P. (ed.) (1971), *Towards Social Change*, SPRO-CAS, Johannesburg.

Randall, P. (ed.) (1972), *Power, Privilege and Poverty*, SPRO-CAS, Johannesburg.

Randall, P. (ed.) (1972), *Apartheid and the Church*, SPRO-CAS, Johannesburg.

Randall, P. (ed.) (1972), *Law, Justice and Society*, SPRO-CAS, Johannesburg.

Randall, P. (ed.) (1973), *South Africa's Political Alternatives*, SPRO-CAS, Johannesburg.

Randall, P. (ed.) (1973), *A Taste of Power*, SPRO-CAS, Johannesburg.

van Rensburg, N.J. (1972), *Population Explosion in Southern Africa?*, privately published.

Rhoodie, N.J. (1969), *Apartheid and Racial Partnership in Southern Africa*, Academica, Pretoria.

Rhoodie, N.J. (ed.) (1972), *South African Dialogue: contrasts in South African thinking on basic race issues*, McGraw-Hill, Johannesburg.

Rhoodie, N.J. and Venter, H.J. (1960), *Apartheid: a socio-historical exposition of the origin and development of the apartheid idea*, De Bussy, Amsterdam.

Sachs, E.S. (1965), *The Anatomy of Apartheid*, Collet's, London.

Selwyn, P. (1975), *Industries in the Southern African Periphery*, Croom Helm, London.

Simons, H.J. and R.E. (1969), *Class and Colour in South Africa 1850–1950*, Penguin, Harmondsworth.

Smith, D.M. (ed.) (1976), *Separation in South Africa: peoples and policies*, Queen Mary College, London, Department of Geography Occasional Paper No. 6. (A further paper is due during 1976, incorporating several contributions.)

Stultz, N.M. (1974), *Afrikaner Politics in South Africa 1934–1948*, University of California Press, Berkeley.

Tatz, C.M. (1962), *Shadow and Substance in South Africa: a study of land and franchise policies 1910–1960*, University of Natal Press, Pietermaritzburg.

Thompson, L.M. (1960), *The Unification of South Africa 1902-1910,* Clarendon Press, Oxford.

Thompson, L. and Butler, J. (eds) (1975), *Change in Contemporary South Africa,* University of California Press, Berkeley.

de Villiers, D. (1970), *The Case for South Africa,* Tom Stacey, London.

Walker, E.A. (1928, 1964), *A History of Southern Africa,* Longman, London.

Wellington, J.H. (1960), *Southern Africa: a geographical study* (2 vols), Cambridge University Press, London.

Wellington, J.H. (1967), *South West Africa and its Human Issues,* Clarendon Press, Oxford.

Welsh, D. (1971), *The Roots of Segregation 1845-1910: Native Policy in colonial Natal,* Oxford University Press, Cape Town.

West, M.E. (1971), *Divided Community: a study of social groups and racial affairs in a South African town,* A.A. Balkema, Cape Town.

Wilson, F. (1972), *Labour in the South African Gold Mines 1911-1969,* Cambridge University Press, London.

Wilson, F. (1972), *Migrant Labour in South Africa,* South African Council of Churches and SPRO-CAS, Johannesburg.

Wilson, F. and Perrot, D. (1973), *Outlook on a Century: South Africa 1870-1970,* Lovedale Press and SPRO-CAS, Lovedale (Cape) and Johannesburg.

Wilson, M. and Thompson, L. (eds), (1969 and 1971), *The Oxford History of South Africa: Vol. I, South Africa to 1870; Vol. II, South Africa 1870-1966,* Clarendon Press, Oxford.

Worrall, D. (ed.) (1971), *South Africa: Government and Politics,* Van Schaik, Pretoria.

Index

Tribal fights 46
Tsonga (Shangaan) 6, 7–8, 149, 202
Tswana 7, 149, 178, 188, 230
Tuberculosis Commission 70
Tugela Location 149, 162
Tugela river 6, 28, 162
Tzaneen 169, 184

Uganda 119
Uitenhage 115
Uitlanders 31
Umkomaas river 28, 162
Umlazi 76, 77, 182, 185, 196, 197
Umtamvuma river 162
Umtata 170, 188, 190, 201, 232
Umtata river 162
Umzimkulu district 205
Umzimkulu river 162
Umzimvubu river 162
Umzinto 111, 120
Unemployment 47, 112, 135, 156, 158,
    159, 207, 228, 243
United Nations 209, 235, 240, 244
United Party 49, 59, 71, 91, 92, 94,
    97, 100, 224–5, 227–8, 229
United States 13, 40, 44, 53, 55, 88,
    120, 236, 238, 240, 241, 245
University of South Africa (UNISA) 112
Upington 65
Urban Africans 43, 46, 49, 57, 59, 67,
    68–9, 70–2, 77–84, 149, 153, 155,
    157–9, 189, 196–7, 220, 225–6, 230
Uranium 53, 68
Urban hierarchy 64–5, 197
Urbanisation 68–9, 77, 88–9, 110, 111,
    124, 126, 142, 182–3, 197, 201, 224
Urban segregation 61–72, 88
Urdu 106

Vaal river 25, 63
Vanadium 178
Vanderbijl Park 55, 58
Vatican 202
Vegetables 28, 110, 124, 169
Venda (homeland) 163–4, 168, 177, 182,
    201, 203, 208
Venda (people) 6, 7, 8, 151, 202
Vereeniging 58,130
'Verkramptes' 90, 228
Verligte Action 227
'Verligtes' 90, 97, 100, 226, 227, 230
'Verswarting' 48
Verulam 113, 118, 120

Verwoerd, Dr Hendrik 207
Victoria Falls talks 240
Vietnam 238
Vines see Wine
Violence 220–1
Voortrekkers 14, 24–8, 124, 126
Vorster, J.B. 142, 239, 244
Vrygrond (Cape Town) 127, 128

Wages 42, 43–7, 49–51, 112, 132, 133–5,
    158, 170, 179, 195, 197, 226, 236
Wages Acts (1925, 1937) 34, 179
Wages Commission 223
Water 154–5, 171, 241
Welfare provision 80–2
Welkom 45, 131
Werkgenot (Cape Town) 127
Western Cape University 136
West Rand 52
Wheat 18, 124, 169
White attitudes 89–90
White Kei river 22
Wilcocks Report 140–1
Windhoek 244
Wine 9, 18, 124, 126
Winterveld 197
Witbank 58, 67, 130, 131
Witsieshoek 187, 201
Witwatersrand 29–31, 34, 63, 83, 84,
    94, 97, 100; see also Pretoria-
    Witwatersrand-Vereeniging
Wool 29, 167
Works and liaison committees 45

Xhosa 4, 6, 23, 24, 80, 123, 149,
    202, 230
Xhosa Development Corporation 168,
    186–7

Yugoslavia 194

Zaïre 39, 240, 242
Zambesi 30, 244
Zambia 154, 239–43
Zeerust 184
Zinc 55
Zulu 6, 8, 14, 26, 27–8, 80, 105, 149,
    230
Zulu–Indian riots 119
Zululand 25, 27–8, 33, 169; see also
    KwaZulu
Zuurbraak 123
Zuurveld 20, 23
Zwelitsha 185

261

The author

Anthony Lemon, MA, DPhil, has been a Fellow and Tutor in Geography at Mansfield College, Oxford since 1970. In 1973 and 1975 he was Visiting Lecturer at the University of Natal, Pietermaritzburg.

Other SAXON HOUSE publications